I0571871

VALKYRJUR, SERVANT OR MASTER?

AN EXPLORATION OF THE VALKYRIES
THROUGHOUT THE MEDIEVAL PERIOD

SIF BROOKES

TLS

ISBN13: 978-1-959350-59-0

Set in: Georgia 8/9/10/11/12/14pt, Kuadrat 24pt

©The Three Little Sisters
USA/CANADA

Contents

ABOUT THE AUTHOR

Sif Brookes is a writer, editor, speaker and artist with academic interests around the Viking Age and the early medieval period. As a reconstructionist Nordic Heathen, she looks to recreate and understand the beliefs of the practitioners of the "old ways", primarily, how they saw the world around them, and how that perspective informed their social structures, culture and religious behaviour.

Central to this pursuit are the Valkyries themselves, with a supplementary academic interest around historical *seiðr*, the role of women in the early medieval period, Viking Age weaponry and armour, and the study of death and burial in pre-Christian Germanic civilisations. As such, the core of her personal practice revolves around Freyja, Hel, Sif, Skadi, Eir, Angrboda, Ran, Saga and the Valkyries.

A large part of her Heathen practice involves community enrichment, at both a local and national level. As of writing, she is on the Committee of Asatru UK as their Marketing Officer, the National LGBTQIA+ Manager for the Pagan Federation and Committee member as one of the Council Representatives, and the Social Media Coordinator and member of the Board of Trustees for PaganAid. She advocates for inclusive Heathenry and Paganism and drives for greater awareness for Paganism within the UK, including within the media and government bodies.

In May 2023, she was grateful to be invited to the *Norse in the North* conference at Leeds University alongside other Pagans, to encourage collaboration and understanding between academic spaces and Pagan practitioners. This remains a prominent focus, including working on an interfaith basis with other religious organisations to promote LGBTQIA+ spaces.

Sif was a founding host of the Heathen Wyrdos podcast, and currently creates content under Valsif on Youtube (a work in progress). She co-authored and illustrated *The Wyrd Less Woven, an Alternative Heathen Prayer Book* with Dan Coultas.

Acknowledgements

Hospitality, kindness, humility, and acceptance should be the words that people associate with all Heathens. It is not our duty to act as a gatekeeper and decide who can and cannot worship the Gods.

'Fire is needful for someone who's come in
And who's chilled to the knee;
Food and clothing are necessary for the man
Who's journeyed over the mountains.'[2]

Our actions and words influence the greater community, as such we should endeavour to leave our mark upon the world, improving it however we can. I dedicate this book to Asatru UK, and especially the committee of Asatru UK; Jack, Rich, Dan, Matt, Jules, Sky, Jonny, Hamish, Ioan, Hayley, Kieran, Sabrina, Josh, Steve, Geoff, Phil – and the greater community et al. To Geoff, Helen and Phil – thank you for your guidance and for being pillars of unending wisdom and support for the Pagan community at large. To Dan, Rich and Ioan for being academic inspirations and for pushing me to pursue my research and obsessions. Dan, I still consider you a mentor. You cannot escape me. You're awesome, and I will not stop in my compliments. Thank you for reading a very early draft of this book and for every draft afterwards.

I also dedicate this book to the Pagan Federation, to Sarah, the Council and the Committee/Board, and the work that the organisation does to further all Pagan paths in the UK. Thank you also to my other half and favourite person, Dan, who has only ever been accepting of my Heathenness. Sorry for my barely coherent, hyper fixated rants on whatever topic I had been reading about that day, as well as your unending patience and support. (Plus, driving me up and down the country with far too much stuff for our little Seat Ibiza, Fin, to carry. Thank you, and sorry).

---

2 Hávamál 3 [Sayings of the High One]. Carolyne Larrington, The Poetic Edda. (Revised Edition) (UK: Oxford University Press, 2014), 13.

I must also thank Jóhanna Katrín Friðriksdóttir, Neil Price, Judith Jesch, Leszek Gardeła, and Luke John Murphy for their continued work when it comes to fleshing out the role of women in the Viking Age and their respective works in relation to the Valkyries.

This is an ever-evolving conversation in academia, and I cannot wait for what the future of Viking Age and early medieval scholarly thought has in store with this groundwork established. Also, because she wanted a mention if I ever wrote a book, Emma, and so follows the rest of my family, Mum, Pete, Tom, and Dad. Love you.

AUTHORS NOTES

Various passages in this book have previously been published in the Pagan Dawn journal created by the Pagan Federation, *Heathenry: An International Journal for Heathen Research* published by Asatru UK, and in the *Heathen Women United Newsletter* distributed by the Facebook page of the same name. Where they appear here, they have been updated and altered to my current understanding of the research I have conducted.

This also applies to the small snippets here and there from any events I have been invited to speak at. This work has been refined and improved several times over the last few years to best reflect my position, snowballing out in various directions to become something much larger than I had originally planned.

I have opted to go down the route of accessibility when it comes to the use of Old Norse or Anglicisation. In the pursuit of that goal, I have mostly used the more recognisable form for the larger potential audience: Valkyries and Valkyrie over Valkyrjur or Valkyrja, Odin over Óðinn, Valhalla over Valhǫll, Angrboda over Angrboða, Skadi over Skaði, and so on. I have chosen to use Old Norse spellings for all of the Valkyries, primarily for clarity and uniformity, as most sources follow that convention too.

Where the Anglicised name is quoted, I will add the Old Norse to avoid potential confusion. A similar approach will be given to quoted material from authors and sources, in that I will default to the stated form in the material used and annotate where necessary. I have left certain titles of poems in the Old Norse where the translation isn't useful for identification, such as *Skáldskaparmál* which is simply *'The Language of Poetry'* or *'Poetic Diction'*, and *Haustlöng* , *'Autumn-Long'*. This also applies to *Heimskringla* , which Snorri named after the first two words of the first saga of the work, *Kringla heimsin.*

Kringla heimsin: [disk/circle/orb - home/world/ earth – "orb of the world"][2]

2 Geir T. Zoëga, A Concise Dictionary of Old Icelandic (Oxford: Clarendon, 1910), 249 & 192.

Essentially, these works are better known by these titles rather than their translated titles. Another exception is *seiðr*, as I've finally taught Microsoft Word to accept that as an actual word. More importantly, in terms of the decision to use the Old Norse there rather than any English alternative, I would suggest that no alternative word would do it justice in terms of encompassing its various and unique manifestations in the source literature. Magic, sorcery and witchcraft, though common replacements, are often used to describe specific actions, or otherwise conjure an image in the reader's head that may depart from the behaviours related to *seiðr* .

Another noteworthy exception will be made with the term *Waelcyrge* to aid in distinguishing these Anglo-Saxon beings from their Nordic cousins. I've also left any non-Anglicised words found in quoted material for consistency on that front. Where sagas have been mentioned, I have included both Old Norse and Anglicised titles once again for clarity. I have chosen to use Chicago-style source citations but have broken with convention when it comes to translated works, most commonly regarding the Eddas, due to a variety of different translations being utilised. In those instances, I have cited the translator rather than, for example, Snorri Sturluson in the shortened format to allow the reader to accurately track references.

I have endeavoured to capture an 'academic-lite' tone across this work, driving for ease of access over anything else. I want this to be a primer on Valkyries for Heathens and interested parties at all ability levels and experience. As a result, some of this may cover well-trodden ground for the well-read amongst you, but I hope to put forth some ideas that, at the very least, spark interest and intrigue with the hope of spawning further discussions down the road.

This work best reflects my current understanding of the topic, and current skill set in being able to tackle the task of exploring it. As I am fully planning on undertaking a postgraduate degree in the near future to further my knowledge and abilities, I do expect to write a revision and further expansion of this book later in life built on the back of a lifelong interest in the Valkyries.

Foreword by Dan Coultas

I first met Sif at the Pagan Federation conference in Bradford in 2022, where I gave a talk on publishing for first-time authors, whilst she gave a talk entitled Valkyries: Servant or Master?, which would later form the foundation of this book. Her talk was fascinating, and afterwards, I spoke to her on her stall, purchased some of her artwork, and said that we must collaborate on something in the future. Over the next year or so, I started listening to Sif's podcasts, and we began speaking online. I found her podcast contributions to be insightful, well-researched and presented in a way that was engaging and accessible, without any hint of the ego that is sadly all too apparent in most other Heathen online influencers.

During the Jorvik Festival 2023, Sif baffled me by telling me she considered me a mentor. I told her at the time that whilst I was honoured, the notion was ridiculous; I very much considered her a peer. Her knowledge, maturity and approach to Heathenry were far beyond that of someone I could consider a mentee; she was teaching me just as much as I was teaching her. The situation has not changed and probably never will.

In 2024, we published The Wyrd Less Woven: An Alternative Heathen Prayer Book together, a work which I am sure will be the first of many collaborations. I was honoured to be asked to write the foreword for this work and have my name attached to it in some small way; because this book is a game-changer.

Sif's passion for the Valkyries is unparalleled. She venerates them as deities in their own right, collectively and individually, and is determined to ensure they receive the recognition they deserve. Her commitment to this cause is evident in her rigorous research, which leaves no primary source unexamined and no relevant secondary material unscrutinised. The bibliography at the end of this book is a testament to the depth and breadth of reading that has brought so many key sources on the Valkyries together and examined them to paint a complete picture of their evolving role through the ages. Nobody writing today is better placed to compile this work. All those who write, present podcasts, or in any other way present information within the Heathen community would do well to learn from this thorough academic approach.

Valkyrjur, Servant or Master? examines the Valkyries from their earliest written attestations, through the Middle Ages and their Victorian revival, right up to their perception in modern popular culture and among modern-day Heathens. While the focus, understandably, is on Old Norse material, the author is not afraid to look further afield for evidence of the Valkyries' role and nature. Old English, Middle High German and even Arabic sources are brought in for points of comparison. Archaeological and linguistic evidence has also been collated to paint the most complete picture of the Valkyries in any research to date.

Whether you are a scholar of Old Norse literature, a Heathen looking to deepen your understanding of these mysterious beings that are so often relegated to the fringes of spiritual practice, or simply someone interested in their historical development through time, this book is sure to be a thoroughly informative, thought-provoking and enjoyable journey through the world of the Valkyries. It brings the Valkyries to the fore. It challenges the dominant yet wildly outdated Wagnerian perception of these complex beings as little more than glorified serving girls, a perception that is sadly perpetuated even by prominent authors within the modern Heathen community. In doing so, it re-opens the debate on their very nature, inviting readers to explore more nuanced understandings.

-Dan Coultas

Introduction

'Helgi assembled a great fleet and went to Frekastein,
and on the ocean they ran into a terribly dangerous storm.
Lightning flashed above them and the ships were struck.
They saw nine Valkyries riding up in the air, and recognised
Sigrun among them.'[3]

There are few beings in Western mythology who hold such a stranglehold on the zeitgeist as the *Valkyrie*. There's something incredibly timeless in the image of the sometimes-winged warrior woman looming over the battlefield and ferrying those chosen dead to their afterlives. Though the Valkyries have evolved and changed over the last millennia to reflect and fulfil various cultural roles, today they remain as muses to creatives and artists, often in ways that echo their later depictions in the medieval period.

The Valkyries remain the crux of my personal religious practice, and beings who fascinate me endlessly in a religious context, as well as a historical and academic one. Yet, there is startlingly little material on them, and even fewer options when it comes to how to approach them from a Heathen or Pagan perspective. I can count on one hand how many books are dedicated to detailing their various appearances and depictions, and fewer still that I would say portray them with any sort of accuracy in line with common modern academic thought.

This is a point that was emphasised by **Luke John Murphy** back in 2013,[4] but remains largely in the same state today. Despite the Valkyries' notoriety in the greater Nordic space, there's very little work being conducted on detailing their various appearances and characterisation. I would state that this is caused by a two-pillared consideration. The first, is that there is a misconception of the "mystery" – or rather, a lack of mystery – around the Valkyries.

---

3 Carolyne Larrington, The Poetic Edda. (Revised Edition) (Oxford: Oxford University Press, 2014), 131.

4 Luke John Murphy, Herjans Dísir: Valkyrjur, Supernatural Feminities, and Elite Warrior Culture in the Late Pre-Christian Iron Age (MA thesis: Háskóla Íslands, 2013), 9-10.

As will be discussed, the literature of the early twentieth century made premature or wholly incorrect conclusions on the role of the Valkyrie that persevered for decades without challenge, and still persevere today. I would argue that no other beings within the corpus are at the mercy of such misinformation, at least to the degree that is afforded to the Valkyries, their role and their duties.

The other pillar is one of hierarchy. In a world with Gods and Goddesses, wights, wyrms and Jotnar [Jötnar], the framing of the Valkyries as "servants of Odin", at times empowered mortal women, has dissuaded further conversation from developing in favour of those beings who are seen as more central or less controversial to Old Norse studies and religion. These two pillars have proven potent in combination.

Unfortunately, this second pillar remains most apparent to the lay reader, with any further research being stymied by the lack of perceived importance within the Nordic world. Framed within this role of 'servant', they are overlooked, or otherwise considered removed from the godly beings we tend to worship as Pagans. In this, a Valkyrie is sometimes seen as synonymous with *Skjaldmær*,[5] a Shield-Maiden,[6] something entirely human, further distorting the conversation. Academia today is still occupied with back-and-forth debates on the validity of Shield-Maidens, which creates another layer of obfuscation.

If the Valkyries are not human, they are servants of Odin, therefore mythological and not relevant to larger discussions on real-world history and archaeology. If they are Shield-Maidens, they are potentially mythological, and irrelevant to larger discussions within the context of real-world history and archaeology. We are in a catch-22 situation.

---

5 Judith Jesch highlights that this is often done "unthinkingly as a synonym", ignoring the nuances between terms. Judith Jesch, "Women, War and Words: a Verbal Archaeology of Shield-maidens", Viking Wars (2021), 129.

6 Just as one example, the Glossary page of Jesse Byock's 1999 translation of 'The Saga of the Volsungs' states "Sigrun... a shield-maiden (i.e. a Valkyrie)". The Saga of the Volsungs. The Norse Epic of Sigurd the Dragon Slayer, trans. Jesse Byock (London: Penguin Classics, 1999), 142.

As it stands, I have been researching the Valkyries for the entirety of my Heathen path and for several years prior. They are evocative beings, and certainly enthralled me before becoming a Pagan. Since then, I would say that my understanding has only been bolstered by my personal gnosis, offering a new (personal) perspective that is absent from current literature. With that in mind, I will clearly label my personal gnosis, so you know where that plays a part over historically based understanding.

I have included a chapter at the end which is dedicated to detailing my personal approach to the Valkyries from a modern Heathen perspective. Today, I lightly consider myself a Valkyric scholar, at least 'in training'. I plummet into anything that mentions the Valkyries, and I'm thoroughly enjoying every second of the journey.

Throughout the course of this book, I will be differentiating between the earliest and later depictions of the Valkyries. I consider the mid-tenth century to herald the beginning of a transitional period for the Valkyries, losing some of their earlier animalistic behaviours and becoming, gradually, domesticated and sanitised. By the twelfth and thirteenth centuries this domestication was in place and agreed with consensus across several written sources.

Then, with this new role of human-born wives of heroes and daughters of Kings, they continued to be romanticised over the eighteenth, nineteenth and twentieth centuries in the shape of a literal romantic figure: a warrior made to repent her warrior ways. This timeline is not linear, and we have attestations later than the mid-tenth century that would seem to align with earlier appearances. This is also noteworthy, hinting at pockets of enduring oral or geographical traditions or lingering elements of older characterisation and behaviour.

In the modern world, the Valkyrie has evolved and adapted once more to embody elements of many of her historical representations of the past, though with more of an emphasis on the later Victorian romanticism. They are supernaturally powered warriors, beautiful and distant in their beauty, objects of lust, love and passion. They are something to be chased, acquired, and made tame. They have a tentative hold on their power, and risk losing it all should they succumb to the temptations presented by the would-be lover.

These representations, alongside post-medieval representations, will not be the core focus of this book. Moving into modernity, the Valkyrie lost the anchor to her roots, becoming more of a literary trope, rather than a cultural and religious figure who was seen as a very real force on the world and in human lives. To clarify then, this work will be focused on analysing material from around the fifth century, from early continental Germanic and Anglo-Saxon sources, through to the fourteenth century, and later Scandinavian sources.

Equally, I do not consider the Valkyries to be a monolith, but in fact for all their depictions within this specific period to hold 'truth' in the way I worship them. We've been gifted the benefit of hindsight, viewing the Valkyries as a relative whole some millennia removed. Of course, the fact remains that the transition from one thing to another took generations. To discount the fourteenth century Valkyries as untrue or otherwise a facsimile in comparison to their earlier, wild appearances would be to draw an arbitrary line in the sand and to discount an evolution that offers crucial insight into the mythological aspects, as well as a culture and civilisation that was changing from one thing to something very different entirely.

To note, I consider the Anglo-Saxon *Waelcyrge* to be an earlier incarnation of the figures we now commonly call Valkyries. While the former has been restricted to a singular schema of behaviour, born from barely a dozen attestations and mostly in the form of glosses, the Valkyries, over the course of their many attestations, were given the freedom to be defined by a plethora of behaviours, sometimes removed from the battlefield, and sometimes not. This has caused some issues in terms of comparison between the two parties, but again, I've combed through the discussion to share my thoughts in the relevant chapter.

The Valkyries are of the battlefield, calling for slaughter and delighting in bloodshed, and they are the more wisdom-driven guardians of heroes we see in the later heroic sagas. I'll detail my thought process in terms of reconciling these appearances within this work. Despite their mortal presentation in the later sources, I do consider them to be Goddesses in their own right, of an importance and station that far removes them from humans, above the generalisation of "spirit", and into the realm of deity.

The language and kennings that are used to describe them suggest they are not of this mortal world and even later depictions lend to this image. **Hilda Roderick Ellis Davidson** calls them, in no uncertain terms, "Battle Goddesses",[7] but this is far from the only example that lends a divine nature to the Valkyries. The "hamingja-woman" mentioned in *Viga-Glum's saga* is described as a "Goddess of the Sword and Spear,"[8] and, as I will discuss in more detail, this surely can only be referring to a Valkyrie. Such descriptions, and similar, occur frequently.

This is a complex topic when we're analysing the literature of the period, namely because we have an ongoing discussion of what defines a God and Goddess in the Nordic sphere in reconciling the archaeological materials of worship with literary representations. While Heathens tend to be more flexible in the definition of what comprises a God in their praxis, the literature itself tends to demarcate those deities described as belonging to the Aesir [Æsir] as being 'worthy' of the title of 'God'. Skadi, for example, is seen to become a 'Goddess' through her marriage to Njordr, who himself becomes a 'God' when he is integrated into the Aesir post-war.

Much of this discourse has functioned to reinforce a dichotomy between the deities that were worshipped, and those that were considered 'other', and so evil, maligned, antagonistic. Indeed, while the Jotnar would seem to fulfil this descriptor– as in being considered evil because they are neither of the Vanir or Aesir - there's flexibility with that definition too. After all, the Aesir Gods often are of Jotunn [Jǫtunn / Jötunn] blood and heritage.

> "His name was Buri. He was beautiful in appearance, big and powerful. He begot a son called Bor. He married a wife called Bestla, daughter of the giant Bolthorn and they had three sons. One was called Odin..."[9]

---

7 Hilda Roderick Ellis Davidson, Myths and Symbols in Pagan Europe. Early Scandinavian and Celtic Religions (Syracuse University Press, 1988), 92.

8 Edmund Walker Head, The Story of Viga-Glum (Illustrated Edition)(1866), 38.

9 Snorri Sturluson, Edda, trans. Anthony Faulkes (London and Vermont: W&N Everyman, 2008), 11. I will be crediting Faulkes in future reference citations for this work.

Odin is far from the only Aesir deity that this applies to, with Thor and Tyr also claiming similar kin, among many others. It may be tempting to go towards literary kennings to justify classification, and regarding the Valkyries, we have numerous kennings that utilise the names of Goddesses to refer to the Valkyries individually.

Ragnarsdrápa [The Lay of Ragnar] has several, including "the Shaking-Sif of Rings"[10] and "the Desiring-Ran of the excessive drying of veins".[11] The tenth century work *Vellekla* [12] by Einar Helgason Skálaglamm has "the Saga of Direful Enmity",[13] while Glúmr Geirason's *Gráfeldardrápa* [The Lay of Harald Grey Cloak] calls a Valkyrie a "Saga of Swords",[14] and so on. This literary tradition also manifests in the kennings for 'agreed Gods' such as Odin, who as an example is called *"Hangatýr"*[15] in *Skáldskaparmál* [16] and *"Hroptatýr"*[17] in *Hákonarmál* [The Song of Hakon].

---

10 Ragnarsdrápa 8. Margaret Clunies Ross "Bragi inn gamli Boddason, Ragnarsdrápa", in Poetry from Treatises on Poetics. Skaldic Poetry of the Scandinavian Middle Ages 3, ed. Kari Ellen Gade and Edith Marold (Turnhout, Belgium: Brepols, 2017), 27.

11 Ragnarsdrápa 8. Ibid.

12 Meaning, roughly, 'Shortage of Gold', so falls into the same category as others presented in the Author's Note at the beginning of the book.

13 Vellekla 29. "dolga Sôgu" – 'Dolga' refers to an enemy, something evil, dangerous, other, hated - leading to 'direful enmity', evoking that sense of hostility. Translation from "Dolg". Zoëga, A Concise Dictionary of Old Icelandic, 89.

14 Gráfeldardrápa 7. Alison Finlay, "Glúmr Geirason, Gráfeldardrápa", in Poetry from the Kings' Sagas 1: From Mythical Times to c. 1035. Skaldic Poetry of the Scandinavian Middle Ages 1, ed. Diana Whaley (Turnhout, Belgium: Brepols, 2012), 245.

15 Tyr is derived from Proto-Germanic Tiwaz meaning 'God', the plural of Tyr is Tivar meaning 'Gods', which drives much of the conversation on Tyr being the 'original' chief of the Gods or holding a more dominant role than he now assumes within Nordic literature. Rudolf Simek, Dictionary of Northern Mythology, trans. Angela Hall (Cambridge: D.S. Brewer, 2007), 337.

16 Faulkes, Edda, 64.

17 Hákonarmál 14.

Equally, Thor is referred to as "the bearing-Tyr of wounds"[18] in the tenth century work *Haustlǫng* by the skald Þjóðólfr of Hvinir, and "the Gautr [Odin] of host-thunder"[19] in Eilífr Goðrúnarson's *Þórsdrápa* [The Lay of Thor], which is an excellent work when it comes to kennings in general.

According to Snorri, this was common practice: "that we speak of Odin or Thor or Tyr or one of the Æsir or elves... I add a term for the attribute of another As...then the latter becomes the one referred to, and not the one that was named".

However, such a tool is used to refer to very human, though often heroic, figures in the literature too, as outlined in Snorri's *Skáldskaparmál* within his Edda. [20]

Perhaps more enlightening is that some Valkyries are given kennings that refer to them with the names of giantesses. *Knútsdrápa* [The Lay of Knut] refers to "the Leikn of Spears"[21] and describes a raven as a "hawk of Leikn of points"[22]. This holds more weight as, staying with and according to *Skáldskaparmál*, mortal women were not referred to with the names of giantesses.

However, I found four examples of women being referred to as giantesses or ogresses in kennings. This is far from common practice and appears reserved towards unflattering portrayals or insults, considering there are some 539 kennings for 'woman' in the literature. In comparison, there are over 200 examples of kennings employing the names of Goddesses, according to The Skaldic Project.[23]

---

18 Haustlǫng 20. Margaret Clunies Ross, "Þjóðólfr ór Hvini, Haustlǫng", in Poetry from Treatises on Poetics. Skaldic Poetry of the Scandinavian Middle Ages 3, ed. Kari Ellen Gade and Edith Marold (Turnhout, Belgium: Brepols, 2017), 431.

19 Þórsdrápa 1. Edith Marold with Vivian Busch, Jana Krüger, Ann-Dörte Kyas and Katharina Seidel, "Eilífr Goðrúnarson, Þórsdrápa", in Poetry from Treatises on Poetics. Skaldic Poetry of the Scandinavian Middle Ages 3, trans. John Foulks, ed. Kari Ellen Gade and Edith Marold (Turnhout, Belgium: Brepols, 2017), 68.

20 "It is also normal to refer to a man using all of the names of Æsir". Faulkes, Edda, 94.

21 Knútsdrápa 6. Matthew Townend, "Hallvarðr háreksblesi, Knútsdrápa", in Poetry from Treatises on Poetics. Skaldic Poetry of the Scandinavian Middle Ages 3, ed. Kari Ellen Gade and Edith Marold (Turnhout, Belgium: Brepols, 2017), 230.

22 Leikn is a Jotunn named by Vetrliði Sumarliðason in his Lausavísa as being killed by Thor.

23 "Kennings for Woman," The Skaldic Project, accessed February 2, 2024, https://skaldic.org/db.php?if=default&table=kenning&val=WOMAN

We may be able to conclude that these names then may be utilised in reference to Snorri's guidance of referring "to him [them] by his [their] deeds or possessions or descent."[24] This assumes the position that Valkyries certainly could be of Jotunn blood, which we see most readily in the Valkyrie Hjlóð.[25] This difficulty and lack of consistency in terms of pinning down a Valkyrie to a singular race has drawn the conclusion that to be a Valkyrie was less a classification akin to Jotnar and Aesir and more a role, an occupation almost, that someone undertook.

They could be giantesses, or mortal, or Goddesses equally, and be of any other ancestry besides. It should be noted that to describe the Jotnar, Aesir and Vanir as separate 'races' would be to present a misrepresentation of the material. They are better presented as tribes or families, distinguished by very vague criteria, and with frequent crossover. These groups were fluid, and one could pass from one group to another through marriage and alliance.

There's fluidity too through the Valkyrie categorisation, which lends to the notion that the Valkyries Þrúðr and Eir are the same as the daughter of Thor and Sif, and the handmaiden of Frigg, respectively. Being a Valkyrie and a handmaiden of Frigg aren't mutually exclusive, but roles Eir could hold equally without conflict or contradiction. If we're to follow that some Valkyries were, at one point or another, offspring of mortal parents, that too reinforces this idea that to be a Valkyrie was a title bestowed or given to an individual, rather than being born into that specific 'race'.

As will be discussed at length in later chapters, the Valkyries exhibit many behaviours that are considered distinctive features of the Jotnar. For instance, with reference to the Valkyries' wild nature, it's far more common for Jotunn figures to be defined as 'of the wild', with all the associating imagery you would expect. This also includes associations with spaces that are inhospitable and outside of civilisation centres, such as mountains, as we see with Qrvar-Odds Saga and the kenning "the Freyja of Cliffs", used to refer to a giantess.

---

24 Faulkes, Edda, 88.

25 Though, I have my personal reservations on whether Hjlóð meets the criteria to be a Valkyrie alongside her attested 'sisters'. My reasoning is included in Appendix B, alongside other disputed and potential Valkyrie figures. It's also interesting that Hjlóð makes for a subservient figure at all, considering her Jotunn roots – Giantesses are not known to display such behaviours in the literature, quite the opposite!

Rock, stone and mountain imagery is thematic of giants and giantesses, with kennings and names often tying those wild places to those figures.[26] This calls back to the giants being born of the primordial entity Ymir, whose flesh was used to fashion the earth – they are 'of' Ymir's flesh. It's also common to see 'troll-women' (or *tröllkonur* or *gýgjar*) as synonymous or at least interchangeable with female Jotnar (and "troll"[27] for male Jotnar).[28]

In *Helgakviða Hundingsbana* [The Lay of Helgi Hundingsbane], wolves are referred to as "the troll-woman's mount". That "troll-woman" would be Sigrún, a Valkyrie. It would also be remiss to overlook the Jotnar's strong association with death[29] in almost all appearances, especially when we're looking at potential Jotunn-born Valkyrie figures.

We should also tackle the misconception of the common translation of Jotnar with the term 'giant'. To note most obviously, not all Jotnar were particularly large, while the by-product of translating 'Jotnar' to 'giant' certainly suggests a 'largeness'. It should be noted that there is a persuasive argument that the conflation between Jotnar, thurs, risi, troll, and giant has actively reinforced a misrepresentation of the material[30] in removing significant distinctions that add a cultural nuance to the Jotnar and their counterparts.

---

26 Maria Kvilhaug, The Maiden with the Mead (Norway: University of Oslo, 2004), 46.

27 "The Giants, or Jotuns, were also known by the names Thursar (þursar), Rime-Thursar (hrimþursar), Ettins (riser), Cliff-Ettins (bergrisar) and Trolls (troll); they persisted in the most evil courses." Spelling taken from the source: Peter Andreas Munch, Norse Mythology. Legends of Gods and Heroes, trans. Sigurd Bernhard Hustvedt (New York: The American-Scandinavian Foundation, 1926), 2.

28 Ármann Jakobsson, 'The Trollish Acts of Þorgrímr the Witch: The Meanings of Troll and Ergi in Medieval Iceland', Saga-Book, 32 (2008), 44. Also in Skáldskaparsmál, "Did Thor achieve any greater exploit in his dealings with trolls?" Faulkes, Edda, 81. & Katja Schulz, Riesen: Von Wissenshütern und Wildnisbewohnern in Edda und Saga. Skandinavistische Arbeiten 20. Heidelberg: Winter (2004), 24-49.

29 Kvilhaug, The Maiden with the Mead, 48.

30 Tom Grant, "A Problem of Giant Proportions: Distinguishing Risar and Jötnar in old Icelandic saga material", in Gripla 30 (2019), 80.

Within this, *Risar* are often described in such terms as to satisfy the translation of 'giants', alongside a non-Scandinavian, alien, origin that separates them from the Jotnar as well.[31] While it's not particularly suitable to use these terms interchangeably as it conjures images and allusions that are not 'true' to the Jotnar's characterisation and appearance, it's become so commonplace it seems easier to continue with that convention here.

It's also not accurate to refer to them as being exclusively *'Frost Giants'* [*hrímþurs*, 'frost-Thurs'] which has become widespread in modern literature, in part due to pop culture, though is used historically on occasion to describe specific Jotnar.

As a non-Valkyrie example, Angrboda is often referred to as a 'troll-woman' across the Eddic material. In *Gylfaginning* [Beguiling of Gylfi], Snorri writes: "A witch dwells to the east of Miðgarðr, in the forest called Ironwood: in that wood dwell the troll-women, who are known as Ironwood-Women (*Iárnvidjur*)".

This aligns with verse 40 in the Völuspá [Voluspa/ Seeress' Prophecy]:

"The giantess old | in Ironwood sat,
In the east, and bore | the brood of Fenrir;
Among these one | in monster's guise
Was soon to steal | the sun from the sky".[32]

Troll-women were seen as possessing magic, ostensibly not of the Aesir or Vanir, and existing in spaces outside of civilisation centres. There's much scholarly discussion[33] on whether these troll-women can be seen as a mythological representation of the attitudes surrounding the Sámi and their culture, a touchstone that the people of the time would have recognised.

---

31 Grant, "A Problem of Giant Proportions", 86. Where giant beings are encountered outside of a strictly Scandinavian setting, we see an increase in the use of the term Risi and Risar. Grant spotlights that Geoffrey of Monmouth's Historia regum Britanniae describes Risar as inhabiting Cornwall – most obviously, the gigantic figure of Goemagog. Ibid, 89.

32 Henry Adams Bellows, The Poetic Edda: The Mythological Poems (Garden City, New York: Dover Publications, 2004), 18. It's not explicitly stated that this is Angrboda, but the similarities in terms of location and description certainly lend to that conclusion.

33 Arwen Thysse, Men and Trolls: A Discussion of Race and the Depiction of the Sámi in the Hrafnistumannasögur (Edmonton, Canada: Scandinavian-Canadian Studies, 2022) https://doi.org/10.29173/scancan221- outlines the various depictions and similarities across a variety of Nordic sources.

For the sake of this book, we'll be classifying them through the criteria shared and deliberated above. This is mostly due to, again, an effort to not incorrectly represent the nature of the beings we are discussing. As one example among many, we have Sigrún called a "troll-woman", but she's presumably not part of any representation of Sámi culture being the daughter of Högni [Hogni], a noted Scandinavian king.

However, it may be useful to consider that potential origination when it comes to rationalising the differences between the Aesir, Vanir and anyone that falls outside of those groups as akin to the Nordic peoples and their relationship with the Sámi. Across time and geography, there was peaceful co-existence and there was incredible hostility. It was not one thing entirely, or the other.

The Jotnar, then, are the unusual, the supernatural, the other, and the wild, contrasting with the established 'norms' of the worlds of Gods and men.[34] They often possess unusual size, or strength,[35] or ability, or monstrous visage that differentiates them from the Aesir and Vanir, but at times, the definition of 'Jotnar' or 'Jotunn' is essentially redundant and indistinguishable from that of the other Gods, such as we see with Gerdr and Skadi.

That's also not to overlook the themes of 'domestication' that persevere through these examples and through the Valkyries themselves. A requirement to put aside wildness to be integrated and accepted into the fold. This 'otherness' presents an innate uncertainty that also colours the greater perspective on the use of magic – a practice that appears to originate outside of the Aesir - alongside the "mysteries of spirituality",[36] a connection to the otherworld and the supernatural.

---

34 John Mckinnell, Meeting the other in Norse myth and legend (Woodbridge, Suffolk: D.S. Brewer, 2005), 4.

35 Faulkes, Edda, 49. The giantess Hyrrokkin possesses strength that outmatches all of the Aesir when she pushes Baldr's funeral boat where they could not, and "all the lands quaked."

36 Ceilidh Elisabeth Burdick, Women of Fate in the Viking Age: Völur, Valkyries, and the Angel of Death (Ma thesis., University of Oslo, 2022), 3.

There's also an element to all of these beings – Aesir, Vanir, Jotunn, Valkyrie – that presents itself as diminishing over time. A gradual stripping away of grandiosity, a stripping away of the mythological and fantastical to better fit the perspective and expectations of the changing audience. The Jotnar, Valkyrie and nebulous 'troll', the wildest of these designations, being the most at the mercy of this degradation.

> Troll: [(in folklore) an ugly creature depicted as either a giant or a dwarf]

Fullvio Ferrari, writing in analysis of *Qrvar-Odds Saga*, states, "The malignant and ugly giants whom Oddr fights against.... Are the same grotesque trolls, deprived of any primeval, mythological greatness, that we find acting in many sagas – especially in *fornaldarsögur* [Ancient Saga], but not only in them – and in folk tales".[37]

For the sake of this argument and the book as a whole, the Valkyries are most often alluded to as akin to Goddesses, but these instances frequently go hand in hand with imagery and descriptions of troll-women and giantesses. They are not, even when given mortal origins, just or simply human. This marks them as fundamentally not synonymous with the 'Shield-Maiden', who fulfil all the criteria and behaviours of 'human' through birth, heritage and, crucially, an absence of supernatural or otherworldly power.

There is one example of a stated Valkyrie – though notably a mortal-born Valkyrie – calling herself a Shield-Maiden: Byrnhildr within *Völsunga saga* [Saga of the Volsungs].

"The day we wed would be our happiest', he said.

"'We're not fated to share our lives together', Brynhild replied. 'I am a shield-maiden, wearing a helmet along with warrior-kings. I help them and I don't find battle distasteful.'"[38]

---

37 Fulvio Ferrari, "Gods, Warlocks and Monsters in Gods, Warlocks and Monsters in Örvar-Odds saga", The Fantastic in Old Norse/Icelandic Literature: Sagas and the British Isles; Preprint Papers of The 13th International Saga Conference; Durham and York, 6th-12th August, 2006, ed. by John McKinnell, David Ashurst and Donata Kick (Durham: The Centre for Medieval and Renaissance Studies, Durham University, 2006), 242.

38 The Saga of the Volsungs, trans. R.G. Finch (Nelson, 1965), 43.

It's a brief reference, Brynhildr is another Valkyrie-figure appearing to be knowledgeable in matters of fate. Brynhildr seems certain here that she is in control of her own fate because of her choices. She cannot be wed, because she has chosen to be a Shield-Maiden.

As highlighted by **Judith Jesch** through **Agneta Ney's** work,[39] it is likely Brynhildr identifies herself as a Shield-Maiden –a label with significant cultural weight - to heighten the later contrast to her metamorphosis into the "courtly maiden engaged in needlework".[40]

All in all, this courtly maiden would have been far more accepted than Byrnhildr's self-described role of Shield-Maiden, which would have been seen as controversial to thirteenth century society. In the above quote, Brynhildr distances herself from her perceived 'womanly duties' by refusing to marry a suitable partner, as she would rather fight in battle. There's a lack of charity coming through with the word choice that would, we can imagine, have been met with disapproval by audiences at the time.

This also puts aside that Brynhildr is explicitly referred to as a former Valkyrie, and she is the only Valkyrie - former or otherwise – that refers to herself as a Shield-Maiden, something entirely human, and stripped of her prior power. With the mortal-born Brynhildr as a shining example, I hold the firm position that the Valkyries were some of the first beings to undergo euhemerism – that is to say, that they were the first causalities of the ante-conversion efforts to make the Nordic Gods and deities more human and mortal.

> Euhemerism is a theory in mythology that states that gods were originally people who were deified for their benefits to humanity

This effort was only exacerbated and solidified in post-conversion writings. Before we had Odin reduced to that of a simple Byzantine wizard given God-like status, we have a well-established tradition of the Valkyries being born to mortal fathers and mothers, though still possessing qualities that would justify their categorisation as 'other'. They are human, then, by birth alone.

---

39 Agneta Ney, "Genus och ideologi i Völsunga saga", Fornaldarsagornas struktur och ideologi, ed. by Ármann Jakobsson, Annette Lassen and Agneta Ney (Uppsala, Uppsala universitet, 2003), 118-20.

40 Jesch, Women, War and Words: a Verbal Archaeology of Shield-maidens, 132.

Imagine an environment that featured powerful feminine figures that ruled over the battlefield. These feminine figures were old, ancient even, but endured still. With the arrival of the written word across the Germanic world came a greater and greater push towards stripping these feminine beings from the source of their power. First, they were assigned a role that made them subservient to another, a satirical piece provided inspiration for others to give them a new role of 'Mead Maiden', then they were made mortal born. Rules were ascribed for them to obey.

Their power became conditional, their appearances described in words tainted with derision. They became fragmented, and the pieces scattered into whatever persevering traditions remained, whether that be a supernatural spirit, or a mortal Shield-Maiden made mythological over time.

You need not imagine; this is the story of the Nordic Valkyrie. A figure with origins no doubt older than Valhalla and the *Einherjar*, but who has become defined by these newer trappings, adornments, and titles. Despite being newer additions, they have dramatically reinvented the Valkyrie over time, greatly contributing to the form she has today.

There's certainly an argument to be made that these additions were vital to her survival in an environment that was becoming less tolerant of feminine power. If period writers hadn't been so enamoured with the past, if they weren't trying to incorporate these traditional figures into their work in a form that was acceptable to the changing culture,[41] if they weren't trying to reconcile the new religion with the old ways... we may not have them at all.

Ultimately, the goal with my greater body of work is to promote further discussion of the Valkyries as we continue to develop our understanding of the Viking Age and early medieval period. We should challenge long held ideas and put forward new perspectives that fall more in line with the latest findings, research and conversations.

This book aims to re-empower the Valkyries away from the labels that are so often attributed to them. These descriptors – servant, minor wight, fragment of the pluralistic soul – are, in my view, incorrect or at the very least, incredibly reductive. They have been used as a bludgeoning tool to dissuade further conversation and to perpetuate misconception.

---

41 Stephen Pollington, Woden, A Historical Companion (London: Uppsala Books, 2024), 390.

Through this revaluation I also want to lower the barriers to entry and invite further discussion. We should question the groundwork for what has been done before, to invite others to the table, and to share ideas to better enrich the academic and Pagan landscapes.

The Last Century and Beyond
A History of Misconception and Bias

If I'm to put forward an altogether diverging perspective of the Valkyries within this book, it's important to examine how they have been perceived over the last century within academia and popular thought. Many of the misconceptions of the Valkyries today stem from works written in the early to mid-twentieth century, and unfortunately remain very persistent in scholarly works and pop-culture. The latter presents a powerful vehicle for propagation among audiences, which in turn feeds into the misinformation cycle.

Guerber's *Myths of the Norsemen* is an influential work dating from 1908, but it's clear from the outset that she herself was far from unbiased in her representation of various deities. Loki is described as "a god of evil",[42] and Ran is as "cruel, greedy and insatiable as her husband."[43] While Hel, Jormungandr and Fenrir are "emblems of pain, sin, and death."[44] Recent re-printings have pushed this book as a source of trusted information for Heathens, which is problematic, steeped as it is in post-Victorian romanticism and Christian values that would not be emblematic of Viking Age beliefs.

The pages dedicated to the Valkyries are riddled with statements made without referencing sources, and so we have the maidens described as "immortal and invulnerable as long as they implicitly obeyed [Odin] and remained virgins".[45] We have the chosen slain receiving "the Valkyrs' kiss of death."[46] They are "young and beautiful, with dazzling white arms and flowing golden hair."[47]

---

42 H.A. Guerber, Myths of the Norsemen (Loki Publishing, 2013), 154. While the work was originally printed in 1908, I primarily utilised a 2013 printing. I compared the wording to earlier printings and found no discrepancies.

43 Ibid, 159.

44 Ibid, 154. This is directly following Julia Clinton Jones: "Loki, like Lucifer fallen from above.... Parent of the Serpent, the Wolf and Hela – Sin, Pain, and Death". J. C. Jones, Valhalla: The Myths of Norseland; a Saga in Twelve Parts (New York: R. Worthington, 1880), 17.

45 Ibid, 146.

46 Ibid.

47 While the Valkyries are often associated with 'bright or fair skin', we rarely get details on hair colour and clothing. In Hrafnsmal we have a description of a "white, bright-haired girl", but that's one of the few descriptions we have that aligns with the description given here.

Their horses were "personification of the clouds....Held in high honour and regard, for the people ascribed to their beneficent influence much of the fruitfulness of the earth, the sweetness of dale and mountain slope, the glory of the pines, and the nourishment of the meadow-land."[48] These words paint a pretty, appealing picture, but much of this cannot be concluded, inferred or found in the literature or archaeology of the early medieval and late Iron Age period. Of course, Guerber is far from alone in this framing and approach of the Nordic deities, Eddas and sagas.

Another prominent misconception lies in the Valkyries' parentage, namely that they are frequently described wholesale as the "daughters of Odin."[49] This is untrue and is only found[50] in **Richard Wagner's** *Der Ring des Nibelungen*, with the Valkyrie Brünnhilde, inspired by the Nordic Brynhildr, reimagined as Wotan's [Odin's] daughter.

It's also here that we first encounter the idea that the Valkyries were given invulnerability and immortality by Odin, with one caveat: they remain virgins. Wagner's work was predominantly based on the thirteenth century *Nibelungenlied*, though here the character of 'Brünhild' [or Prünhilt] is not described as a Valkyrie or in words that would otherwise suggest that role, but as the Queen of Iceland who has "great strength". She loses this prestigious strength upon losing her virginity, with the image made more complete by the theft of her golden ring and belt by Sivrit.[51]

---

48 Guerber, Myths of the Norsemen, 146.

49 There are numerous instances of this being quoted, but as one example, "In Norse Mythology, daughters of the principal god Odin, often called Odin's maidens, were called the Valkyries". The version of the entry dedicated to 'Scholars' omits this detail. "Valkyries," Britannica Kids, accessed November 18, 2023, https://kids.britannica.com/students/article/Valkyries/313973

50 A note should be made here that Lee Hollander translates a section of Viga-Glums saga with the kenning "Oðinn's daughter" to describe the mountainous hamingja-woman Glum witnesses in a dream. The verse is absent in other translations. See Appendix A for that verse

51 The Nibelungenlied; The Lay of the Nibelungs, trans. Cyril Edwards (Oxford World Classics, Oxford University Press, 2010), 65. The entire event is problematic by modern standards.

This situation strongly evokes the classical story of Heracles and Hippolyta, with the latter possessing a "girdle" that granted her superhuman strength that the former was tasked with acquiring. Wagner incorporates these elements, alongside *Völsunga saga* [Saga of the Volsungs], into *Der Ring des Nibelungen*, creating his character of Brünnhilde, a Valkyrie who loses her immortality and power by defying her father [Wotan/Odin] to save Siegfried's father, Sigmund. There's a well-documented and persistent theme across these stories of the feminine figure being depowered and stripped of her strength out of love or from trickery and deceit.

Equally, as Brünhild is better identified as akin to an Icelandic Hippolyta, and not in terms of being a Valkyrie or with any of the roles and duties of the Valkyrie, I won't be touching on the *Nibelungenlied* in more detail than is presented here.

The Valkyries, as a whole, are depicted as obedient and subservient to the king of the Gods, with Brünnhilde being the leader among them. Much here is now presented as archetypal of the Viking Age Valkyrie, rather than an invention or adaptation of a later time. Moving a few years further into the nineteenth century, Bulfinch's Mythology once again repeats the notion that the Valkyries are all virgins by nature and definition.

"The Valkyrie are warlike virgins, mounted upon horses and armed with helmets and spears. Odin, who is desirous to collect a great many heroes in Valhalla to be able to meet the giants in a day when the final contest must come, sends down to every battle–field to make choice of those who shall be slain."[52]

We can presume that **Thomas Bulfinch** was more familiar here with Wagner than the Eddas and sagas, which again, contains no such explicit detail. The focus on the Valkyries' virginal status, or loss of virginity, is a trend that has endured in the decades since, lending itself to proclamations of promiscuity and sexual activity. I have seen declarations on social media that the Valkyries are primarily "Goddesses of Promiscuity", alongside confident descriptions of engaging in sexual intercourse with the *Einherjar*, or Odin, in Valhalla.

---

52 Thomas Bulfinch, Bulfinch's Mythology: The Age of Fable or Stories of Gods and Heroes (Boston: Sanborn, Carter, and Bazin, 1855), 180.

Neither statement correlates with period literature and seems entirely based on works spun out from the Wagnerian image of the Valkyrie into modern fiction.[53] Instead, within the literature, there exists a trend for the Valkyrie figure to be uninterested in men, resistant to attempts towards domestication or social normative behaviour. Indeed, in what is agreed to be her first surviving appearance: "The valkyrja thought herself wise, [the] pleasures of men are not so to the flashing-eyed [one], who knew the language of birds."[54]

The "Valkyrie as a love interest" archetype appears within the later heroic sagas and was not characteristic of her earliest attestations. In other ways, Wagner's perspective on the material endures in books throughout the twentieth century, as can be seen in Guerber's book, but in others too. **Padraic Colum's** 1920 work, *The Children of Odin*, utilises Wagner's interpretations throughout.

"Youngest of all the battle-maidens was Brynhild. Nevertheless, to her Odin All-Father has shown more of the Runes of Wisdom that he had shown to any of her sisters."[55] In *Völsunga saga* [Saga of the Volsungs], Brynhildr speaks to Sigurd about runes, but there's no indication that Brynhildr is particularly exceptional compared to her Valkyrie sisters. Sigrdrifa expresses a similar expertise within *Sigrdrífumál* [The Lay of Sigrdrifa]. Brynhildr's apparent exceptionality exists only in Wagner's material.

Like much of the work done in this period, there's a lack of language that hedges descriptions and points delivered. Statements are made as though undisputed fact, alongside flowery additions that create an evocative image of the Gods but remain, largely, inventions of the author. Interestingly, many of the additions seen in Guerber's book seem to originate from J.C. Jones' 1880 piece, *Valhalla: The Myths of Norseland; A Saga, in Twelve Parts*, which is far from an academic work.

---

53 Needless to say, there's a staggering amount of romantic fiction based around Valkyries and their 'chosen warriors'.

54 Hrafnsmal 2. Translation by Luke John Murphy. Murphy, Herjans Dísir, 129.

55 Padraic Colum, The Children of Odin (New York: Macmillan, 1920), 177.

Not to mention steeped in the sort of Nordicist language one would expect from a work published amid the Germanic romanticist movement. The preface opens with a lament that the English-speaking world has been enamoured by classical antiquity rather than the "far purer and truer religion of the North".[56]

Otherwise, Guerber seems influenced from later folkloric additions, with little distinction on the 'true' myths of the Norseman, or rather, information solely drawing from Eddic sources. With the ever-present understanding that we can conclude relatively little about actual Viking Age beliefs and practices, outside of an image of fluidity and inconsistency. Before we go too far down this road, I want to emphasise that I have no issue with fictional retellings or additions, only that those additions should be clarified from the outset lest they improperly influence things for decades to come.

As it is, modern parties are faced with the reality of having to wade through years of such material looking for the slither of historical attestation. This practice has muddied the waters immeasurably for those wanting to base their religious practice in firm foundations, or more commonly, students of history eager for accuracy.

Regarding common misconceptions, we should also touch on the iconography of a winged Valkyrie. Though modern depictions of Valkyries are often, if not always, winged, this is drawn from inference, with no explicit attestations of the sort. We are told frequently that the Valkyries "fly overhead", for example, but no descriptions of *how* they flew overhead.

When the Gods fly they take on animal forms, or otherwise utilise animals that apparently possess the power of flight. Of the latter, the most well-known example lies in Thor's chariot pulled by the goats Tanngrisnir and Tanngnjostr,[57] with the assumption that the magic lies in the animals themselves, not the chariot. As the Valkyries are often described as riding various mounts, the assumption is then made that they are riding on *flying* mounts. If we imagine that the Valkyrie could fly on wings, it was in the form of a swan, as I will discuss in later chapters.

---

56 Jones, Valhalla: The Myths of Norseland, 7.
57 Gylfaginning, chapter 21. Faulkes, Edda, 22.

The image of the protective, winged Valkyrie seamlessly fits into the mould of the Christian 'Guardian Angel' archetype, which is likely an inspiration for that continued imagery. That being said, I am personally not opposed to the winged depiction of the Valkyrie as, again, we do not have any descriptions that explicitly deny that interpretation. It can be a useful sort of pictorial shorthand to denote a Valkyrie from the mortal Shield-Maiden. Within my own artwork I have depicted the Valkyrie as being winged.

Like much in this period, classical and Christian influences had a large role in skewing the image of the 'old ways' towards elements that could be more easily synchronised, when needed. The Valkyries have been at the mercy of this influence, partnered with the biases of predominantly masculine writers, and moulded to become whatever was required of them in the centuries after conversion. Wagner, of course, being the most obvious example, but far, *far* from the only example. I will break down these areas of potential biases below.

Modern academia has often dismissed further discussion of the Valkyries on a platform defined by a refusal, either consciously or unconsciously, to give credibility to their existence beyond that of being, simply, skaldic tools. Despite offering one of the most thorough breakdowns of the Valkyries in terms of attestations, **Rudolf Simek** dismisses further commentary by stating that the names of Valkyries, and thus the Valkyries themselves, are used to personify the chaos of battle.[58]

Not to mention that, for reasons I will discuss in more detail, this position doesn't maintain its apparent integrity when we look at attestations of Valkyries outside of the environment of battle and war. This, as you might imagine, is not an uncommon statement in the field of research, but I would argue that by framing the narrative from a place of fiction and superstition distances the Valkyries as religious figures within the early medieval period and unnecessarily biases any further discussion to be had. More simply, if we state from the outset that the Valkyries are just skaldic tools, any further comment to the contrary is undermined and undercut. It stymies discussion.

---

58 Throughout Simek, Dictionary of Northern Mythology.

That's also where I hope to distinguish this work. I worship the Valkyries as a modern Heathen, and I'm framing my discussion from a position that, first and foremost, sees the Valkyries as real beings. This starts the conversation from a place that aligns the commentary with the beliefs of the pre-Christian people of the time, rather than working against those beliefs. Ultimately, I'm of the opinion that the dissemination of information should consider the potential influence of said information. If you present yourself as an expert or in a position of authority, as is often inferred at the publication of a book or paper, you should recognise the impact of that. Or at the very least, make some sort of comment to help the reader distinguish pure fiction from historical commentary.

That has been far from standard practice over the last one hundred years, and there may be an argument for it being unnecessary outside of academic spaces. However, as the barrier for entry can be so high for attaining academic literature and scholarly works, it becomes a valid point when we're discussing available materials for modern Heathens. With the current state of such literature being those sourced from global ecommerce sites with little in the way of vetting - at the mercy of poorly researched works and AI written materials - we're at a point of misinformation saturation.

Misinformation breeds misinformation, and clarity should be important to allow readers to individually form their own practices and opinions based on the materials accurately presented to them. Unfortunately, what is done is done on Guerber and her contemporaries' part, with misconceptions stubbornly persevering today. Although, those very same misconceptions ultimately led to the creation of this book.

The Valkyries appeared to me as a juxtaposition, at once utterly untameable in their earliest depictions, yet appearing to don the costuming of a noble servant in others. They were wild, blood-thirsty, feral and beautiful, aristocratic, restrained. They were, and in some ways still are, confusing, but forged into something multifaceted, evolving over the timeline of their attestations, through the conversion period and beyond.

In summary, the discussion on the Valkyries has been incredibly mixed over the last century and beyond, creating a distorted image that would likely look very alien to the people of the Viking Age. Few authors and academics have explored the nature of this transformation, or otherwise tackled the issue of misconception acting to warp and twist the field of view for interested parties looking to obtain information on the Valkyries within the early medieval period.

Above, sky-born stallions ride,
High over clouds, bloodfield bound,
The sound of their sundering hoof falls a war drum
Beating a march of death, bearing down
A herald for what is to come, the frenzy
The furious host, howling into the night.
The Valkyries are coming, called to war
By the clash of spear and shield.
Let free their fury, to sow strife
And claim necessity.

SOURCES

As with all material pertaining to this period of history, it's worth demarcating and analysing the sources I will be using throughout this book to lay the groundwork on potential biases and points of interest. All sources will contain bias within them as that's the nature of the historical record. No one is truly unbiased in their perspective. When we're analysing sources in the early medieval period, we're faced with an undeniable aspect of bias that manifests in a variety of ways. Nonetheless, those biases can themselves be valuable and interesting, revealing an undercurrent of social, cultural and geographical variables that might otherwise go unexamined, unnoticed and unexplored.

The nature of the Viking Age being as it is, much of what we have available to us in the modern age has been recorded hundreds of years after conversion to Christianity. As such, we can't take any representation of Heathen beliefs, society or culture at face value, and must always have the thought in mind that this record could be many times removed from context, or otherwise be framed through political and religious motivations that may, at times, be obvious, and at others not so obvious to our modern eyes. What we can do, is compare, rationalise and question the provenance of the material: who wrote it, why they wrote it, who they wrote it for, and when they wrote it.

Heathens today are aware of the Christian influence on our core texts. I think, at times, the extent of this bias can be understated as much as it can be overstated by various parties and individuals. But the truth of the matter, as bitter a pill as it is to swallow, is that we won't ever know the extent to which such perspectives influenced the historical record. Moreover, there is no centralised 'objective truth' when it comes to Heathen beliefs. It was never a cohesive whole, but rather a sporadic, unorganised, changeable set of religious behaviours and traditions that could differ dramatically from region to region and person to person.

The people of the Viking Age and prior didn't even have a name for their beliefs, only to refer to it as the 'old ways' relative to the new incoming wave of dogmatic and organised religion. The primary texts I will be referencing will be the *Poetic Edda*, the *Prose Edda*, **Saxo Grammaticus'** *Gesta Danorum* [History of the Danes], *Heimskringla*, and numerous sagas from the tenth century through to the fourteenth. I will be utilising a variety of translations to offer several approaches to the texts, alongside academic material to analyse the historical. I will also denote personal gnosis where appropriate and frame context where necessary.

The unique biases of the Eddas, *Gesta Danorum*, and *Heimskringla* are well documented at this point. **Snorri Sturluson's** motivations for composing *Heimskringla* were mostly political in nature, reaffirming the position of his political allies through his writings.[59] In his Edda, otherwise known as the *Prose Edda*, he wrote to guide others looking to write in the skaldic tradition, sharing what he knew in terms of kennings and, at that time, the stories of the old Nordic Gods.

In this, Snorri's *Skáldskaparmál* is best seen as a poetic treatise for interested parties born from the scholar's fascination with the skaldic tradition and in preserving that tradition for the future. With Snorri's Christian bias in mind, it would be wise to consider that he was working within very specific parameters. Too 'Pagan-friendly', and his work would be criticised by the Church for promoting the 'old ways'. Too much in the opposite direction, and he would dilute the topic of discussion to such a degree as to be useless.

In terms of Snorri's credentials in writing on this topic, it's important to note that he was working primarily from existing sources, such as *Eiriksmal*, material that didn't survive to the modern day, and memory. As **Anthony Faulkes** discusses, "the poems Snorri quotes and the prose stories he retells were probably all known to him from oral tradition".[60]

---

59 Sverre Bagge, Society and Politics in Snorri Sturluson's Heimskringla (Berkeley: University of California Press, 1991), 6-7. This work breaks down Heimskringla as a political piece, and an analysis of society and politics in early thirteenth century Norway and Iceland.

60 Anthony Faulkes, "The sources of Skáldskaparmál: Snorri's intellectual background", in Snorri Sturluson. Kolloquium anläßlich der 750. Wiederkehr seines Todestages. ScriptOralia volume 51, ed. by Alois Wolf (Gunter Narr Verlag, 1993), 2.

Which all add a layer of obfuscation, in their own way. Snorri certainly shouldn't be considered infallible, especially regarding the beliefs of the Viking Age people, beings that 'oppose the Gods' such as the Jotnar, or in portraying the relationship between the Gods and the Jotnar with any accuracy. These are the elements that would have been most unknown to Snorri, or we can argue, would have been the most likely to be altered to fit in line with a more Christianised 'good vs evil' dichotomy.

Especially, as **Jon Hnefill Aðalsteinsson** explains, Snorri's *Prose Edda* "contains a great deal of material that has been drawn from the world of folk belief and folk tale that existed during the first centuries after the Conversion, material that Snorri often dresses up so artistically that on the surface it has the appearance of being ancient and original."[61] Like Saxo, Snorri peppers in classical references alongside his euhemerisation of the Nordic Gods, claiming, for instance, that the devastating *Ragnarök* was actually the Trojan War.[62]

In many ways, Saxo Grammaticus presents his work in a way that is easier to highlight his biases. Saxo often utilises a euhemerised view of the material, and so we have examples such as, "at that time there was a man called Odin who was believed throughout Europe, though falsely, to be a god."[63]

Unlike Snorri, Saxo was even less incentivised to keep accuracy regarding pre-Christian religious elements, and indeed we frequently see how he alters and adapts material to fit into his personal ideological framework. This tendency towards euhemerism and demonising Pagan deities far extends beyond Saxo and Snorri, and was an early strategy employed by the Church at the time of the conversion[64] and perseveres throughout the literature.

Ultimately, where there are instances of idol parody, mockery, demonisation and euhemerism, we can safely conclude that these depictions deviate from authentic Old Norse practices and better reflect an effort of the Church to strip the divine nature of the old Nordic Gods.[65]

---

61 Jon Hnefill Aðalsteinsson, A Piece of Horse Liver: Myth, Ritual and Folklore in Old Icelandic Sources (Iceland: Haskolautgafan, 2012), 16.

62 Faulkes, Edda, 65.

63 Saxo Grammaticus, The History of the Danes, Books I – IX, trans. Peter Fisher, ed. Hilda Ellis Davidson (UK: D.S. Brewer, 2008), 25. I will be citing Fisher for this work moving forwards.

64 Jonas Wellendorf, Gods and Humans in Medieval Scandinavia: Retying the Bonds (Cambridge: Cambridge University Press, 2018), 4-5.

65 Ibid, 23-5.

Where Saxo is particularly useful is where he diverts away from obvious Christian insertions or offers brief descriptions of topics that are otherwise absent from other sources. It's clear that these aren't entirely invented by Saxo, so we can gather that he had some sort of source that hasn't survived its journey through time. In the former and in comparison to Snorri, Saxo describes Hel in a less negative light.

"First they penetrated a smoky veil of darkness, then walked along a path worn away by long ages of travellers, and glimpsed persons in rich robes and nobles dressed in purple; passing these by they eventually came upon a sunny region ...having advanced further they stumbled on a river of black-blue water...they crossed it by a bridge and saw two strongly matched armies encountering one another."[66] Interestingly, Saxo adds a detail that these armies are men who "met their death by a sword".[67]

Which is worthy of note considering the normally stated criteria for entering Hel being those who died of sickness or old age, and categorically not those who had died in combat. A similar exception is made within *Hjaðningavíg* [Battle of the Heodenings] in *Ragnarsdrápa* [Ragnar's Poem], as will be discussed.

Compare this to Snorri's allegorical description of a place defined by misery, "her dish Hunger", "her knife Famine", "her bed Sick-Bed".[68] Hel's hall is *Éljúðnir* [Eljudnir], which **Jesse Byock** translates to "sprayed with snowstorms".[69] Saxo's presentation of the underworld is one that doesn't reflect the Christian Hell, which would have been an easy and obvious insertion to make. Instead, he presents a landscape of intrigue, almost as if the character of Hading is being taken on an *Alice in Wonderland* style adventure into a place of magic and wonder.

---

66 Fisher, The History of the Danes, Books I-IX, 30-1.
67 Ibid,31.
68 All from Faulkes, Edda, 27.
69 Snorri Sturluson, The Prose Edda, trans. Jesse Byock. (London: Penguin Books Ltd, 2005), 39.

If Saxo is notable in one aspect, it is his view of women and, by extension, Goddesses, who he often reduces to "helpless princess"[70] figures or omits entirely, as is the case with Freyja. Despite that, I have opted to use the material Saxo presents regarding 'Shield-Maidens' and like figures, as he often presents the most detail, but also because – in light of the aforementioned misogyny – it's interesting that he dedicates much time to them at all in this context. Of course, these comments are always going to be skewed towards presenting an unflattering portrait of the people and societies in question, but it would equally be remiss to push those excerpts aside entirely.

When viewed together, Snorri and Saxo present a fascinating collage of the political and religious landscape of their respective focuses, even with consideration of the various biases each presents through their writings. Within these spheres lies opportunity to compare any similarities – where crossover occurs, we can conclude elements to be more reflective of Viking Age beliefs, or at the very least, born from a central source of inspiration.

The *Poetic Edda* [or Elder Edda] is often mistakenly stated as being an older source than Snorri's Edda, which is often unhelpfully referred to as the *'Younger Edda'*, due to a persevering seventeenth century misunderstanding. Namely, that an Icelandic bishop, Brynjolfur Sveinsson (1605-1675), believed that the *Codex Regius* [King's Book], in which much of the *Poetic Edda* is retrieved from, was written by Saemundr Sigfusson.[71] As this writer predates Snorri, it was widely concluded that he must have used that manuscript to compose his *Prose Edda*. This is not the conclusion made today, with many understanding that Snorri and the anonymous author(s) of the *Codex Regius* were utilising similar, if not largely the same, source materials for their respective works.[72]

---

70 To use a phrase presented in "Gesta Danorum in English Translations" by Joseph S. Hopkins, Mimisbrunnr, accessed November 27, 2023. https://shorturl.at/pVKoD. This article also frames Saxo's general approach to describing women and Goddesses well.

71 Born 1056, died 1133. There is a version of Benjamin Thorpe's translation that is entitled, "The Eldar Eddas of Saemund Sigfusson", which showcases the enduring nature of this belief into the nineteenth century.

72 Paul Acker and Carolyne Larrington, The Poetic Edda: Essays on Old Norse Mythology (New York and London: Routledge, 2002), 13.

As of writing, no conclusions have been satisfactorily met in terms of determining who composed the various poems found in the *Poetic Edda*, though we can safely conclude that it wasn't the work of one individual but many, due to stylistic variances across the poems. This, however, also presents a useful basis for comparison.

If we're to follow that the *Poetic Edda* was the work of numerous authors, then any similarities between poems – and indeed any similarity between the *Poetic Edda* and the *Prose Edda* - would reinforce the period 'accuracy' of the story and its elements. It creates a benchmark in a discussion with few such benchmarks. We simply don't have access to unbiased material, and everything we do have access to is tinted through the lens of varying perspectives and ideologies.

Saying that, no source can be stated to be entirely fabricated, but referencing earlier oral traditions or written sources, refracted and twisted though they may be in the form presented to us today. As such, every attestation of the Valkyries, every image that they are presented alongside, every kenning, every character they interact with, and every line of dialogue should be comprehensively considered within the stated period of interest.

SHIELD-MAIDENS

"There were once women in Denmark who dressed themselves like men and spent almost every minute cultivating soldiers' skills.... loathing a dainty way of living, they would harden body and mind with toil and endurance...compelling their womanish spirits to act with a virile ruthlessness."[73]

It remains a highly controversial statement to say that women were or even could be deemed warriors in the Viking Age. In any book tackling the Valkyries as a whole, it stands to reason to start in a place that anchors discussion to the human female warriors we call *Skjaldmeyjar*, Shield-Maidens. There are numerous trusted sources that claim outright that women could not be warriors in the Viking Age.[74]

Yet, we also have a consistent presentation of women warriors within the early medieval period, and indeed prior, with classical historians making mention of Germanic warrior women. It is unlikely that such a tradition would have been eliminated by the Viking Age.[75] I am ultimately of the opinion that it's still premature to make such broad stroke conclusions, especially as we're in the process of revisiting long-held academic and archaeological practices to better reflect and represent our understanding of the period.

First and foremost, if we're to look singularly at the literature, we have several prominent individuals who would fulfil the image of the 'Shield-Maiden' as it is often defined – a female warrior who is shown typically or occasionally to wear armour and exhibits a proficiency or propensity for wielding weapons. In the current environment, Lagertha would perhaps be the most immediate example in mind due to modern popular media.

---

73 Fisher, The History of the Danes, 212.

74 "War was certainly a part of Viking life, but women warriors must be classed as Viking legend." Judith Jesch, "Viking women, warriors, and Valkyries", The British Museum, published April 19, 2014. https://shorturl.at/krrsu. Similar conclusions were the default position of twentieth century works.

75 Jenny Jochens, Old Norse Images of Women (Philadelphia: University of Pennsylvania Press, 1996), 107.

"perita bellandi femina, quae virilem in virgine animum gerens, immisso humeris capillitio, prima inter promptissimos dimicabat."

"A woman skilled in warfare, who, though a maiden, fought in the front among the bravest, with the courage of a man, and her hair loose over her shoulders".[76]

It is in *Gesta Danorum* that we find this description of Lagertha, with Saxo emphasising that "though a maiden" – *despite* her womanhood or virginity – she exhibits courage and bravery befitting that of a man. This is unusual praise coming from the scholar, piquing interest and offering a thread of connectivity to other attestations of like figures, suggesting a central truth that these stories were inspired by.

Worthy of note is Saxo's use of the descriptor of "virgin", which **Dan Coultas** – and a majority of modern writers - translates to 'Maiden'. There's notable confusion around the nature of the word 'Maiden' in relation to Shield-Maidens and like figures that has, it can be soundly concluded, also influenced the discussion around the virgin status of Valkyries.

The Old Norse *mær* or the plural, *meyjar*, can be used to infer virginity as it is used to denote a 'girl' but is also used to describe daughters and young women equally. If we're to discuss this example and translate it literally, Lagertha is a warrior despite being a virgin. Here then, Saxo frames her virginity as an obstacle. Compare this to Wagner who describes the Valkyries as losing their power when their virginity is taken from them.

---

76 Translation from Dan Coultas, Perceptions of Male Queerness in Early Medieval Scandinavia (MA Diss., University of Leeds, 2023), 41.

Within kennings, we mostly have Valkyries described as 'women', rather than young virgins as can be implied with the word 'maiden,' such as we see with the kenning *"Valmeyjar"* [Carnage-Maidens/Maidens of the Slain/ Death-Maidens].[77] *"Almdrósar"*[78] [bow woman], *"Valdrósar"*[79] [Slaughter-Woman], *"vífs Mistar"*[80] [Woman of Mist]. In *Vellekla* we have both *"Valmey"*[81] [Maiden of the Slain/Maiden of Slaughter] and *"Vífs Odda"*[82] [Women of Weapon Points] used to describe a Valkyrie.

Consider also that there's a persevering theme of female sexual freedom and expression, most seen through ecstatic practices, being tied to the attainment of power and agency - even if that power and agency is viewed as deviant behaviour - in Old Norse literature[83] which seems at odds with these positions. It has long been proposed that the practice of *seiðr* may have involved sexual elements or the imitation of sexual acts over the course of the 'ceremony'.

"One might venture, however, that the seiðr ceremony imitated heterosexual intercourse where the woman played her accustomed role of receiving, not the male member, by its substitute, the staff which was always the standard equipment of the human vǫlur in charge of magic."[84] Otherwise, it is believed that the practice involved some aspect of 'receiving', being submissive, or passivity that were considered feminine qualities, the perceived antithesis of masculinity.[85]

77 Snorri refers to the 'Valmeyjar' in his Edda. Faulkes translates it to Death-Maidens. Faulkes, Edda, 118.

78 Hákonardrápa 2.

79 Hrafnsmal 4.

80 Hákonardrápa 1. Russell Poole, "Guthormr sindri, Hákonardrápa 1", in Poetry from the Kings' Sagas 1: From Mythical Times to c. 1035. Skaldic Poetry of the Scandinavian Middle Ages 1, ed. Diana Whaley (Turnhout, Belgium: Brepols, 2012), 157.

81 Vellekla 20.

82 Vellekla 7. Edith Marold, "Einarr skálaglamm Helgason, Vellekla 7", in Poetry from the Kings' Sagas 1: From Mythical Times to c. 1035. Skaldic Poetry of the Scandinavian Middle Ages 1, ed. Diana Whaley (Turnhout, Belgium: Brepols, 2012), 291

83 "Identifying the origins of seidr, a prophetic magic unique to women… accounting for the greatest source of women's power, and also providing further insight into the ways in which such power was first feared by, and then claimed by, men." Erin M. Caffey, Femininity in Medieval Scandinavia: How Paganism Forged Gender Equality (grad diss.,Winthrop University, 2023), 20.

84 Jochens, Old Norse images of women, 74.

85 Jenny Blain and Robert J. Wallis, "The 'Ergi' Seidman: Contestations of Gender, Shamanism and Sexuality in Northern Religion Past and Present", Journal of Contemporary Religion Vol 15, 3 (2000), 402-3.

In exploring *seiðr's* ties to textiles, **Leszek Gardeła** offers a simpler explanation, that *seiðr* had a connection to tasks that belonged to the domestic sphere of women,[86] though **Eldar Heide** argues that, with the extreme nature of the insult of *'ergi'*,[87] there must have been more to the practice than simply doing what was considered women's work.[88]

We may also turn then to the sexual connotations held within certain ritualistic behaviours, such as those we see in *Völsa þáttr* [Volsa Thattr / Volsi Yarn][89] and the treatment of the horse phallus as an emblem of fertility, which are quite explicit. These examples offer several rationalisations for why the practice of *seiðr* was seen as particularly effeminate and dishonourable for a man to partake in. With *seiðr* being so varied in its utility within the sagas, it's possible that all of these may have had a role to play across regions and time.

These altogether lend to the conclusion that the association of virginity with warrior women is a post-conversion cultural insertion with word choice that has influenced interpretations and translations. As will be discussed, we have Shield-Maiden figures that are decidedly not virgins. There is, of course, another interpretation here that lends itself to the suggestion that some Valkyries, at times described as uninterested in men, are lesbians or asexual, and maintain 'maidenhood' as a result, as sex without penetration was largely, if not entirely, unrecognised in medieval societies.[90]

I remain unconvinced of any implied collective 'maidenhood' possessed by the Valkyries and maintain that this would not have been an understood characteristic of their number during the Viking Age. This is a position that remains steadfast within modern academia too: **Heather O'Donoghue** dismisses the Valkyrie's virgin status as entirely born of classicisation.[91]

---

86 Leszek Gardeła, "Into Viking Minds: Reinterpreting the Staffs of Sorcery and Unravelling Seiðr," Viking and Medieval Scandinavia 4 (2008), 45–84.

87 'unmanliness' – this word will be explored more thoroughly in a later chapter.

88 Eldar Heide, "Spinning Seiðr", in Old Norse Religion in Long-Term Perspectives: Origins, Changes, and Interactions, ed. by Anders Andrén, Kristina Jennbert, and Catharina Raudvere (Lund, Sweden: Nordic Academic Press, 2004), 167.

89 A 'Yarn' here would be referring to a story/tale.

90 Judith Bennett and Ruth Karras, ed., The Oxford Handbook of Women and Gender in Medieval Europe (Oxford: Oxford University Press, 2013), 11.

91 Heather O'Donoghue, From Asgard to Valhalla. The Remarkable History of the Norse Myths (2nd Edition) (London, UK: Bloomsbury Academic, 2024), 110. "the Valkyries, classicised as virgins"

As it stands, if the assumption holds any weight at all, it is because of post-period insertions based on later interpretations of the Valkyrie as, essentially, a reward for those chosen dead who arrive in Valhalla. However, it does fall perfectly in line with the characterisation and behaviours presented in more modern writings, sanitised and pure, though sexually available and lustful. For the sake of future discussion within this work, it may be best to define 'maiden' as 'young woman' or, even more traditionally, 'woman of marriageable age'.

Unfortunately, it is highly likely that Lagertha herself was an entirely fictitious figure of folkloric origin,[92] or otherwise an amalgam of known figures at the time, either born from contemporary works or from antiquity. Moreover, Saxo never uses the term 'Shield-Maiden', but rather focuses on emphasising their womanhood, perhaps in an effort to exaggerate the divergent behaviour of the women in question rather than offer them any sort of avenues for justification by utilising a collective descriptor.[93]

This, no doubt, has influenced the framing of these women, alienating these figures as totally anomalous within Saxo's writings, rather than contributing to a larger trend. Yet, they appear frequently throughout his work regardless. In Book II of *Gesta Danorum* the character of Frothi disguises himself "as a young female warrior and went to the town as a deserter, shedding his masculine appearance and impersonating a woman".[94] This almost offhand remark adds credence to the existence of female warriors, something that wouldn't be too unusual or rare as to draw unwanted attention to Frothi in his effort to remain unnoticed.

Take also the characters of Rusla,[95] considered to be the same

---

92 Terri L. Barnes, "The Intrigue of the Female Warrior: Lagertha, Joan of Arc, and Matilda of Tuscany", Medieval Warfare (2019), 43.

93 Judith Jesch, Women in the Viking Age (Woodbridge: Boydell, 1991), 176-80.

94 Fisher, History of the Danes, 42.

95 Meaning 'Red'.

figure as Rusila within Saxo's work, and her companion, Stikla.

"After Dan, Fridlef, named 'the Swift', took power. While he was on the throne Hvirvil, lord of Oland, leagued himself with the Danes and assaulted Norway. This man by his endeavours achieved no small accession of renown, for he fought and overthrew the maid Rusila, who in her military ardour had aspired to arms, and collected manly fame from his female adversary."[96]

"In order to preserve her chastity the girl Stikla stole away from her fatherland, preferring the sphere of war to that of marriage."[97]

"-he heard that a struggle over the kingdom must occur between Olaf, king of the Thronds, and two women, Stikla and Rusila; utterly enraged at such female brashness, he went to the king unobserved and, assuming apparel which would obscure his long teeth, made an attack on the amazons.[98] Each of them was quashed and he bequeathed to twin harbours a name related to theirs."[99]

Rusla's story ends in a rather dramatic and gory manner, with Saxo taking the opportunity to frame the whole affair as a cautionary tale against women moving into masculine pursuits, delivered by way of a moral. An inevitable end to her chosen path.

"At that same time the maiden Rusila, surpassing a woman's temperament in her strenuous military activities, had had frequent clashes with her brother Thrond for the throne of Norway...she declared war on all who had given their allegiance to the Danes."
'When a messenger informed Omund of this, he selected his finest soldiers to quell the rising. But Rusila overcame them

---

96 Fisher, History of the Danes, 110.

97 Ibid, 150.

98 Not the first time Saxo's familiarity with classical antiquity becomes apparent.

99 Fisher, History of the Danes, 227.

and, waxing proud from her victory...she set her sights on nothing less than the sovereignty of Denmark.

"While his sister was steering clear of the Danes, Thrond confronted her with his troops, but suffered defeat and was robbed of his whole army.

"Rusila, however, slipped away with a small number of other vessels, her boat, rowed at high speed, furrowing the waves. While managing to evade the Danes, she ran into her brother, who cut her to pieces. Unforeseen dangers often have more power to harm us, and in many cases chance makes the evils we fear less more perilous than those we feel threatened by."[100]

Rusla's story is potentially given more depth within the Irish Annals, specifically *Cogadh Gaedhel re Gallaibh* [The War of the Gaedhil with the Gaill].[101]

"There came there also, the fleet of Oiberd and the fleet of Oduinn..... and lastly the fleet of the Inghen Ruaidh."[102]

The translator, **James Henthorn Todd**, comments, "Inghen Ruaidh: i.e. the red-haired maiden",[103] continuing:

"And assuredly the evil which Erinn had hitherto suffered was nothing compared to the evil inflicted by these parties. The entire of Mumhain, without distinction, was plundered by them, on all sides, and devastated."

What follows is a lengthy section dedicated to detailing just how devastated Mumhain became at the hands of these "furious,

---

100 All quotes from Fisher, History of the Danes, 246.

101 Also known as 'The invasions of Ireland by the Danes and other Norsemen'.

102 Cogadh Gaedhel re Gallaibh: The War of the Gaedhil with the Gaill Or, The Invasions of Ireland by the Danes and Other Norsemen, trans. James Henthorn Todd (London: Longmans, Green, Reader, and Dyer, 1867), 41.

103 Ibid.

ferocious, pagan, ruthless, wrathful people".[104] It seems this 'red maiden' was every bit as ruthless as her compatriots, murdering without discrimination, and creating fortresses and landing ports so that "there was no place in Erinn without numerous fleets of Danes and pirates."[105]

Alexander Brugge argues that the famed "inghen ruadh" [Red Maiden/Woman] described here is a distortion of the original text and is instead describing the actions of Rollo, the conqueror of Normandy. Brugge comments that Rollo's "Anglo-Saxon name was Rodla. Because of the ending -a this name has been taken as feminine, and the Irish have transformed the celebrated hero into a heroine."[106]

If we put this possibility aside, Rusla is a Shield-Maiden figure that appears in two very different sources, a powerful statement to her potential existence, in one form or another. Another familiar figure to modern audiences would be Freydis Eiriksdottir, the daughter of Eirik the Red, sister to Leif Eiriksson, and an early colonist of North America, if we're to accept the narrative presented by the *Vinland Sagas*. Despite often being included in the discussion of Shield-Maiden figures in the literature,[107] Freydis arguably doesn't fulfil the criteria of that description.

She is never stated to be proficient in handling weaponry, only killing an unarmed woman when no other would act. Putting aside one event in which she acts in a fearless manner, Freydis is otherwise shown to use underhanded tactics, and often incites others to do 'her dirty work' through threats of divorce or discontent. Another woman who is commonly stated to fulfil the criteria of the Shield-Maiden archetype, though displays behaviours similar to Freydis, is Audr Ketilsdottir.

She does, however, seem to enjoy bucking social convention and challenging the boundaries of acceptable behaviour. Within

---

104 Henthorn Todd, Cogadh Gaedhel re Gallaibh: The War of the Gaedhil with the Gaill Or, The Invasions of Ireland by the Danes and Other Norsemen, 43.

105 Ibid, 41.

106 Duald MacFirbis, "On the Fomorians and the Norsemen, trans. Alexander Brugge (Norway: J. C. Gundersens bogtrykkeri, 1966), 21 -2.

107 Leszek Gardeła, Women and Weapons in the Viking World: Amazons of the North (Oxford: Oxbow Books, 2021), 30.

Laxdæla saga [The Saga of the People of Laxárdalur] she is depicted as a Heathen woman, while other sagas in which Audr appears go to great lengths to emphasise her pious Christian nature. In the former, she dons the mask of reprobate, commonly causing controversy within her small world. The reason?

She dares to wear breeches, long leggings and a codpiece! Her husband, Thordr [Þórðr] doesn't appear to notice until an object of his affection, Gudrun, comments negatively on his wife's appearance. Anticipating an opportunity, he responds in a manner that offers insight into the perceived boundaries of gender expression of the time:

> "If women go about dressed as men, they invite the same treatment as do men who wear shirts cut so low that the nipples of the breast may be seen – both are grounds for divorce."[108]

Thordr promptly asks for a divorce on these grounds and proceeds to marry Gudrun. In doing so, Audr realises that her choice of clothing had been a mere excuse for his actions, and not a driving motivator. In anger, she decides to arm herself.

> "She drew her short-sword and struck him with a great wound on his right arm which cut across both breasts. She struck with such force that the sword lodged in the wood of the bed. Auðr then returned to her horse, sprang into the saddle and rode home. Roused by the attack, Þórðr tried to get to his feet, but was weakened by the wound and loss of blood."[109]

It may be expected that Audr would be seen as the antagonistic force in this situation, but the reaction of the greater community suggests a belief that she was justified in her actions, and indeed Thordr doesn't seek further compensation considering his injury. **Leszek Gardeła** suggests that when Audr wields a sword she, in essence, becomes a man[110] and acts in such a way as to effeminate her husband.

Acting in a masculine manner, she is not shamed, but Thordr – acting in the submissive woman's role – is. There was evidently

---

108 Translation by Leszek Gardeła in Gardeła, *Women and Weapons in the Viking World: Amazons of the North*, 32.
109 Ibid.
110 Ibid.

some cultural nuance in women embodying masculine features, in wielding weaponry, enacting revenge for lost honour, and holding power over another. As will be discussed in more detail in later chapters, the practice of magic - most commonly *seiðr* – is also associated with gender-role-breaking behaviours across masculine and feminine practitioners equally. In *Ljósvetninga saga*, a sorceress named Thorhildr [Þórhildur] dons breeches and a helmet while wielding an axe to perform magic.

There's something inherently liminal in this, and similar, presentations of magic that remain outside of the definitions of 'Shield-Maiden' though suggest a sort of liminality to those that do meet the definition outlined. They are unusual, and often co-exist in stories that incorporate supernatural elements. Where magic and the supernatural exists, so too do examples of breaking established gender boundaries.

Chief among those instances is Hervor Bjarmarsdottir, a key figure of *Hervarar saga ok Heiðreks* [The Saga of Hervor and Heidrek]. Within this saga is the poem *Hervararkviða* [The Lay of Hervor, though often published under 'The Waking of Angantyr'][111] in which Hervor speaks to her deceased father in order to lay claim to his cursed sword Tyrfingr. Hervor is also noteworthy for other examples of gender nonconformity, donning the masculine name of Hervard and 'gender appropriate' clothing over the course of the saga.

There is much debate on whether this is indicative of Hervor/Hervard being better identified as transgender to modern audiences, whether this falls into a motif of highlighting the figure's troublemaking and convention-breaking behaviour,[112] or otherwise being an example of a feminine figure finding more comfort or preference in being seen as masculine to avoid derision, or for concerns of safety.[113]

Of course, the 'truth' could also sit somewhere in between, or be another reason entirely. There is also a suggestion that Hervor/

---

111 Which is often included in various compiled works of the Poetic Edda.

112 Lena Norrman, Woman or Warrior? The Construction of Gender in Old Norse Myth, 11th International Saga Conference (2000), 377.

113 John McKinnell, "The Trouble with Father: Hervararkviða and the Adaptation of Traditional Story-Patterns", Essays on Eddic Poetry, ed. by Donata Kick and John D. Shafer (Toronto: University of Toronto Press, 2014), 301.

Hervard's cross-dressing is as an aspect of perceived social function, with them becoming, in essence, a "functional son" to lay claim to their inheritance and heritage. "So powerful is the principle of male inheritance that when it necessarily passes through a female, she must become, in legend if not in life, a 'functional son.'"[114]

Though others state that such justification falls apart once we examine the supernatural elements, with no need for assuming a masculine identity or attire when confronted with beings and forces that sit outside of social convention.[115] Indeed, Hervor drops the identity of Hervard when speaking to her father. Ultimately, as with much in the study of early medieval literature, the answer would seem to lie entirely in personal interpretation in the absence of further cultural context.

Throughout the saga, Hervor/Hervard remains in a place of liminality, not quite fully moving to the masculine identity, but also remaining resistant to fulfilling the accepted roles of womanhood in contemporary society. At the end of the saga there is an apparent acceptance of 'female arts', with Hervor adopting embroidery. This acceptance is certainly reminiscent of a sort of concession on Hervor/Hervard's side, the empowerment of the earlier actions giving way to a return to perceived social acceptance. Though **Lena Norrman** suggests a more innocuous reading, that Hervor becomes "weary of being out with a band of Vikings"[116], a decision driven by agency rather than defeat.

Crucially, Hervor/Hervard contrasts with the Valkyries we'll be moving on to discuss as the latter never adopts masculine identities or exhibits preferences towards another gender identity or descriptor other than 'woman'. There is an understanding that they are capable warriors, not despite of their womanhood, but effortlessly in tandem with it. Made magnified and noteworthy because of their perceived gender and all the associations it would have held within the period.

---

114 Carol J. Clover, "Maiden Warriors and Other Sons", Journal of English and Germanic Philology 85, 1 (1986), 39.

115 Miriam Mayburd, "Helzt þóttumk nú heima í millim..." A reassessment of Hervör in light of seiðr's supernatural gender dynamics', Arkiv för nordisk filologi, Vol 129 (2014), 125.

116 Norrman, Woman or Warrior?, 381.

Hervor's Death painted by Peter Nicolai Arbo.
[Public Domain]

Less ambiguous in this conversation is Hervor's granddaughter, also called Hervor, who also appears within *Hervarar saga ok Heiðreks.*

"On the plains stood a fair stronghold, over which Hervör, the sister of Hlöd and Angantyr, had command, together with Ormar her foster father; they were set there to defend the land against the army of the Huns, and they had a strong garrison.
  One morning at sunrise Hervör stood on a watchtower above the fortress-gate, and she saw a great cloud of dust from horses' hooves rising southwards towards the forest... Hervör went down swiftly and called her trumpeter, and ordered him to blow a summons to the host: and then she said, 'Take you weapons and make ready for battle; but do you, Ormar, ride to meet the Huns, and challenge them to battle before the south fate of the stronghold.'"[117]

---

117 Christopher Tolkien, The Saga of King Heidrek the Wise (London: Thomas Nelson and Sons Ltd, 1960), 52-3. This is a translation of a saga dated to the thirteenth century from several separate manuscripts of varying provenance.

Upon Ormar's return: "Hervör was ready, and all her army. They rode out of the stronghold with all the garrison to meet the Huns; and there a most mighty battle arose. But since the Huns had by far the larger army the slaughter became heavier in Hervör's host; and at last Hervör fell, and a great company around her."[118]

Hervor presents one of the least debated 'Shield-Maiden' figures in the literature. She is a commander and leader on the battlefield, with notable authority. She shows great bravery in face of the "far.. larger army", though is eventually overwhelmed by it. There is no controversy around that leadership, lacking the derogatory tone that Saxo and his peers adopt when describing other feminine warriors of the type. It is depicted as a matter of fact and without further comment. Hervor is also unmarried, which no doubt had an influence on the tone with which she is depicted here.

There's freedom and greater social acceptance in feminine figures without partners acting in more masculine roles. We've already established that there was flexibility in women moving into masculine roles than the reverse, as **Neil Price** explains: "Women could, on occasion, take on the social roles of men....For men, there was no such blurring of boundaries, and it was not condoned for a man to take on any aspect of women's lives and duties."[119] Women without partners would not be at risk of emasculating another due to their actions, so there was presumably more acceptance for those behaviours than those conducted by their married counterparts.

---

118 Ibid, 53.
119 Neil Price, The Children of Ash & Elm. A History of the Vikings (UK: Penguin Random House, 2020), 172.

"Interestingly, however, Þorhildr's case, like those of Auðr or Freydis, involves the absence of a husband.[120] Þorhildr is a widow, Audr is divorced, and Freydis appears to be contemplating divorce. Without a husband, the woman can no longer be labeled as a wife, with all the subordinating baggage that attends the designation. Through adoption of male dress, the woman, in effect, appropriates to herself the power of the dominant stratum while also displacing her own sexual identity, with the effect that she is free to act in ways never open to her as a woman. The absence of the husband, then, removes the limitations imposed by male control and thus permits the reassignment of female identity."[121]

Grave Goods and Archaeology

Judith Jesch reasoned "that the very few women buried with weapons were warrior women in life seems the least likely explanation of all."[122] While I understand the need to hedge statements in light of the sheer weight of the total archaeological work done in this area, I would disagree slightly here with the noted academic Jesch, in that the attitudes and 'best practices' of the past have unnecessarily biased our understanding of the role of women in the Viking age.

We simply don't know how, for lack of a better word, damaging that assuming the sex of skeletal remains because of grave goods has been to our understanding of the period at this moment in time. We're faced with an unknown quantity of discovered – and undiscovered – grave sites that potentially contain female remains alongside armour or weaponry.

---

120 Note the other figures discussed within this chapter and the absence of relationships with men.

121 Kirsten Wolf, Transvestism in the Sagas of the Icelanders (Ontario: University of Manitoba, 1997), 680.

122 Judith Jesch, The Viking Diaspora (UK: Routledge, 2015), 107. Earlier in this work, on page 104, Jesch does state that "the people in the Viking Age and its aftermath were perfectly capable of imagining women as warriors...doubtless it did occur in real life...but the strong emphasis on gender distinctions in Viking Age society ... suggests it did not happen very often." The excerpt quoted in the text is her sceptical, hedged concluding remark.

Of course, we have the additional consideration of concluding whether the presence of such weaponry indicated that the person was a warrior, or not. All with the very present caveat in mind that we will likely never actually know the lives and occupations of most of those buried.

We're working with an unknown quantity on top of numerous unknown quantities. As summarised by **Marianne Moen** in 2021, "a tendency remains to rely on stereotypes of 'gender appropriate' behaviour and roles in archaeological narratives, at times not considering whether this reflects the material record.... The result of this is incomplete and potentially inaccurate depictions of the past..."[123] This is a colossal issue that we've only been working to challenge and rectify in recent history, with the image being far from complete.

In all of this ongoing discussion, I'm reminded of a conclusion drawn by **Marguerita Spence** and **Marian E. Everatt** in their 1948 work *A Short History of York*, in which the following statement is made. "In Clifford Street... have been found a variety of combs, glass beads, jet and articles of bone. These, with the stonework in the churches, some Saxon crosses, and the placenames are all that remain of York from the fifth century to 1066."[124] What was considered fact can quickly be turned on its head, and I remain resolute that the role of women in the period will undergo a similar development to that experienced by York with the Coppergate excavations. We could just be one more discovery away from a colossal paradigm shift in our understanding of the period.

The realities of living in such a world would lend itself to the conclusion that there were women trained in the art of warfare and would have some degree of ability to defend the community. The appearance of such women in the literature, with varying provenance, acts to strengthen such a statement. Surely, we cannot simply dismiss all of these instances as mere fantasy? If we're to break this down to its most basic components, we're talking about half the population never being given the freedom to fight and defend at a time when such behaviours may have been necessary for survival.

---

123 Marianne Moen and Matthew J. Walsh, "Agents of Death: Reassessing Social Agency and Gendered Narratives of Human Sacrifice in the Viking Age", Cambridge Archeological Journal (2021), 597-8.

124 Marguerita Spence and Marian E. Everatt, A Short History of York (London: A. Brown & Sons LTD, 1948), 14-15.

Special consideration should also be given to Birka grave **BJ 581**, which has been well-documented as of writing.[125] Once described as an exemplar of a male warrior grave of the tenth century, the greater landscape was flipped on its head when, in 2017, analysis of the bones discovered they belonged to a female. This warrior had been assumed male due to the nature of the grave goods – a rich gathering of weaponry and equine remains. Compare this to a statement made just a decade earlier, that such goods were a "widely recognised symbolic language of lordship, one that was unquestionably masculine."[126]

This unquestionable statement is now very much drawn into question. The legacy of **BJ 581**, rather than being unquestionable evidence for the validity of warrior women, may be that it has encapsulated the unsteady ground that defined nineteenth and twentieth century work within Viking Age archaeological pursuits.

However, a commonly stated conclusion with that grave in current discourse – that it couldn't have belonged to a warrior because of a lack of trauma to the skeletal remains – is not accurate. The skeletal remains are "too poorly preserved to allow any assessment of physical strength or battle trauma".[127] As such, it also cannot be used as a lightning rod towards any outright conclusions against the validity of female warriors in the period.

---

125 Courtesy of Charlotte Hedenstierna-Jonson et al., 'A female Viking Warrior Confirmed by Genomics', American Journal of Physical Anthropology, 164.4 (2017), 853–60.

126 Dawn Hadley, "Ethnicity and Identity in Context: The Material Culture of Scandinavian Settlement in England in the Ninth and Tenth Centuries", in Identité et ethnicité: concepts, débats historiographiques, exemples (Ve-XIIe siècles), ed. V. Gazeau and P. Badouin (Caen: Publications du Centre de Recherches Archéologiques et Historiques Médiévales, 2008), 172.

127 William Short and Reynir Óskarson, Men of Terror: A Comprehensive Analysis of Viking Combat (USA: Westholme Publishing, 2021), 191. This has also been reaffirmed by Anna Kjellström in C.M Surrisi, The Bones of Birka: Unravelling the Mystery of a Female Viking Warrior (US: Chicago Review Press, 2023), 60.

The questions remain and the pattern presented continues regardless, beyond (I would say) pure coincidence. As Moen states, "I do not believe we can continue to argue for women on the margins when faced with clear evidence … of women buried alongside men, in the same types of locations, and with the same types of material remains as well as remains of the same types of rituals."[128]

If the evidence continues to point towards a certain flexibility in gender roles, then the theory must adapt to the evidence. To remain rigid and unmoving would be to become unscientific in our collective approach, especially as the foundation for the original conclusion was based on faulty reasoning to begin with – as was the case with grave **BJ 581** and potentially many others of the sort.

Indeed, there's an argument for the warrior identity of these figures to be considered as a sort of 'third gender' both between and entirely separate from the presumed genders we've associated with them today.[129] A similar proposition has been made in regard to the practice of *seiðr*, with practitioners potentially also being classified on a third gender basis.[130] Elsewhere, this model has been criticised for reinforcing a rigid, universal binary system of gender identity.[131]

It must also be said that our understanding and perception of gender and identity today is different from the world of fifty years ago, different from the 1600s, and in turn, different from the Viking Age. As a social construct, the perception of gender is entirely at the whim of specific cultural norms and expectations.

---

128 Marianne Moen, The Gendered Landscape, A discussion on gender, status and power expressed in the Viking Age mortuary landscape (Oslo, Norway: University of Oslo, 2010), 78.

129 Kathleen M. Self, "The Valkyrie's Gender: Old Norse Shield-Maidens and Valkyries as a Third Gender", Feminist Foundations Vol. 26, No. 1 (2014), 143 -72.

130 Brit Solli, "The Norse God Odin and "Holy White Stones": A Queer Interpretation", in Facets of Archaeology: Essays in Honour of Lotte Hedeager on her 60th Birthday, ed. Konstantinos Chilidis, Julie Lund and Christopher Prescott, Oslo Archaeological Series, 10 (Oslo: Unipub, 2008), 275-89

131 Amy Jefford Franks, "Valfǫðr, Vǫlur, and Valkyrjur: Óðinn as a Queer Deity Mediating the Warrior Halls of Viking Age Scandinavia", Scandia, 2 (2019), 33.

"Gender is a multidimensional construct that refers to the different roles, responsibilities, limitations, and experiences provided to individuals based on presenting sex/gender.... these categories are social constructed...ideas about gender and culturally/temporally specific and subject to change."[132]

The structure which we use now – tending towards a flexible, fluid arrangement - would seem rather alien to our ancestors, as would their understanding seem alien to us. It's important to keep that in mind, and in not simply assuming that the long-standing European idea in the dichotomy between 'male' and 'female' was archetypal of the Viking Age. As has been discussed, women, in many ways, were given more freedom within their gender identity and expression than men.

The latter was prescribed to strict social behaviours or otherwise would be at risk of severe judgement. Masculinity seems to have been something more absolute, a measuring stick for which all male deeds and words were judged and reinforced through peers. It was to be physically strong, wilfully strong, and distinctly lacking in perceived feminine qualities and all the ways that could manifest. Without a doubt, the relatively recent past has dramatically influenced and dramatically damaged our modern perception of the period. Take an item that has become synonymous with Viking Age women: the key.

Often described as a feminine status symbol,[133] the key is often raised up as the feminine equivalent of the sword, its presence as a grave good acting as a crucial identifier of gender identity. Using **Anne-Sofie Gräslund's** 2001 work on the same subject as scaffolding to his research, **Antonio Redon** writes that "keys are almost exclusively found in female graves as women have been seen as the head of the households."[134]

132 Joy L. Johnson and Robin Repta, "Sex and Gender: Beyond the Binaries", Sociology (2012), 20-1.

133 Anne-Sofie Gräslund, "The position of Iron age Scandinavian women: Evidence from graves and rune stones", Gender and the archaeology of death, ed. Bettina Arnold and Nancy L. Wicker (Walnut Creek, CA: Altamira Press, 2001), 93.

134 Antonio Redon, Females Warriors of the Viking Age: Fact or Fiction (MA diss., Iceland: University of Iceland School of Humanities, 2017), 44.

Conversely, in a study conducted two years earlier, **Heidi Lund Berg** refutes that position, arguing that there is no correlation between gender and the presence of keys as a grave good – persuasively and conclusively arguing that keys are equally present in assumed male graves.[135]

Earlier still, **Pernille Pantmann** dismisses the association of keys to female status as a "misinterpretation...which comes from a disregard for earlier archaeological ideas and, not least, documentary sources."[136] It is possible to conclude that this association was born, like many things in this period of history, from Victorian romanticism, where keys were indicative of upper-class women and their role in managing the household, not representative of women in the Viking Age.[137]

There has been an ongoing assumption that the beliefs of the present wholly reflect the beliefs of the past, and that has influenced so much of the academic work we have available to us today. I concede that, if women could be recognised as noted warriors, they were relatively few, at least compared to their masculine counterparts. Regardless, it is fascinating that we have literary feminine entities who were seen as being significant agents on the battlefield. The above list is far from exhaustive, but merely the most obvious and distinct examples among many, many others.[138]

It is highly likely that the image of the Shield-Maiden and the Valkyrie influenced each other greatly, and perhaps if we're to discount the former entirely as fantastical, the latter eventually became the literary human Shield-Maiden due to greater and greater erosion and euhemerism. If the former existed, those human women could very well have fuelled the enduring legend of the Valkyrie, becoming the embodiments of their perceived cultural power.

---

135 Heidi Lund Berg, "'Truth' and reproduction of knowledge. Critical thoughts on the interpretation and understanding of Iron-Age keys", in Viking Worlds. Things, Spaces and Movement, ed. Marianne Hem Eriksen, Unn Pedersen, Berndt Rundberget, Irmelin Axelsen and Heidi Lund Berg (Oxford and Philadelphia: Oxbow Books, 2015), 129-31.

136 Pernille Pantmann, "The symbolism of keys in female graves on Zealand during the Viking Age", in The Iron Age on Zealand, Status and Perspectives, ed. by Linda Boye (Royal Society of Northern Antiquities, 2011), 75.

137 Nancy Marie Brown, The Real Valkyrie. The Hidden History of Viking Warrior Women (New York: St. Martin's Press, 2021), 6.

138 Nancy Marie Brown states "I can name twenty warrior women from sagas and histories, another fifty-three in poems and myths." Ibid.

At numerous instances, we're reminded that these Shield-Maiden figures were just as ruthless as their masculine counterparts, acting in ways that were not befitting of their 'womanly' nature. Ruthlessness also absolutely defines the Valkyries, as they put aside gender expectations entirely, unbound as they were and are to the world of mortal-born social convention.

THE VALKYRIE, THE CHOOSER OF THE SLAIN

*"Methought I was standing out of doors, and that I saw two
women who had a trough between them, and they took their
stations at Hrisateig and sprinkled the whole district with blood.....
Then I sung these verses--*

*The gods--methought, they swept along
Across the path of men.
the clash of swords and the javelins song
We shall hear full soon again.*

*I saw the maids of carnage stand,
In grim and vengeful mood,
As the battle raged, and they drenched the land
In slaughtered warriors blood."*[139]

Forming the foundation of this book is a question: Are the
Valkyries servants?

Within that question, there are numerous others we must
consider: Do they fulfil the characteristics of servitude in status,
behaviour and role? Are these characteristics consistent over time
and geography? Was the Valkyrie believed to only be a servant over
the Viking Age, prior and beyond, or were their notable deviations
from this image?

Whatever the answer to these questions may be, we are faced
with a landscape today that wholeheartedly frames them within this
descriptor with few deviating narratives. In pursuit of an answer to
that question, I will explore how the Valkyries have been portrayed
and perceived over the medieval period, utilising surviving literature
and archaeology as the cornerstone of that analysis.

---

[139] Chapter 21 of Víga-Glúms saga. Edmund Walker Head, The Story of
Viga-Glum (Illustrated Edition) (1866), 77-8.

In ways that will become clear, I am personally disheartened by the all-too common approach that describes the Valkyries as being only servants, acting as mindless drones of Odin to carry out his will. It's an easy trap to fall into, with scholarly works of past centuries feeding into this paradigm, forging Odin into the image of an omni-God meting out his whims through his hordes of supernaturally powered women[140] on the battlefield.

As there's little in the way of material challenging that image, it has propagated. Yet, I propose, that very image is far from accurate if we are to refer to the Eddas and sagas themselves. Within these works we're faced with a complex tapestry of various characterisations and appearances, rich with nuance and variation.

I would like, then, for you to imagine a Valkyrie. What do you see? Do you see the noble Valkyrie, riding high on horseback? Do you see the winged 'angel of death' flying above the blood grounds? Do you see the image of the mead maiden, mingling among the *Einherjar*? Or, maybe, a Wagneresque woman wearing a bronze breastplate and a horned helmet, with long, blonde hair draped over her shoulders in plaits?

> Wagneresque: resembling or suggesting in style and treatment the work of Wagner

Today's image of the Valkyrie is based on historical record and modern inspirations equally, becoming a very different creature than would be recognised by the people of the Viking Age and early medieval period. Convoluting the matter is that these 'historical Valkyries' often present themselves in apparent contradiction. They appear at once to be dignified cupbearers in Valhalla, as women in shining armour, and as the guardians of heroes, alongside depictions of bloodthirsty battle-lusted monsters who gleefully twist and pull men's intestines on the field of war.

---

140 Appearing to be so much like the avenging angels of Christian mythology. The comparisons are obvious and many play into that available and known imagery.

The Valkyries are all these descriptions seemingly at once, appearing here and there in a plethora of guises and forms. Over the course of the following chapters, I will unravel these contradictions and present to you instead, a story of *evolution*. A story of a 'survival of the fittest', adjusting to best fit into an environment that was changing in ways that could not sustain the Valkyrie in her original forms. This is a story of an adaptation over time to fulfil various roles, breaking beyond their core duty to 'choose the slain', and acting as a mirror to reflect the ever-revolving political, religious and societal landscape.

Let's start then at a simpler point devoid of contradiction: a name. Valkyrie. In the old Norse, *Valkyrja*, a portmanteau comprised of two Old Norse words: *Valr* and *Kyrja*. *Valr* meaning 'slain/ killed in battle', and *Kyrja* coming from *Kiosa*, 'to choose', with *Kyrja* being 'chooser'. Together, 'Chooser of the Slain'.

This is their central role, though even that comes with some confusion when we consider the various ways in which that phrase has been interpreted over the years. It's common, for instance, to remove the Valkyries' agency in creating the battle slain and describe them as passive observers plucking those scattered lifelessly across the battlefield to take them to Valhalla. Here, they have no say or decision in who dies, only in choosing from among the dead who is worthy to be taken to Odin's Hall over or after the natural course of the battle.

Instead, what reveals itself in the literature is a far more active role on the battlefield, with the Valkyries choosing from those present who are going to die, and who are going to live, and further still, who will win the battle and who will lose. It might seem from the outset like a simple re-framing, but it's one that elevates the Valkyrie significantly from simple psychopomp to crucial agent of fate doling out death and sparing life equally.

An example of this can be seen in *Heimskringla* quoting *Hákonarmál* [The Lay/Words of Hakon] with Odin sending Göndul and Skögul to "choose among King's kinsmen"[141] who should die and join him in Valhalla. King Hakon and many of his men die in that battle, with the king asking Skögul why he was not given victory. Skögul responds "Tis owing to us that the issue was won and your foemen fled."[142] Victory, after all, is rarely secured without loss. The king died, but his enemies were routed. From the godly perspective, his presence on the mortal realm was deemed no longer necessary and the Valkyries decreed that he would join Odin's host.

Let's push this framing to an extreme to make my point and overall position more apparent. Say this battle was the culmination of a colossal years long war, with the fate of settlements, kingdoms, regions and countries on the line. By choosing the slain, the Valkyries are manipulating fate to their own drives and desires. It is *their* choice. This is a realm that they are innately familiar with, a space that they are associated with from their earliest attestations.

Of course, we have the oft-stated example to the contrary, that in Sigrdrifa and/or Brynhildr being punished for going against Odin's wishes, but this is notably the only such example of the type. We have many more examples that frame the Valkyries as independent agents working to fulfil their own choices, often without mention of Odin. To avoid confusion here, Brynhildr and Sigrdrifa are punished for going against Odin's choice of victor. I have seen it incorrectly stated on numerous occasions that Sigrdrifa/Brynhildr is punished for not marrying Odin's preferred partner. That is not the reason given in the appropriate sources.

The respective stories -*Fáfnismál* [Fafnir's Sayings], *Sigrdrífumál* [The Lay of Sigrdrifa], and *Völsunga saga* [Saga of the Volsungs] - contain details that are so similar in the modern day it's easy to conclude that they are, or were at least on occasion historically, seen as the same figure. *Grípisspá* [Gripir's Prophecy] appears to distinguish the two as individual figures by inferring Sigrdrifa is the reincarnated Sváva who has been sleeping in the mountain since Helgi's previous death. Meanwhile, Brynhildr is given explicit parentage, is not associated with the reincarnating Valkyrie figures, and is placed in the mountain as punishment by Odin.

---

141 Snorri Sturluson, Heimskringla: History of the Kings of Norway, trans. Lee Milton Hollander (USA: University of Texas Press, 2007), 125.

142 Ibid, 126.

"A prince's daughter, bright in her mail-shirt,
sleeps on the mountain after the killing of Helgi;
You must strike with your sharp sword,
Slit the mail-shirt with Fafnir's slayer."[143]

Fáfnismál uses Sigrdrifa's name but includes Brynhildr's punishment for opposing Odin's choice of victor. This is likely indicative of regional variation within the oral tradition.

Sigrdrífumál and *Völsunga saga* describe a "great light"[144] that looks like a fire burning on the mountain that contains Sigrdrifa/Brynhildr, while *Fafnismal* states that fire "plays above her" through the kenning "terror of linden".

"I know on the mountain the battle-wise one sleeps,
and the terror of the linden plays above her;
Odin stabbed her with a thorn;
The goddess of flax had brought down
A different fighter from the one he wanted.

Young man, you shall see the girl under the helmet,
Who rode away from battle on Vingskornir.
Sigrdrifa's sleep may not be broken,
By a princely youth, except by the norns' decree."[145]

Brynhildr places herself in a hall surrounded by fire after Sigurd is made to forget her later in *Völsunga saga*: "They found the hall and the fire, and there saw a golden-roofed fortress with fire burning around the outside."[146]

It is also worth considering that the beliefs of the Viking Age can never be defined by consistency, and nearly all conclusions we can draw have exceptions due to the nature of a belief system based on an oral tradition, with no centralised material to base those practices on.

---

143 Larrington, The Poetic Edda (Revised Edition), 141.
144 Ibid, 162.
145 Ibid, 161.
146 Byock, The Saga of the Volsungs, 80.

The people themselves were often far travelling, taking inspiration as they moved, and so the stories changed in turn. Snorri, Saxo and the skalds of old are recording the stories and history they are familiar with, and so inconsistencies are to be expected, presenting a margin of error. Add the possibility of scribal error due to copying texts before the invention of the printing press, as well as secondary scholarly analysis where the original manuscripts have been lost, and we have numerous obstacles barricading the way to clarity and objectivity.

As noted by **Pernille Hermann** in 2009: "Medieval writers remembered the past in more than one way, and their recording of memories also involved a dynamic and creative dimension that not only saved memories from oblivion, but also organized memories according to present needs."[147]

Even so, if we're to include Brynhildr/Sigrdrifa within that consideration, that example highlights that Odin seemingly has no active control over the battlefield in ensuring his choices come to fruition. Why would he not intervene, to overpower the Valkyries? As I will outline further, the Valkyries hold significant power over the battlefield, more so than Odin is ever stated to actively wield. A controversial statement, I'm sure!

Odin reaffirms in *Gylfaginning* [The Beguiling of Gylfi] that while he sends them to every battle, it's the Valkyries themselves who "allot death to men and govern victory."[148] It is in this verse too that we have Snorri writing that Skuld, the "Youngest Norn", is considered among their ranks.[149] The idea of them being entirely beholden to Odin and to his whims and decisions just doesn't hold up to scrutiny, even from surface readings.

Which is interesting considering **Edward Petit**, in his translation of the *Poetic Edda*, often emphasises Odin's role in choosing the slain over the Valkyries. "Elsewhere in Norse myth, valkyries choose the slain by taking fallen warriors, whom Óðinn has selected, to his hall to join the unique champions" and "The einherjar 'unique/only champions' are fallen male warriors who, having been chosen by Óðinn, are (elsewhere at least) brought to his hall by Valkyries."[150]

---

147 Pernille Hermann, "Concepts of Memory. Approaches to the Past in Medieval Icelandic Literature", Scandinavian Studies, 81:3 (2009), 293.

148 Faulkes, Edda, 31.

149 An important clarification that will be addressed in a later chapter.

150 Edward Petit, The Poetic Edda: Dual Language Translation (Open Book Publishers, 2023), 162.

As will be laid out over the extent of this book, the Valkyries are deciders of fate on a scale we rarely see in the literature outside of the *Nornir*, yet, that aspect of them so often goes unnoticed or undermined. They are often hand-waved away as passively working in the background, ferrying the dead to Valhalla and Folkvangr and serving them mead. That last one is important in the historical sense, but when seen through a modern lens by some groups and individuals is watered down to essentially mean 'bar wench', for lack of a better term. It's a role that is frequently removed from vital historical context and historical importance.

Regardless, there's far more to their attestations than can be summarised in that language. For many, we had pieced together the Valkyries into what we thought was a cohesive whole and filed them away. We collectively decided that they were *just* Nordic psychopomps, bridging the gap between the world of the Gods and our own mortal world.

Yet, significant questions remain. The categorisation of Psychopomp ignores much of the material we have on these supernatural warrior women, reducing their complexities. As such, I assert that we haven't yet solved the mystery of the Valkyries, not by any measure.

There was one question which to my eyes appeared glaring, shining bright and obvious among the shades of grey and sheer weight of the corpus in front of me, right back at the beginning of my Heathen journey.

It was a question that seemed completely at odds with this image of the Valkyries I have presented within the available literature – that they are servants of Odin, and Odin alone. If the Valkyries can only be described as Odin's servants, why does Freyja get half of the chosen dead? This is heavily inferred in *Grimnismal* [The Lay of Grimnir] verse 14 of the *Poetic Edda*:

"The ninth is Folkvang, where Freya decrees
Who shall have seats in the hall;
The half of the dead each day does she choose,
And half does Othin have."[151]

---

151 Henry Adams Bellows, The Poetic Edda: The Mythological Poems (UK: Dover Publications Inc, 2004), 90-1.

There are ways of interpreting these lines, and many have[152] as Freyja getting first pick of the chosen dead delivered by the Valkyries. First pick of the Valkyrie chosen, or indeed any percentage of the chosen dead, acts as a potent contradiction to the prevalent idea of these maidens being Odin's servants only. Snorri echoes this image in *Gylfaginning* [The Beguiling of Gylfi]. "Freyja is the most glorious of the Asynjur. She has a dwelling in heaven called Folkvangar, and wheresoever she rides to battle she gets half the slain, and the other half Odin....[153]"

What is interesting here is the specific word choice in *Grimnismal*, "half of the dead each day does she choose", which positions Freyja in a role aligned with the Valkyries as a literal 'Chooser of the Slain' though without the complimenting iconography and the environmental context of the latter. There's something in the wording within *Grimnismal* that almost supersedes Odin's traditional role as 'Master of the Valkyries' as it is often portrayed, with Freyja decreeing who shall have seats in the hall, as if she was deciding who the Valkyries would choose from the outset. Note too, that Odin is cast as a receiver here, without language that infers a role in choosing or killing the slain. However, the Valkyries are removed from the equation, unnamed and unmentioned.

An earlier verse adds an element of confusion:
"Gladsheim a fifth is called,
there gold-bright Valhall extends out widely;
there Odin chooses every day
those dead in combat."[154]

To use the Bellows translation to compare:
"The fifth is Glathsheim, | and gold-bright there
Stands Valhall stretching wide;
And there does Othin | each day choose
The men who have fallen in fight."[155]

---

152 Patricia.M. Lafayllve, Freyja, Lady, Vanadis (USA: Outskirts Press, 2006), 28. Lafayllve briefly discusses both sides of the interpretation here.

153 Faulkes, Edda, 24.

154 Larrington, The Poetic Edda (Revised Edition), 49.

155 Bellows, The Poetic Edda: The Mythological Poems, 89.

I would suggest that this wording does not contradict the position put forward in *Gylfaginning*, that the Valkyries oversee and govern the battlefield. Rather, that Odin here is choosing from among the dead who shall have seats in Valhalla, as Freyja chooses who should have seats in her hall. The wording is "men who have fallen" and "those dead in combat", both suggesting that the Valkyries have already chosen and claimed them. This poem, then, presents Freyja and Odin as essentially equals, each receiving half of the dead, with no inference on mastery or ownership over the Valkyries themselves.

There is a prominent alternative interpretation that, while Freyja chooses half the slain for her hall, the Valkyries choose the remaining half for Odin.[156] I would argue that this is an entirely retroactive approach to the material, trying to justify and maintain the Valkyries as being solely beholden to Odin, rather than exploring any alternative perspectives. The first line of *Hákonarmál* [The Lay of Hakon] reinforces this approach:

"The god of the Gautar [Odin] sent Gǫndul and Skǫgul to choose among kings, which of the kin of Yngvi should go with Óðinn and live in Valhǫll."[157]

There is no reference here to Odin preferring one side to win over another, or otherwise choosing prior to the battle. Instead, the Valkyries "found Bjorn's brother [Hakon]",[158] and observed as he donned his mail-shirt and prepared for battle. After Hakon is killed (to emphasise here, *by their decree*), the Valkyries proclaim that they will ride "through the green abodes of the gods, to say to Óðinn that now a supreme ruler will come to look on him in person".[159]

---

156 "The goddess Freyja presided over Fólkvangr and chose half the dead on the battlefield for her realm; Valkyries chose the other half for Odin." "Valkyrie", World History Encyclopedia, accessed January 24, 2024, https://www.worldhistory.org/Valkyrie/

157 R.D. Fulk, "Eyvindr skáldaspillir Finnsson, Hákonarmál", in Poetry from the Kings' Sagas 1: From Mythical Times to c. 1035. Skaldic Poetry of the Scandinavian Middle Ages 1, ed. Diana Whaley (Turnhout, Belgium: Brepols, 2012), 171.

158 Ibid.

159 Ibid.

None of this suggests that Odin is fully knowledgeable about exactly who will be arriving at his hall, about who has lost the battle, or who has won. They are cast in the role of 'informer' here, passing on information that Odin would otherwise not know. This instance is notable in that they do exhibit a behavioural similarity to Odin's information gatherers, Huginn and Muninn. These two ravens, in turn, emphasise that Odin is not omniscient, but must rely on informants to see where he cannot. There are limits to his power, and his oversight.

Conversely, Snorri essentially presents Freyja acting as a Valkyrie, positioning her as – on occasion at least – flying out to battlefields to pick of the slain. The yield of this action is apparently half hers, half Odin's. Once again, there are no other mentions of Valkyries, almost implying that Freyja acts alone as a death-bringer figure on the battlefield, even if this isn't a permanent or even frequent arrangement ("wheresoever she rides to battle").

There's also a potential inference, born from the lack of Valkyrie mentions here, that this was an occurrence of the 'mythic past', which works with the suggestion that Freyja could be understood to be the proto-Valkyrie,[160] the mould on which the Valkyrie would emerge fully forged as an agent of the Gods, choosing the slain that would be granted admission to the halls of the warrior dead.

Within the eighth century *Historia Langobardorum* [History of the Lombards] we have an interaction between Godan (essentially, Odin) and his wife, Frea (essentially Freyja, though identified with Frigg here as was often the case within continental Germanic mythologies).

---

160 Richard North, Heathen Gods in Old English Literature (Cambridge and New York: Cambridge University Press, 1997), 108.

"Then Ambri and Assi, that is the leaders of the Wandals, asked Godan that he should give them the victory over the Winniles. Godan answered, saying: 'Whom I shall first see when at sunrise, to them I shall give the victory.' At that time, Gambara with her two sons, besought Frea, the wife of Godan, to be propitious to the Winniles. Then Frea gave counsel that at sunrise the Winniles should come, and that their women, with their hair let down around their face in the likeness of a beard, should also come with their husbands. Then when it became bright, while the sun was rising, Frea, the wife of Godan, turned around the bed where her husband was lying and put his face toward the east, and awakened him. And he, looking at them, saw the Winniles and their women heaving their hair let down around their face. And he says: " Who are these longbeards?" Then spoke Frea to Godan: "My lord, thou hast given them the name, now give them also the victory." And he gave them victory, so that they should defend themselves according to his counsel and obtain victory. From that time, the Winniles were called Langobards."[161]

While Godan is given ultimate control over this decision, Frea is cast in the role of 'chooser', manipulating the situation to ensure her favourites prevail. This contrasts with the passive role that Godan undertakes, leaving the result to circumstance rather than his own agency or decision. Except for the 'Brynhildr incident' in which Odin voices a preference, he is otherwise shown to act in much the same way as this Godan figure.

This markedly contrasts with the behaviour of the Valkyries, who echo Frea's actions here, but elevated – they ultimately decide and enact their vision rather than act through an intermediary. In these examples, we're faced with an inferred association of Freyja's duties as being aligned with the Valkyries, either in acting as akin to Odin in receiving half of the dead or acting as a Valkyrie in actively collecting or choosing the dead.

---

161 Historia Langobardorum, trans. William Dudley Foulke (1907). "Historia Langobardorum", Germanic Mythology, accessed March 19, 2024 https://germanicmythology.com/works/HistoriaLangobardum.html

Either way, the commonality cannot be ignored. There is some sort of connection between Freyja and the Valkyries, the detail of which was probably common knowledge as part of skaldic tradition, and as such, not worth the dedicated page space to explain. Today, that tacit knowledge has been lost, leaving strands of thought and written statement frayed and dangling. From the material we have available, it is evident that the Goddesses in the Eddas play very diluted roles.[162]

As a key example, no Goddess is mentioned over the course of the events of *Ragnarök*, though the Valkyries are mentioned, albeit briefly. There's a bias here that comes from the time it was written, and it would be easy to imagine that details were omitted, on top of the natural filtration due to time, the nature of the oral tradition, and memory. The fact that they were included at all gives insight into a potentially greater image. If this was recorded even with the bias of removing or diminishing the role of the Goddesses, what wasn't mentioned? What else could there have been in terms of Freyja's connection to the Valkyries and the dead?

> *"Then a light shone from Logafell,*
> *And from that light came lightning-bolts;*
> *Wearing helmets at Himinvangi [came the Valkyries]*
> *Their byrnies were drenched in blood;*
> *And beams blazed from their spears."*[163]

There's a robust motif of many of the Nordic Goddesses and giantesses having a control or influence over life, fate and death. Freyja, Eir, Ran, Hel, Gullveig, Gefjon, and the Valkyries all play a role in this consideration, and with reference to the above-stated relative scarcity of Goddesses in the applicable literature, this association is brought into greater focus.

---

162 Kurt Hohmann, Skaði and Freyja: Females of Power amongst the Aesir, 1. Academia.edu, accessed May 3, 2024. https://www.academia.edu/15301723/Ska%C3%B0i_and_Freyja_Females_of_Power_amongst_the_Aesir

163 Helgakviða Hundingsbana I. Larrington, The Poetic Edda (Revised Edition), 112.

Above, a silver figurine from Tissø depicting a feminine figure.Her mouth appears to be open, with sharpened teeth. Her arms are entangled in her hair with fierce-looking eyes.

As **David Varley** emphasises, Odin "appears to be the only male figure who actively interferes in the workings of destiny and death, in which Freyja, Hel, the Valkyries and the norns all have important roles."[164] This is an area otherwise dominated by feminine figures, with Odin being the apparent outlier.

While Odin is almost exclusively discussed in relation to the Valkyries, we need to frame the importance of one Goddess who is so frequently associated with them, whether by inference, explicit reference or behavioural similarity. Freyja, the Vanic Goddess so commonly associated with love and beauty, who possesses multitudes and apparent contradictions. She is a fertility Goddess who is tied to death, battle, and the afterlife.

Still, we encounter some difficulty in fully defining Freyja's connection to the Valkyries, as the relationship between these two entities is not one thoroughly explored within early medieval literature, despite notable similarities in presentation, associations and behaviour. Was she believed to be a sort of Valkyrie, choosing those who were to die and enter her halls? At what point did Freyja incorporate those behaviours and characteristics, and why? If we're to follow that the Nordic Valkyries had a much older origin, then how did Freyja become entangled within their larger role?

---

164 David Hugh Varley, The whirling wheel: the male construction of empowered female identities in Old Norse myth and legend (Durham theses, Durham University, 2015), 227.

With reference to the Tissø, Denmark[165] figurine, I find myself considering that Freyja may have herself emerged from the blood-thirsty Valkyrie like figures into explicit Goddess-hood. As she is only thoroughly attested through Scandinavian sources, it may stand to reason that she emerged from the Nordic Valkyrie archetype, growing to mingle among the other Gods and snowballing to be identified with like beings, developing her own cult alongside to the point we see her today, distinct from Valkyries.

While I'm far from married to this idea, it presents itself as a compelling possibility, one of many. This figure may also, simply, be a Valkyrie, all teeth and frenzy. We so often find ourselves using archaeological finds as a mirror to the literature, trying to find the best match among many possibilities.

A more widely stated position is that Freyja was understood to have been the 'Queen of the Valkyries'.

It's a view suggested by **Jackson Crawford,**[166] among other academics, and is a position you'd generally see stated as fact in a plethora of materials. It is used as an easy answer to reconcile Freyja's relationship with the Valkyries considering no other forthcoming answer, especially when it comes to modern popular content.

---

165 A prominent potential Valkyrie figure was discovered in the same locale.

166 Jackson Crawford, "Valkyries (Valkyrjur)," Jan 23, 2019, YouTube video, 29:14, https://www.youtube.com/watch?v=VMrYEq_jNVs - born from a conflation between Göndul and Freyja in Sörla þáttr [Sorli's Yarn/Story]. This will be discussed further below, but for brevity, I do not personally hold that this would have been a consistent element in the literature. Compiled in the fourteenth century, it was a time where the Valkyries were understood to be less defined by supernatural behaviours, allowing the freedom for Freyja to assume those behaviours in their stead.

For example, the 2018 God of War game by Santa Monica Studio[167] depicted Freyja as the previous Queen of the Valkyries, their current Queen being Sigrún, with Gna taking on that role in the sequel.[168] It was an interpretation that worked within the framework of that reimagining, borrowing other elements from the literature to reinforce the image presented, such as Frigg and Freyja being the same Goddess,[169] with the former being the adopted Aesir name for the latter due to the negative connotations of the Vanir within the Asgardian social system.[170]

I will add a caveat here that I'm certainly not against such descriptions, and only wish we had more conclusive evidence to make the connection. As it stands, we're working mostly on inference, the weight of the association leaning on one heiti, *Valfreyja*,[171] the agreement that Freyja is a prominent Goddess – therefore, it has been presumed, above the status of normal Valkyries – her possession of a hall of the dead, and her larger associations with battle.

Many Freyja devotees outright reject or disapprove of this idea of positioning the Vanir Goddess as a Valkyrie, either as being among their roster, their 'Queen' or leader. **Patricia Lafayllve**, a noted Heathen regarding this topic, writes that describing Freyja as a Valkyrie or anything similar reduces her perceived power. As "we know that Freyja was a very important goddess in her own right. The Valkyries.... were Odin's servants. They served the warriors who entered Valhalla mead and meat all night long.

---

167 Santa Monica Studio, God of War, PlayStation 4 (Sony Interactive Entertainment, 2018)

168 Santa Monica Studio, God of War Ragnarök, PlayStation 5 (Sony Interactive Entertainment, 2022).

169 A theory called the 'Common Origin Hypothesis' states that Frigg and Freyja are descended from a single common Proto-Germanic figure. Freyja makes no appearance outside of Scandinavia, with her qualities being subsumed into Frigg's characterisation.

170 I also very much appreciated how the Valkyries were depicted in the game and its sequel. It achieved a representation of their most prominent depictions – noble woman and feral warrior – that had internal logic to that representation. Another recommendation comes by way of Kate Heartfield's The Valkyrie, a retelling of the Saga of the Volsungs, which incorporated the Valkyrie mythos in new, interesting ways.

171 Personally, I hold that this heiti is referencing Freyja's possession of a hall of the dead and her associations with battle, rather than a more explicit connection to the Valkyries via the 'Val' prefix., i.e. 'Freyja of the Slain'. Odin has several similar titles including Valfǫðr [Valfodr] 'Father of the Slain'.

Therefore, it stands to reason that Freyja - certainly never mentioned as a servant to any other deity – would not be a Valkyrie. Her rank, high among the gods of the Norse, assures this."[172] Altogether, that seems to be a common approach, in having to lower Freyja to the Valkyries' level of servitude to allow the association to work at all. In many ways, this narrative has hindered any sort of reconsideration of the Valkyries and their role in the literature. I posit that we should work instead to elevate the slaughter maidens from the image of servant, and further towards the position posed in this book: as crucial agents of fate and beings of notable independent power.

It would also be appropriate to mention that there are many other differing, often contradictory opinions and theories when it comes to Freyja and her connection to the Valkyries. We have on one side, the Lafayllve idea that lowering Freyja to the level of the Valkyries does her a disservice as a powerful Goddess in her own right. While on the other side, we have **Maria Kvilhaug** who believes Göndul,[173] Gefjon, and Hildr are Freyja, alongside the mysterious Gullveig.

"Another name for Freyia is Gondul [The Magician][174] ...it is certainly possible to suggest that [both Frigg and] Freyja are identifiable as the ancient witch who tells the world's history in the Völuspá and is the first being."[175] She refers to Freyja as *Gullveigr-Heiðr*, the "three times born,"[176] "the first Völva ...the first to conquer death."[177]

Kvilhaug is far from the first to suggest that Gullveig is Freyja in another form. **Edward Oswald Gabriel Turville-Petre**, better known as **Gabriel Turville-Petre**, drew the same conclusion, writing: "If Gullveig appears in one strophe as the 'power' or the 'drunkenness of gold', and in the next as the glittering, seductive witch, her place in the myth is less obscure. She is one of the Vanir, who were gods at once of riches and of that evil form of magic called seiðr....If we may be more precise, Gullveig can hardly be other than Freyja."[178]

---

172 Lafayllve, Freyja, Lady, Vanadis, 31.
173 A noted Valkyrie.
174 Parentheses are that of Kvilhaug.
175 Maria Christine Kvilhaug, The Seed of Yggdrasill: Deciphering the Hidden Messages in Old Norse Myths (Whyte Tracks, 2015), 87.
176 Ibid, 214.
177 Kvilhaug, The Seed of Yggdrasil, 214.
178 E.O.G. Turville-Petre, Myth and Religion of the North: The Religion of

It would be relevant to note here that, despite writing a rather comprehensive study of Old Norse religion in 'Myth and Religion in the North', Turville-Petre doesn't make a single reference to Valkyries over the course of some 340 pages. That is not a rare occurrence.

Equally, Turville-Petre's translation of Gullveig to mean "drunkenness of gold", as Kvilhaug points out, has remained stubbornly persistent in relevant discussions since. Instead, she translates Gullveig to mean "Gold Power Drink",[179] drawing connections away from negative modern qualities and towards those associated with "precious mead" or "mead of memory."[180] Something special and of the Gods.

With Kvilhaug's approach to the material in mind, Gullveig then represents secret knowledge and wisdom. From there, you can see how Freyja's, and the Vanir's, secret knowledge and power, most apparently *seiðr*, could be a cause for the 'Great War of the Gods'. Odin has never been one to shy away from the draw of hidden knowledge, wisdom and power, with the lure of *seiðr* – that "art which contained the most power"[181] – being all too strong to ignore. Further, for Freyja to, potentially, be sharing that power among the human populace without sharing it with the Aesir themselves may be the cause of significant attrition.[182]

Gold is a frequent motif in the literature, invoking fire, fertility, wealth, mead and, perhaps crucially, warfare. **Stephen Pollington** describes how the appearance of gold in Germanic literature often evokes imagery of armour and weaponry. "Descriptions of these women... emphasise that their appearance is metallic – *goldhroden* – 'encased in gold', *beahhroden* 'encased in rings', *goldegehyrsted* 'armoured/decorated with gold'. The language is deliberately ambiguous."[183]

Ancient Scandinavia (Westport, Connecticut, USA: Greenwood Press, 1964), 159.

179 Kvilhaug, The Seed of Yggdrasill, 196.

180 Ibid, 197.

181 Maria Kvilhaug, The Maiden with the Mead (Norway: University of Oslo, 2004), 51.

182 I will discuss this in more detail in the chapter Inheritors of Divine Seiðr, Magic in the Nordic World.

183 Stephen Pollington, The Elder Gods: The Otherworld of Early England (Ely, Cambridgeshire: Anglo-Saxon Books, 2022), 314.

Freyja too has many connections to gold, as do the Vanir as a collective, and perhaps here we have an underlying theme of the Vanir being warrior-like, or alternatively, reinforcing Freyja's propensity for warfare through the otherwise innocuous-seeming associations with gold and other metals. Unsurprisingly, some Valkyries are described in ways that reflect the above also. Sigrún is described as a "gold-adorned lady" (gold-adorned, *gullvarið*),[184] and a "ring-adorned woman" (ring-adorned, *baugvarið*).[185] While Sváva is described as "sea-golden" (*margullin*)[186] in *Helgakviða Hjörvarðssonar* [The Poem of Helgi Hjorvardsson]. Once again, the language is ambiguous, lending, at first read, to the image of nobility possessed by these supernaturally empowered women.

But to be "ring-adorned" could also be referring to mail shirts, shields and chainmaille. A kenning for warriors found in *Erfidrápa Óláfs Tryggvasonar* [Funeral Lay of Olaf Tryggvasonar] is "Wounded workers of the mighty shirt of the ring of point-harm", with the "mighty shirt of the ring" being a mail shirt. As above, a kenning for a Valkyrie was "the shaking-Sif of Rings",[187] evoking the noise of chainmaille in battle. The language around being adorned in armour, and being adorned in finery is nebulous, offering an enticing look at the crossover between the Valkyries' later depictions as being high-born individuals, while also pursuing a warriors' path.

The imagery is consistent and paints an image of a war-like and war-ready noble class, who, of course, were often the target of significant Valkyrie interest, especially in the later manifestations of their character. Strictly speaking, it was also largely expected for those in power to be engaged in acts of warfare, or prepared for acts of war, and capable of fighting to protect what was theirs. While violence is often exaggerated in terms of its prevalence in Viking Age Scandinavia, it certainly played a role within its social structure. As **Jesse Byock** explains, in comparison to Viking Age Iceland, "The mother culture, Viking Age Scandinavia, was a society of regional groupings and warlords."[188]

---

184 Larrington, The Poetic Edda (Revised Edition), 136.
185 Ibid, 134.
186 Ibid, 124.
187 Found in Ragnarsdrápa.
188 Jesse Byock, "Feuding in Viking-Age Iceland's great village", in Conflict in Medieval Europe: Changing Perspective in Society and Culture, ed. W.C Brown and P. Gorecki (Aldershot: Ashgate, 2003), 230.

Gold – wealth – was a pathway to power. It could be distributed in the form of rings, and favours, gifted to favoured peoples to strengthen positions of power. This power came through the reinforcement of a social position, with wealth being shared to solidify friendships and loyalties.[189] Generosity was a good quality for leaders to possess, with poor leadership being defined by greed and miserly behaviours.[190]

Writing in reference to *Beowulf*, **Patricie Silber** holds the position that gold plays a crucial, symbolic and evolving role over the events of the story. Its first appearance, however, is tied to the imagery of warfare: "Boar figures shone over cheekguards, adorned with gold, shining and fire-hardened."[191] This image is subsequently reinforced through repeated associations with gold-decorated weaponry, and to gold-adorned people.[192] Within *Oxarflokkr*[193] 3, composed by Einar Skulason, we have a similar concept delivered by way of a complex kenning which once again unites Freyja with a prominent image of war. *"Freys nipt brá driptir"* or "Freyr's [female relative/niece][194] eyelash rain." Hnoss cries the golden tears of her mother, Freyja, and those tears decorate an ornate axe.[195]

It was not unusual for higher social status to be attained and maintained through violence.[196] Equally, the cost of armour, not to mention the cost of creating a sword, was prohibitive and reserved for those of higher status, while wealth was a product – a reward - of violent activity and threat during the period. Consider the entire premise of Danegeld, the Danish Tax that was used to pay tribute to Viking raiders to placate them and dissuade violence.

---

189 Tamás Reinicke, Bound by Gold and Blood: Power Structure in the Viking Age (Norway: University of Oslo, 2017), 9.

190 In a concept many Heathens would be familiar with, the 'gifting cycle' was also crucial to the mechanisms behind social hierarchies within the period.

191 Patricie Silber, "Gold and its Significance in Beowulf", Annuale Medievale, vol.18 (1977), 9.

192 Ibid.

193 Unhelpfully, "Poem about an Axe", though it's far more commonly known by the Old Norse considering its vague nature.

194 Hnoss is referenced earlier in the verse as the glory-child of Horn (Freyja).

195 Anthony Faulkes, Poetical Inspiration in Old Norse and Old English Poetry (London: University College London, 1997), 27-8.

196 Kirstina Williams, Of Thralls and Freemen: Norse social structure during the Viking Age (Seattle, USA: University of Washington, 2015) DOI: 10.13140/RG.2.1.3161.5209.

All of this adds a porous nature to the imagery of nobility, wealth and warfare, with frequent crossover in terms of the language utilised.

> Hail to the gold ring adorned goddess,
> From noble-birth given divine duty
> To deliver the heroic dead to Havi's hall
> Silvered skin shining through Sol's grace,
> Cast in swan-cloak, with veins of iron and steel,
> she rides resplendent.

Valkyries and the Disir, Hamingjur and Fylgjur

While my primary area of interest revolves closely around the Valkyries, I also have a larger fascination with "supernatural feminities,"[197] with both elements combating against the otherwise perfect image of patriarchy perceived to be held by Viking Age peoples. When it comes to matters of life, death, and fate, Goddesses, giantesses and feminine spirits appear to reign supreme, while Odin works to navigate around them.

The *Nornir*, the *Disir*, the *Fylgjur*, the *Hamingjur* and the Valkyries all operate prominently in a space dictated by life, death and the protection from death, or otherwise prophesying or predicting when a life will end.

The common thread is having some role to play in 'fate'; allotting fate, protection from a premature death, dealing out death, predicting death. The Valkyries themselves, at one point or another, arguably fulfil all of these roles. Frustratingly this similarity has led to confusion, with some labels being used interchangeably across various sagas due to semantic weakening over time.

'*Dis*' is often used interchangeably with 'Goddess', though the term 'Valkyrie' seems to be used in a very specific context, with characteristics and iconography that were collectively understood to be distinct. Much of this comes down to the etymology of the title – the choosers of the slain are unique through their duty and associations to Odin, to the battlefield and to the dead primarily within the literature. Though we do have the Valkyries being called and identified as '*Dis*' too,[198] if not perceived to be thematic cousins to the *Disir* through various connective threads.

---

197 To use Luke John Murphy's phrasing in his 2013 work, Herjans Dísir: Valkyrjur, Supernatural Feminities, and Elite Warrior Culture in the Late Pre-Christian Iron Age.

198 Viga Glum 12 we have a kenning of "mens dreyra disar" – 'of the dis of the jewel of blood', which describes a Valkyrie. Guðrúnarkviða I [The First Lay of Gudrun] includes "Herjans Disi", which Larrington translates to "Odin's ladies". Larrington, The Poetic Edda (Revised Edition), 174.

"In both their benevolent and malevolent aspects, the Valkyries are related to a generic group of half-mortal, half-supernatural beings called *idisi* in Old High German, *ides* in Old English, and *dis* in Old Norse...they are armed, powerful, priestly. They function as arrangers of destinies and intermediaries between men and the deity."[199]

The semantic weakening of the term *'Dis'* from what we can gather was its original incarnation resulted in it being another catch-all skaldic tool to mean, in vague terms, feminine figure of supernatural persuasion. Within kennings, then, it became similar to the convention of using names of Goddesses as a shorthand for 'Goddess' and supernatural feminine figure, or to emphasise exceptionality relative to the general human population. While a common practice in kennings, the specific Goddesses used in these instances raises points of intrigue.

Of the ones I have sourced, the majority are names connected with Freyja, including Gefn[200] and Syr, alongside Saga, Fulla, Gna, Var, Gerdr, Sif, Ran, and the names understood to belong to other Valkyries, such as Eir, Þrúðr, and Hildr. **Rudolf Simek** suggests that Saga and Var "should probably be seen as female protective goddesses,"[201] with the criteria to that designation being those Goddesses who are "not closer defined Asynjur."[202] Gna, like many of the Valkyries themselves, traverses between worlds and across realms on horse-back. Ran is a Goddess associated with death, and the kennings she is used alongside draw on that imagery ("the desiring-Rán of the excessive drying of veins", as mentioned above).

199 Helen Damico, "The Valkyrie Reflex in Old English Literature", in New Readings on Women in Old English Literature, (USA: Indiana University Press, 1990), 176.

200 Though, there's some debate as to whether this is Gefjon, a separate Goddess.

201 Simek, Dictionary of Northern Mythology, 274.

202 Ibid.

Snorri names Ran among the Asynjur [Goddesses] in *Skáldskaparsmál* – and without the marriage to a recognised member of the Aesir, like Skadi or Gerdr - though it's not uncommon for her to be assumed Jotnar due to her name and associations. It's never explicitly clarified in the period literature.

Sif, Gerdr and Fulla are, in various ways, associated with the earth, though Fulla too has connections with healing, like Eir, and to gold. The association with healing comes to us by way of identification with Volla in one of the Merseburg Charms. "Then Friia sang charms, and Volla her sister; Then Wodan sang charms, as he well could: be it bone-sprain, be it blood-sprain, be it limb-sprain: bone to bone, blood to blood, limb to limb, so be they glued together".[203]

In *Grimnismal* [The Lay of Grimnir], Fulla is tasked by Frigg to warn King Geirrod that he will be visited by a wizard (Odin). "[Fulla] told the king to beware lest a wizard, who had come into the country, should bewitch him, and he said he could be known by this sign: that no dog was so fierce that it would leap on him."[204] In this role, she is not unlike the protective *Hamingjur* and *Fylgjur* as they are presented in later literature, acting to warn an individual of incoming danger.

Fulla's associations with gold[205] are found in kennings in *Skáldskaparmál* in the *Prose Edda*, "How shall gold be referred to? By calling it Aegir's fire and Glasir's foliage, Sif's hair, Fulla's snood, Freyja's weeping..."[206]

With reference to Sif, Gerdr and Fulla[207] respectively, and their connections to abundance, harvest, fertility and the natural world, it is interesting that **Stephen Glosecki** suggests that the *Disir* and Valkyries can potentially be seen as "earth-spirits".[208]

---

203 John Lindow, Norse Mythology: A Guide to Gods, Heroes, Rituals, and Beliefs (Oxford: Oxford University Press, 2001), 227.

204 Larrington, The Poetic Edda (Revised Edition), 48.

205 The nebulous associations of gold with armour and weaponry appear above.

206 Faulkes, Edda, 94.

207 Snorri suggests in Skáldskaparmál that Fulla may be another name for Frigg. Faulkes, Edda, 86.

208 Stephen O. Glosecki, Shamanism and Old English Poetry (New York: Garland Publishing, 1989), 66.

Though this would seem to conflict with other interpretations of the Valkyries being less of the earth and more associated with the air and sky in reference to their connections to flight and storms. The association with storms is one of the lesser featured attributes of the Valkyrie, despite its prevalence in the material. Storms are chaotic, and frequently used in kennings to describe the destruction caused by those on the battlefield. Battles[209] are called "blizzards of arrows",[210] the "furious rain of sword points",[211] "metal-rain",[212] and the "storm of shields".[213]

Valkyrie names are mentioned alongside this imagery, including "the strongest roaring wind of Gǫndul"[214], "Hrist's storm-time"[215] and "Skǫgul's wind."[216] Battle is chaotic, unpredictable, an overwhelming force akin to a natural phenomenon. It's an otherworldly space, defined by the sound of metal against metal, and relentless arrow-rain. Similarly, the Valkyries seem to be associated with lightning, at least within the *Poetic Edda*.

---

209 A relevant note here is that battle can also be referred to as "the judgement of Gǫndul", as seen in Hákonardrápa 5. Another point of evidence that highlights contemporary acknowledgment of the role and importance of the Valkyrie. Russell Poole, "Tindr Hallkelsson, Hákonardrápa 5", in Poetry from the Kings' Sagas 1: From Mythical Times to c. 1035. Skaldic Poetry of the Scandinavian Middle Ages 1, ed. Diana Whaley (Turnhout, Belgium: Brepols, 2012), 347.

210 Magnússdrápa 14, from Judy Quinn, "The 'Wind of the Giantess': Snorri Sturluson, Rudolf Meissner, and the Interpretation of Mythological Kennings along Taxonomic Lines", Viking and Medieval Scandinavia 8 (2012), 219.

211 Gyðingsvísur 5. Katrina Attwood, 'Anonymous Poems, Gyðingsvísur 5', ed. by Margaret Clunies Ross, Poetry on Christian Subjects. Skaldic Poetry of the Scandinavian Middle Ages 7 (Turnhout, Belgium: Brepols,2007), 521-2.

212 Liðsmannaflokkr 1. Russell Poole, 'Anonymous Poems, Liðsmannaflokkr 1', in Poetry from the Kings' Sagas 1: From Mythical Times to c. 1035. Skaldic Poetry of the Scandinavian Middle Ages 1, ed. Diana Whaley (Turnhout, Belgium: Brepols, 2012), 1016.

213 Óláfs drápa Tryggvasonar 8. Kate Heslop, Anonymous Poems, Óláfs drápa Tryggvasonar 8', in Poetry from the Kings' Sagas 1: From Mythical Times to c. 1035. Skaldic Poetry of the Scandinavian Middle Ages 1, ed. Diana Whaley (Turnhout, Belgium: Brepols, 2012), 1039.

214 Kari Ellen Gade, "Einarr Skúlason, Fragments 4", in Poetry from Treatises on Poetics. Skaldic Poetry of the Scandinavian Middle Ages 3, ed. Kari Ellen Gade and Edith Marold (Turnhout, Belgium: Brepols, 2017), 155.

215 Háttatal 59. Faulkes, Edda, 201.

216 Háttatal 54. Ibid, 198.

"Lightning flashed above them and ships were struck. They saw nine Valkyries riding up in the air, and recognised Sigrun among them."[217]

-"And from that light came lightning-bolts;
Wearing helmets at Himinvangi [came the Valkyries]"[218]

Yet, that categorisation of earth spirit would better fit in line with Valkyries that we can presume to have Jotunn heritage, with reference to their ties to the earth, mountains and stone. In a reference to the kenning, 'Wind of the Giantess', **Judy Quinn**[219] posits that there was an understanding within the mythology that giantesses, supernatural female figures, were tied to the storm because it represented their power over men's fates. This is framed as a fight against a landscape-changing atmospheric force that was potent and powerful and unpredictable. A warrior being able to 'weather the storm' and find victory against the odds would be a significant marker of virility and fighting ability.

Kennings that evoke the imagery of storms generate "imagined sensations, visual, aural, and tactile, that are evoked through the interaction of moving air and another force: a valkyrie sweeping past the warrior or swords slicing through the air."[220] No doubt, the way that the Valkyrie invisibly manipulates the battlefield holds an importance within these examples. It wouldn't be difficult to see a strong wind as the Valkyrie herself, or weather summoned by the Corpse-Chooser.

There is a particularly intriguing kenning associated with Sif that perseveres in *Eiríksflokkr* [Poem about Eirik] "lítt vas Sóti Sifjar svang" – "the wolf was hardly hungry."[221] Here, a wolf is being described as "the horse of Sif / *Sóti Sifjar*". This falls far outside of the sources that mention Sif, as limited as they admittedly are. Of course, the Valkyries too are described as riding wolves.

---

217 Larrington, The Poetic Edda (Revised Edition), 131.
218 Ibid, 112.
219 Quinn, The 'Wind of the Giantess', 207 -59.
220 Ibid, 215.
221 Kari Ellen Gade, 'Halldórr ókristni, Eiríksflokkr', in Poetry from the Kings' Sagas 1: From Mythical Times to c. 1035. Skaldic Poetry of the Scandinavian Middle Ages 1, ed. Diana Whaley (Turnhout, Belgium: Brepols, 2012), 469

The Rök runestone includes the line, "I say this the twelfth, where the horse of Gunnr sees fodder on the battlefield, where twenty kings lie."[222] Gunnr has numerous attestations across the tenth century to the thirteenth century that reinforce her position and role as a Valkyrie,[223] often appearing in tandem with wolves or wolf imagery. Elsewhere, wolves are frequently described as the "horse of the trollwoman"[224] or "horse/steed of the giantess/giant."[225]

"So they sent to Giantland for a giantess called Hyrrokkin. And when she arrived, riding a wolf and using vipers as reins, she dismounted from her steed..."[226]

This description falls in line with the idea of the wolf being 'of the wild', unlike the domesticated horse, and being utilised by those that dwell in wild spaces, like giants and troll-women, if they can indeed be accurately described as different entities. As I will discuss further, the Valkyries exhibit an interesting duality of being both of the wild and of civilised spaces across their various appearances, with a rough correlation of the earlier attestations showcasing wild behaviours, and later attestations comparatively civilised.

Sif's association with wolf-riders and Valkyries then raises questions, suggesting potential Jotnar roots that have been lost over the centuries. In wolf kennings that include names, we only have names of giantesses and troll-women (Varðrún [Vardrun], Gjálp, Jarnsaxa,[227] Imð [Imd], Leikn and Gríðr [Gridr]), two instances of heiti of Odin (Gauti and Yggr) and one of a giant (Geitir).[228] Sif would seem to be the anomaly, with no associations with wolves such as that possessed by Odin, and no outright attestations as being a Jotunn, or a troll-woman.

222 Runic inscription Ög 136 in Scandinavian Runic-text Database, Department of Scandinavian Languages, Uppsala University, accessed November 20, 2024. https://bit.ly/3LUrkod

223 Neil Price, The Viking Way: Religion and War in Late Iron Age Scandinavia (Revised Edition) (Uppsala, Sweden: Uppsala University, 2019), 281.

224 In Gyðingsvísur 8, Óláfs drápa Tryggvasonar 24, Valþjófsflokkr 1.

225 In Kálfsflokkr 1, Sigtryggsdrápa 3, and Sigurðardrápa 3, and others.

226 Faulkes, Edda, 49.

227 "He reddened with gore the chops of the dark-looking steed of Jarnsaxa." Faulkes, Edda, 138.

228 All references from "Kenning of type WOLF", The Skaldic Project, accessed November 19, 2023 https://skaldic.org/db.php?if=default&table=kenning&val=90&view=meiss

This kenning is one reason why I strongly suggest that Sif is a Jotunn or has Jotunn parentage, and possibly has a martial background, perhaps even stories in which she took on a more 'warrior-like' role, potentially that of a Valkyrie, or stories that explicitly involved her wielding magic. A potential answer to her previous identity lies in the confusion around the giantess Jarnsaxa, the mother to Thor's son, Magni, who is either called the 'Rival of Sif' or is otherwise another name for Sif herself.[229] Jarnsaxa's name means, essentially, 'Iron Sword' which certainly speaks to a martial background, associations, or proficiency.

While Sif's name refers to a relationship, most commonly to a relation by marriage[230] which offers another avenue of justification, almost as if it is a given title after she has been incorporated into the Aesir. She may have been stripped of her prior identity, and her history erased.

Altogether, she is a mysterious Goddess, having, we presume, a previous relationship outside of Thor, and a son in Ullr, with no story detailing his – or her- origin. We know nothing of her parents, or her life outside of her marriage to 'the Thunderer'. Considering that Ullr shares notable similarities with Skadi, herself a Jotunn, though with connections to oaths and oath-giving, it wouldn't be a colossal inference to see how Ullr would be a unification between Jotunn wildness and Aesir 'order'.

Further, Sif is notably absent from the list of Asynjur in Snorri's *Skáldskaparmál*.[231] While it is likely that this is a simple omission, it is a noteworthy omission nonetheless, considering her position as wife to one of the most frequently attested Aesir Gods.

---

229 Varying on translation, highlighted by Simek, Dictionary of Northern Mythology, 178.

230 Simek, Dictionary of Northern Mythology, 283.

231 Within Nafnaþulur . It would otherwise be a natural inference to say that Sif not being included here would be potential evidence of Snorri working from source material that perhaps listed her among the Jotnar, but we do have Jotunn listed here too, including Gerdr.

DEMARCATING THE DISIR, HAMINGJUR AND FYLGJUR FROM THE VALKYRIE

In *Valkyrie, the Women of the Viking World*, **Jóhanna Katrín Friðriksdóttir** states that the *Disir* are female spirits or minor Goddesses who give and withhold life, as well as dispense protection and prosperity. In essence, they are "guardians and takers of life."[232] This certainly brings to mind the Valkyries, even if modern academia has worked to further demarcate the *Disir* from the Valkyries in the last couple of decades.[233]

The *Disir* are perhaps most commonly perceived as ancestral women that oversee births within the framework of "giving life". Within this role they may also have been seen as identical to the Norns who allot fate at a life's beginning.

"Aid runes shall you learn
If you would grant assistance
To bring the child from the mother.
Cut them in her palm
And hold her hand in yours.
And bid the Disir not to fail."[234]

In their aspect as ancestral beings, the *Disir* were believed to have once been mortal, but were now very much not of the living world, as can be observed in *Atlamál* [The Greenlandic Lay of Atli].

"I thought that dead women came here tonight,
they were not badly decked out, they wanted to choose you,
invite you very soon to their benches;
I declare that your disir are powerless to help you."[235]

For clarity moving forwards, I would demarcate the *Disir* as, originally, ancestral feminine cult figures who were seen to grant protection, or blessings or good will. They *were* mortal but became of the 'otherworld' once they passed over the threshold from life into death.

---

232 Jóhanna Katrín Friðriksdóttir, Valkyrie, the Women of the Viking World (UK: Bloomsbury Academic, 2020), 191.

233 See Karen Bek-Pedersen, The Norns in Old Norse Mythology (Scotland, UK: Dunedin Academic Press, 2011), 41-56.

234 Byock, The Saga of the Volsungs, 69.

235 Larrington, The Poetic Edda (Revised Edition), 214.

With that in mind, it is easy to see how the *Disir* and the Valkyries became entangled when we consider that certain Valkyries were eventually given human lineages and human offspring, living apparently mortal lives.

Here there was a potential for a mortal born Valkyrie to be a venerated ancestor, protecting descendants at times of need. The character of Gudrun, for instance, in *Laxdæla saga* [The Saga of the People of Laxárdalur] is said to be descended from a Valkyrie.[236] This is where I would state the confusion ultimately lies, in that the delineation between *Dis* and Valkyrie seems to have been, at one point, based on mortality and ancestor relations. When the Valkyrie moved further into euhemerism, the line became irrevocably blurred.

As the Valkyrie became incorporated into the image of the *Disir*, the *Disir* adopted more Valkyric behaviours. The language used in the above excerpt from the *Atlamál* - 'to choose' - is illuminating, though it must be said, ultimately unsuccessful. When the Valkyries ride, they claim their chosen without interference. Their strike is unavoidable. The *Disir* would appear to have more restrictions on their actions when it comes to their influence on the mortal world, reinforcing a power differential between the *Disir* and the Valkyrie, at least at one point within their histories.

I would posit that *Atlamál* presents another notable demarcating factor between the *Disir* and the Valkyries at the point that they were seen as wholly separate entities. The *Disir* are frequently described as ancestral spirits of the dead, coming from a place of the dead. Valkyries are not described as dead. They are often monstrous, and troll-like, but never dead. With the one exception being Brynhildr, explicitly framed as a former Valkyrie, they are undying. Even in their mortal presentations, they endure through reincarnation.

---

236 Later in the book I will discuss how Gudrun herself takes on characteristics of the Disir.

Outside of that, they are immortal, supernatural, and godly. They are not said to inhabit the afterlife spaces defined by absolute death, such as *Nástrǫnd*[237] and Hel's hall, but in a place devoid of absolute life and absolute death: Valhalla, a hall on the threshold between those worlds. There's something that rings of 'interference' with the Valkyrie's actions, intervening in the natural order to achieve a specific outcome, while the *Dísir* follow that order.

The Valkyries experience a fracturing as they move beyond the conversion and firmly into the medieval period. As touched on above, they become incorporated into other entities and figures, becoming malicious spirits, or conflated with other aspects within the Nordic or Germanic spheres.

In this way, the focus of defining the Valkyrie as a 'Chooser of the Slain' and mead-bearer singularly has worked to both unnecessarily minimise the Valkyries role, while also being a crucial lifeline for trying to distinguish the Valkyrie from so many similar figures.

The evidence of *Dísir* worship or veneration, seen most apparently in the *Dísablót*, has also been used to distance the classification between these ancestral guardians with the Valkyries and *Fylgjur*, despite evidence for fluidity between terms, perhaps an artefact of regional differences and time.

> "It must suffice to say that these beings bear close similarities to the figure of the Scandinavian Fylgjur (fetches) and valkyrjur (Valkyries) both of which were personal spirits that followed and sometimes protected individuals....Unlike the other two types of beings, however, the Disir sometimes receive sacrifices, have place names dedicated to them, and appear to protect not only individuals but also families and even nations...."[238]

---

237 See above, Gudrun is stated to be from Nástrǫnd in her Disir guise.
238 Terry Gunnell, "The Season of the Dísir: The Winter Nights and the Dísarblót in Early Scandinavian Belief", Cosmos, 16 (2005), 130.

While this has been used as a framework for analysis, I would disagree with the nature of the classification of the Valkyries as being simply personal spirits, when they are so frequently described with a duty and importance that aligns them with the *Nornir*, rather than lesser than the *Disir*. This classification ignores much of the information presented on the Valkyrie over the literature, with most not being tied to a single person at all.

How would the Valkyrie as a personal spirit be reconciled with their core duty of choosing who wins and dies on all battlefields? Their scope is expansive, not singular or focused on specific individuals. Where that occurs most prominently it is firmly within the euhemerised aspect of the human-born Valkyrie of the heroic sagas or within the dreamscapes archetypal of the works of the thirteenth century and beyond.

Regarding the latter, the characterisation of the *Fylgjur*, and by extension the *Hamingjur*, would seem quite distinct from the Valkyries, but even there we have witnessed significant conflation within the literature. In Chapter 9 of *Víga-Glúms* saga, a thirteenth century work, we encounter the figure of Glum,[239] who dreams of a gigantic woman striding towards him.

"It is said that Glum had a dream one night, in which he seemed to be standing out in front of his dwelling, looking towards the firth; and he thought he saw the form of a woman stalking up straight through the district from the sea towards Thverá. She was of such height and size that her shoulders touched the mountains on each side, and he seemed to go out of the homestead to meet her and asked her to come to his house; and then he woke up. This appeared very strange to everyone, but he said, The dream is no doubt a very remarkable one, and I interpret it thus--My grandfather, Vigfuss, must be dead, and that woman who was taller than the mountains, must be his guardian spirit, for he too was far beyond other men in honour and in most things, and his spirit must have been looking for a place of rest where I am. But in the summer, when the ships arrived, the news of Vigfusss death became known, and then Glum sang as follows--

---

239 This saga was mentioned earlier in the opening chapters of the book. It is one of the most creative in its presentation of Valkyries and potential Valkyrie-like figures and remains an interesting resource in the larger discussion.

At dead of night, beneath the sky,[240]
Upon the banks of Eyjafirth,
I saw the spirit stalking by,
In giant stature over the earth.
The goddess of the sword and spear
Stood, in my dream, upon this ground;
And whilst the valley shook with fear,
She towered above the mountains round."[241]

He interprets this woman as his ancestral, protective *hamingja*, his guardian spirit. It is noteworthy that this woman, as Glum describes her in song, is a "goddess of the sword and spear". As part of the pluralistic soul, it seems anomalous to refer to this "hamingja-woman" as a "Goddess", and indeed "of the sword and spear" could surely only be referring to a Valkyrie. This description of a mountainous being evokes the image of Skögul ['Shaker' or 'High-Towering'], with **Hilda Ellis Davidson** reasoning that the translation of the name, specifically, 'High-Towering', "might be a reference to the gigantic size of these beings."[242]

We have at least one potential Valkyrie being a Jotunn in Hljóð, who appears in the *Saga of the Volsungs*, despite being referred to as a "wish maiden" of Odin rather than as a Valkyrie outright. Scholarly consensus is that 'wish maiden' is a kenning, or otherwise a reference to a Valkyrie.[243] As discussed in this chapter, the Jotnar are often presented as being wolf-riders too, which would suggest that some Valkyries may have similar heritages.

---

240 As mentioned above, Lee Hollander uses an alternative verse in his translation. I've included that verse in Appendix A.

241 Edmund Walker Head, The Story of Viga-Glum (Illustrated Edition) (1866), 38.

242 Hilda Roderick Ellis Davidson, Myths and Symbols in Pagan Europe. Early Scandinavian and Celtic Religions (Syracuse, USA: Syracuse University Press, 1988), 96.

243 Andy Orchard, Dictionary of Norse Myth and Legend (Great Britain: Cassell, 1997), 198. In Appendix B I comment on my scepticism of this inference in relation to the characterisation and personality of Hljóð in comparison to her Valkyrie and Jotunn sisters.

While Davidson's comment infers that all Valkyries may have shared a gigantic stature, or the ability to change size, we can make no comment or inference on whether this ability was consistent across their number. Indeed, it's far from consistent across the examples we have of the Jotnar themselves. If we're to accept the literal translation of *Hamingja* to mean, in essence, 'luck', then we can consider another interpretation that lends evidence to this being a Valkyrie.

The image of the reincarnating Valkyrie protecting a family line, as presented in the heroic sagas, could be equated as this aspect of 'luck' personified, dictating fortune, and steering the individual away from danger. Such a protected individual would then have extraordinary 'luck' in battle and in life equally through manipulation and interference from the protective Valkyrie. The image works even if we remove the reincarnation element, though this is how it most commonly presents itself in the material.

We are then, potentially, seeing an amalgamation of the image of the Valkyrie with the elements of the *Hamingja*, in being able to be passed from one person to another through a sort of inheritance or sense of preserving duty to the familial line on behalf of the Valkyrie figure. A similar scenario plays out in *Hallfreðar saga Vandræðaskálds* [Hallfredar saga], with a "tall" woman wearing a mail-coat walking over the waves "as if she was on dry land."[244] Here, however, the titular Hallfred recognises her as a *"Fylgja-woman"*. From both examples, those that see the dream figure perceive it as an ill-omen of death, either recently occurred or imminent. Whatever guise they are presented in, Valkyrie figures cannot shake their associations with death, fate and destruction.

Maria Kvilhaug presents a framework regarding the *Fylgja* when she states that they "walk[s] before her person on the path of life."[245] This wording would seem to give some internal logic on how the *Fylgja* were seen to be an omen when the life was to end. The "path of life" comes to a halt and the person catches up with the fetch, meeting at the end of the road. By being in a position 'ahead' of the person, or otherwise in a liminal space that allows for exposure to future events, they act as a sort of 'canary in the mineshaft'.

---

244 Ibid, 123.
245 Kvilhaug, The Seed of Yggdrasill, 175.

This is made more interesting when she states, a couple of pages later, that the Valkyries "are Oðin's Fylgjur, the Fylgjur of the warrior and the king."[246] The Valkyries, after all, are often tied closely to human royalty by birth or through marriage within the heroic sagas, acting as a guide and guardian for those who have great potential ahead of them. However, I remain sceptical of this statement, as it further reduces the Valkyries to be an element of Odin, a part of his soul, while additionally, contradicting a variety of key attestations.

Where would Brynhildr, Sigrún, Kara and Sváva sit within this paradigm, being Valkyries presented as mortal in origin? Not to mention other Valkyries given explicit parentage. There's a lack of consistency here with the agreed role of the *Fylgjur* and how the Valkyries appear in the literature. Further, Sigrún and Sváva are never directly associated with Odin over the course of their respective appearances.[247] It's a conclusion drawn entirely from the image of a servant and ignores the Valkyries' role of dictating life and death on the battlefield that permeates their attestations.

This statement naturally also leads into further discussion on whether the Gods possess souls comparable to mortals, and how this would impact the greater cosmology. If we're to follow that they were perceived as possessing souls, and thus the various elements of the 'multi-part' or 'pluralistic' soul, then **Alexandra Sanmark** follows with the suggestion that Huginn and Muninn ["thought" and "memory"] are representations of Odin's travelling *hugr*[248] - a logical conclusion that aligns with these creatures' agreed role and function.

Nonetheless, we cannot avoid the consistent conflation between the presentation of the *Disir*, alongside the feminine *Fylgjur* and *Hamnigjur*, with the Valkyrie. I posit that the evolution of the latter away from roles that were singularly 'choosing the slain', but nonetheless tied to death and the supernatural world, lent itself to syncretisation to similar beings.

---

246 Ibid, 177. Neil Price makes a similar statement too, calling them semi-distinct aspects of Odin. Price, The Viking Way, 334.

247 Amanda. L. Green, Knocking on Death's Door. A Re-examination of the Old Norse Worlds of Death (Iceland: Háskóla Íslands, 2022), 212.

248 Alexandra Sanmark, "Living On: Ancestors and the Soul", in Signals of Belief in Early England: Anglo-Saxon Paganism Revisited, ed. Martin Carver et al., (Oxford and Philadelphia: Oxbow Books,2010), 161.

Of course, we also must consider that there was no central glossary that these skalds and scholars were all working from, with words such as *'Dis'* being used to describe, at times, normal mortal women and Goddesses, as well as those we would commonly associate with the *Disir* as demarcated by Bek-Pedersen.[249]

Even when identified with the Swan Maiden, as will be discussed in a later chapter, and the *Disir*, the Valkyrie almost[250] exclusively appear individually[251], in pairs, or multiples of three. Interestingly, **Else Mundal** also states that people have a limited number of "visible *Fylgja*", with the clarification of their number being "2-3-9",[252] elsewhere clarifying that the *Fylgja* was on "one side is a helpful counsellor, protective and luck-bringing, on the other hand she is a bringer of death.

Before battles or violent deaths *fylgjur* appear as grim-looking ogresses."[253] Again, these *Fylgjur* seem, by all appearances, to be Valkyries in all but name. We cannot ignore that Odin's association with the Valkyries has also acted as a crucial defining factor. Where Odin is absent, it has often been assumed that similar figures simply cannot be Valkyries if not mentioned explicitly. He has, in many ways, become their crucial identifier.

In *Darraðarljoð* within *Njal's Saga*, we are told that twelve women arrive outside the *dyngja* before departing, six to the north, six to the south.[254] The importance of the specification of north and south has been lost, though we may follow that this has something to do with the location of Asgard/Valhalla and, potentially, Hel's realm. This imagery is evoked in the fourteenth century 'Story of Thidrand and Thorhall' in *Flateyjarbók* [Book of Flatey]:

---

249 Aforementioned; see Karen Bek-Pedersen, The Norns in Old Norse Mythology, 41-56.

250 Helreið Byrnhildar [Brynhildr's Hel-Ride] makes an ambiguous reference to eight sisters, though it's unclear whether that's referring to eight plus Brynhildr or not.

251 Exclusively in the later Heroic sagas, with Sigrdrifa and Brynhildr as key examples.

252 Maria Kvilhaug's translation, Else Mundal, Fylgjemotiva i norrøn litteratur (Oslo: Universitetsforlaget, 1974). "Fylgjur – Guardian Spirits and Ancestral Mothers," accessed December 1, 2023. https://bladehoner.wordpress.com/2020/01/29/fylgjur-guardian-spirits-and-ancestral-mothers/

253 Ibid.

254 I will be discussing this in more detail in the chapter on seiðr.

"But suddenly someone knocked at the door; the noise was repeated twice. Thidrand drew his sword and stepped outside. He saw two troops of nine women, one clad in white, riding white horses arriving from the south, the other clad in black and riding black steeds, coming from the north. Attacked, Thidrand valiantly defended himself, but he was mortally wounded and it was believed that the Disir had sought revenge on him for being neglected and that they had come to take him as a sacrificial victim."[255]

While they are named as *Disir* in this excerpt, they don the appearance and behaviour of the Valkyrie: riding horses, arriving from the north and south, and demanding bloodshed. By the late fourteenth century then, it appears that the supernatural Valkyrie and *Disir* had become largely equated with each other, the former being overshadowed with the name and identity of the latter.

Whatever demarcation we can state in the modern day, the sources at the time saw notable conflation between these elements, with descriptions and behaviours seeming to overlap frequently. What I would suggest is that the *Fylgjur* and *Hamingjur* incorporated elements of the earlier Valkyrie at a time when the later Valkyries were becoming less defined by their supernatural elements, and more in line with the image of the 'noble warrior woman'. There's a diversion presented here, a fork in the road, with the Valkyrie becoming less supernatural while their presentation and behaviour remains disembodied to be collected into persevering supernatural elements and folk belief.

If one were to imagine a hypothetical Valkyrie existing throughout the course of this change, we would witness a being who is bloodthirsty, entirely supernatural and otherworldly. As we move through time, she becomes less supernatural and less liminal. She would splinter into various depictions, most prominently to the noble Valkyrie with mortal origins, reincarnating to protect heroic individuals. One splintered path would double down on the image of the Valkyrie as 'other', resulting in the depiction of a vengeful spirit used in curses. Something old and of the old world, left behind at the point of conversion.

---

255 Claude Lecouteux, Phantom Armies of the Night, The Wild Hunt and the Ghostly Processions of the Undead (USA: Inner Traditions, 2011), 20-1.

What wasn't able be incorporated into these branches would seemingly be dissolved into the *Disir*, *Haminjur* and *Fylgjur* over hundreds of years. A sort of watered-down image of protective ancestral guardians – still dealing in fate, and so easily incorporated into the existing lore of these beings. Whatever was left, could merge into the human Valkyrie come Shield-Maiden, occasionally possessing supernatural gifts, and other times, not.

Hail to the honoured ancestors,
To the Mothers, Grand-Mothers, Sisters and Daughters
Protectors, Guardians and Guides.

SKULD AND NORDIC FATE

"They played chequers in the meadow,
they were merry –
for them there was no
want of gold-
until there came three
ogres' daughters,
of redoubtable strength,
from Giant Realms."[256]

In the midst of this supposed idyll, the most prominent *Nornir* arrive[257]– Urdr, Verdandi and Skuld - three by number, Jotunn by heritage.

With their arrival, they bring upheaval to, what apparently was, an altogether pleasant and peaceful world. This was a world without consequence or death, where nothing was wanted, and nothing was needed. It was a world without constraint or limitation. A world without conflict but built on the back of it, through blood and toil.

The Jotnar have commonly been seen as emblematic of upheaval, acting as both harbinger and bringer of chaos, with the appearance of these three *Nornir* representing considerable change for the established order. From the earliest of days, the Jotnar have been consistently positioned as in apparent opposition to the Aesir and those that align themselves with them.

---

256 Ursula Dronke, The Poetic Edda: Volume II: Mythological Poems (Oxford: Oxford University Press, 1997), 9.

257 The identity of these figures is a matter of current consensus, as outlined by Bek-Pedersen, The Norns in Old Norse Mythology, 82.

However, while the Jotnar are seen as chaos, conflict and disorder incarnate,[258] there is a degree of a façade to this characterisation, with many of their attestations and appearances seeming in contradiction to that representation.[259] They often possess wisdom[260] that Odin craves, or otherwise incredible power and ability that marks them as notably distinct from the Gods themselves.

The *Nornir* certainly fall into this latter category, acting as the embodiment of order and law, stabilising the cosmic chaos into a rigid, readable structure. They are frequently described as agents of 'fate', of *Urðr*, determining a life's course and a life's end.

> "Thence come the maidens mighty in wisdom,
> Three from the dwelling down 'neath the tree;
> Urth is one named, Verthandi the next, —
> On the wood they scored, — and Skuld the third.
> Laws they made there, and life allotted
> To the sons of men, and set their fates"[261]

As such, when individuals suffer poor circumstances in period literature, they blame the *Nornir*, either the three main *Nornir*, or presumably the plethora of others who are said to exist within the greater cosmos.[262]

> "You've not been given entirely good luck, alien creature,
> yet I declare that the Nornir caused this, in part[263]

> -

> "The words I say now, I shall regret after this;
> his wife is Guðrún, and I am Gunnarr's;
> loathsome Nornir shaped long sufferings for us!"[264]

> -

---

258 M. Clunies Ross, Prolonged echoes: Old Norse myths in Medieval Northern Society (Odense, 1994), 144-86.

259 Ármann Jakobsson, "A contest of cosmic fathers: God and giant in Vafþrúðnismál", Neophilologus 92 (2008), 263-77. See also examples of marriage between Aesir and Jotnar.

260 As seen most prominently in Vafþrúðnismál [Lay of Vafthrudnir].

261 Bellows, The Poetic Edda, The Mythological Poems, 9.

262 "There are also other norns who visit everyone when they are born to shape their lives." Faulkes, Edda, 18. The vagueness around the descriptors of 'Nornir' could lead to a conclusion that the Valkyries fall into this category in terms of being tied to fate, alongside numerous others – including the Disir.

263 Edward Petit, The Poetic Edda: A Dual-Language Edition (Open Book Publishers,2023), 443.

264 Ibid, 573.

"His head were now off | if Erp were living,
The brother so keen | whom we killed on our road,
The warrior noble,-- | 'twas the Norns that drove me
The hero to slay | who in fight should be holy."[265]

They are said to manage every aspect of our lives, whether that involves misfortune, good fortune, or otherwise. Depicted as these grand architects, they are often equated with the Hellenic *Moirai*, the Greek Sisters of Fate. Yet, the image presented in the literature is far more nuanced than the stated similarity between the *Nornir* and *Moirai* often lends itself to.

The Nordic understanding of fate is not deterministic,[266] but rather cumulative and ever evolving. In this, Skuld, who is said to represent 'future' within this point of comparison, possesses a name that is often translated to mean 'Debt',[267] 'to owe', or 'should be',[268] all far from conveying a sense of absolute certainty.

Considering this, Skuld doesn't fit neatly into the comparison of a Nordic *Atropos*, one of the 'Sisters of Fate' who was known as "the Inflexible One"[269] and responsible for cutting the thread of life. So, what then does she represent?

It is in the common translation to 'Debt' that inspires a possible answer to that question. What, after all, is the payment for a life lived? We all have a debt to pay in the end: we live our lives, we enjoy our moment on the earth, but – at the end of it all – we all must pay our dues. This wording is used in verse 119 of *Njal's Saga*, suggesting it was an understood metaphor of the time:

"Snorri spoke: 'I see you are fierce and daunting, and yet my guess is that your good luck is at an end and that you have only a short time to live.'

---

265 Verse 28. Henry Adams Bellows. The Ballad of Hamther (1936). "The Ballad of Hamther", Sacred Texts, Accessed April 3, 2024, https://sacred-texts.com/neu/poe/poe37.htm

266 Declan Taggert, "Fate and Cosmogony in Völuspá: Shaping History in a Moment", Northern Studies vol 44 (2013), 31.

267 Orchard, Dictionary of Norse Myth and Legend, 169.

268 "Shall," Online Etymology Dictionary, accessed January 2, 2024. https://www.etymonline.com/word/shall

269 Clement of Alexandria, The Exhortation to the Greeks. The Rich Man's Salvation. To the Newly Baptized, trans. G. W. Butterworth, Loeb Classical Library 92 (Cambridge, MA: Harvard University Press, 1919), 52-3.

'Good,' said Sharphedin, 'because that's a debt we all have to pay. But you need to be avenging your father rather than predicting my fate."[270]

It is within this framework that I reconcile Skuld's position as a Valkyrie. Also within *Njal's Saga*, which I will go on to discuss in more detail, we have the phrase, "the Valkyries have their choice of the slain."[271] Its implication is that the Valkyries are given total mastery and choice over those that enter their blood grounds. A warrior's debt is a death on the battlefield. While the *Nornir* have their role to play in how a life plays out, Skuld may be there to collect.

In this, she may best be seen as akin to a death deity, or even the personification of death itself. Death within Nordic literature is, at once, impermanent, goal driven and crucially, cyclical. It is often the result of machinations and calculations, akin to the exchange of chess pieces on a board. It is a realm that is strongly associated with Odin, though from a more disembodied aspect: he oversees, he receives, he has the dead dedicated to him, and he exists on the line between life and death as the 'Gallow's Burden' [*Farmr galga*], revelling in that liminal position.

Freyja occupies a similar role as the result of her implied possession of a hall of the dead, and, on occasion, fulfilling a role akin to or aligned with the Valkyries as a 'Chooser of the Slain'. Hel and Ran are hosts to the dead through their possession of afterlife halls, but there is not an obvious embodiment of death as we see with other pantheons, like Thanatos within the Hellenic belief structure. The Nordic world is not unfamiliar with such concepts, as we have beings such as Jord, Dagr and Nott, embodying the earth, day and night, respectively.

---

270 Njal's Saga, trans. Robert Cook (Penguin Classics, 2001), 201. This work will be referenced via Cook moving forwards.

271 Bek-Pedersen, The Norns in Old Norse Mythology, 137. I suggest that this has ritualistic, sacrificial undertones, a point I will be addressing in more detail below with consideration of the common iconography and presentation of the Valkyrie.

Alongside my suggestion of Skuld being the personification of death and endings, the other *Nornir* would fit into the mould of beginnings and continuation, and all that those words would represent within that schema. This would also help 'solve' the issue of demarcation when it comes to the 'three main *Nornir*' and the plethora of others that are said to exist within the cosmology, which at times also includes the Valkyries themselves.

While the framing of Skuld being the Nordic equivalent of the Hellenic Atropos may be misaligned, there's certainly an element of certainty when it comes to how our stories all end, in that they *must* end. **Neil Price** suggests that Skuld could mean "must be",[272] and while he is one of the few to suggest this translation, I would argue that it becomes more justified if we see Skuld less of a representation of 'future', and more of 'an end'.[273] Death is a necessity, necessary for the continuation of life itself to thrive and grow. It is the "universal constant, the one experience that everything that lives shares."[274]

'There are yet others, Odin's maids, Hild and Gondul, Hlokk, Mist, Skogul. Then are listed Hrund and Eir, Hrist, Skuld. They are called norns that shape necessity.'[275]

The Nordic ideas around fate offer room to manoeuvre, grey areas to navigate.[276] In this, consider that Skuld isn't setting the path for us to walk on, nor necessarily the time or the place of our death, only that we *do* die. Fate is created in real time, dictated in part by our actions on the world, shifting in response to those actions and rippling across the people we surround ourselves with, altering their paths in turn.

---

272 Price, The Viking Way, 283.

273 Jackson Crawford also suggests a translation of 'necessity', which I again argue fits into this paradigm. Jackson Crawford, "Valkyries (Valkyrjur)," Jan 23, 2019, YouTube video, 21:54, https://www.youtube.com/watch?v=VMrYEq_jNVs

274 Meredith Catherine Moore, Dread Sisterhood: Conceptions of the Feminine in Norse Depictions of Death (MA thesis., Háskóli Íslands, 2015), 4.

275 Faulkes, Edda, 157. Hildr, a Valkyrie figure we will go on to discuss in more detail in a later chapter, creates a distorted nightmare of this imagery through her creation of a never-ending battle. It's carrying this duty to its most extreme end point - a place only defined by death, continuous and eternal.

276 Rudolf Simek posits that the Valkyrie Svipul's name refers to the changeable nature of fate, emphasising once again that fluidity that is absent in other common cultural comparisons. Simek, Dictionary of Northern Mythology, 308.

While the concept of a linear thread is common when discussing 'fate' outside of the Nordic sphere, it may be easier to think of fate as a web within it, or a tapestry. With innumerable threads stemming from ancestors and their actions on the world, something we inherit and shape. The combined image is better presented as not one thread alone travelling in the ether, but a network. Colliding and crossing with various others, intertwining and diverting according to our actions and words.

This image is also commonly analogised to a weave comprised of a warp and weft, infinitely crisscrossing. While the *Nornir* are said to weave or spin fate, there are few attestations that invoke textile imagery alongside their various appearances. *Helgakviða Hundingsbana I* [The First Poem of Helgi Hundingsbani] contains one of the few explicit mentions of fate strands, *örlögþáttu* [orlogthatto], producing the image of a landscape-spanning textile work, with its edges 'tucked into the corners' of the territory.

> "Night fell on the estate, then came norns,
> Those who shaped fate for the prince;
> They said the war-leader should be most famous
> And that he'd appear the best of princes.
>
> They plied very strongly the strand of fate,[277]
> As strongholds were breaking in Bralund;
> They prepared the golden threads
> And fastened it in the middle under the moon's hall.[278]
> East and west they concealed its ends,
> The prince possessed all the lands between;
> Neri's kinswoman to the north
> Threw one fastening; she said it would hold for ever."[279]

---

277 Bellows translates this as a 'web of fate'.
278 Presumably in the sky, orientating the action to one reaching from the sky to the ground. The imagery created is not unlike the image of the drop spindle, with the production of textiles being associated with the practice of seiðr – as detailed by Eldar Heide.
279 Larrington, The Poetic Edda (Revised Edition), 110-11.

Of note is the word choice in the second verse presented here that falls in line with **Karen Bek-Pedersen's** explanation of the *Nornir's* actions in this piece. "The verbs used to describe what the Nornir do with these örlögþáttu [fate threads] are snúa, 'to twist',[280] greiða, 'to comb out, arrange', and bregða, 'to braid, throw across'.

Were the intention to unequivocally portray spinning, one would have expected the word *spinna* to be employed.... Three threads are too many for spinning...and too few for weaving. Instead, it seems that three strands are plied or twisted into one thread."[281] The *Nornir* are never shown weaving or spinning thread. They are only shown *plying* thread, acting in such a way as to strengthen and stabilise rather than in a manner that can be seen as pure creation.

Bek-Pedersen, utilising work by **Henning Kure**,[282] notes that this image of three strands being plied top-down, leaving three individual strands heading in different directions, is not unsimilar to the common image of Yggdrasil. Below ground, three roots extend in three directions, while above ground, those three roots/threads are united into a singular, strong, trunk.[283] With this in mind, the *Nornir* may be better stated to be the anchors of 'order' stabilising the various threads. Directing and utilising what has already been created or already exists to form and shape what is to come into cohesion.

It's an act of unification. In the example above within *Helgakviða Hundingsbana I* we're seeing the Norns mark out the physical land with these threads that the prince is directed to inherit and "possess". A similar result is also declared by Sigrún later in verses 55 and 56 once Helgi has gained her favour.

"Unscathed, prince, you'll unleash men,
Upholder of Yngvi's line, and enjoy your life,
Since you have brought low the king who scorns flight,
The one who dealt death to the dread-bringing man'.

---

280 Larrington, also chose the word "plied" in the verse quoted above, following this reasoning.

281 Bek-Pedersen, The Norns in Old Norse Mythology, 129.

282 Henning Kure, I begyndelsen var skriget -- Vikingetidens myter om skabelsen (København: Gyldendal, 2010), 308-9.

283 Bek-Pedersen, The Norns in Old Norse Mythology, 130.

'And it's fitting, lord, that you should have
Both red-gold rings and the powerful girl;
Unscathed, lord, you'll enjoy both
Hogni's daughter and Hringstadir,
Lands and victory, now the battle is over."[284]

This conflicts slightly with a conclusion drawn by **David Varley,** namely that the Valkyrie's power lies only in a restricted landscape, the battlefield, while the Norns showcase power over a more expansive landscape from the outset. "The norns are implied to have a near-omnipotent degree of power over the fates of all things, as evidenced by their maintenance of the world-tree and their establishing of fate for gods and men in Voluspa, whilst the valkyries express their power only in the context of the battlefield."[285]

Here, Sigrún implies that she can achieve a similar result, granting Helgi lands and power through her influence and protection. The battlefield is a crucible where titles, land, people and resources are exchanged, making the Valkyries' mastery over this space far more critical than is often concluded. Further, with the Valkyries having control over the results of the battlefield space, it implies that the *Nornir* as a collective do not, acting to restrict their power over the fate of an individual. This reinforces the notion that Skuld is a death deity, as the future is in constant shift and out of the control of the other *Nornir* who rely, so often, on the Valkyries to decide one way or another.

The *Nornir* may have influence up to a certain point, the moment a warrior steps over the threshold into war, and at that moment precisely the Valkyries take over with the future being undecided, undictated, and untold. This also helps inform the connection between Odin and the Valkyries as an attempt to circumnavigate the *Nornir* through this undecided and uncertain future. A behaviour that is often ascribed to Odin and his constant, unsatiated pursuit of wisdom and power – a means to take control of his own destiny.

---

284 Larrington, The Poetic Edda (Revised Edition), 118.
285 Varley, The whirling wheel, 237-8.

Equally, this point also lends weight to the overall thematic image of the 'tamed Valkyrie' "being a means through which a hero can obtain mastery of his fate through independence and absolute self-governance."[286] The hero who marries a Valkyrie is one that escapes the *Nornir's* influence, and instead relies on her protection and guidance to dictate his own future - in a way gaining mastery over his own fate.

Consider also that Skuld is listed, by Snorri in his Edda, among the Valkyries themselves, which seems a curious inclusion at first glance.

"These are called valkyries. Odin sends them to every battle. They allot death to men and govern victory. Gunn and Rota and the youngest norn, called Skuld, always ride to choose who shall be slain and to govern the killings."[287]

This is a role that very much puts Skuld's death-allotting aspect to the forefront, associating her with a force that sits explicitly and comfortably within that realm. This is an environment that the *Nornir* as a collective would appear to have no control over, except for Skuld alone, who "always ride[s] to choose who shall be slain."

The image painted is one that evokes the Biblical 'Four Horsemen of the Apocalypse', with the Valkyries representing victory, war, frenzy and death, with Skuld especially personifying the latter, the inevitable end that people 'owe'. Skuld could be seen as a collector of that debt, joining the slaughter maidens as they ride out to reap their share of the dead, but also operating beyond their jurisdiction, dealing out death across the greater landscape, wherever it manifests. All of this, ultimately, aids in the possibility of Skuld being seen more as an 'end', rather than 'future'. With all lives having a beginning moment, an intermediary period, and an end. That's the order within the greater chaos.

---

286 Ibid, 249.
287 Faulkes, Edda, 31.

That's the *Nornir's* role to play, acting as they do in ways to nurture and feed the continual cycle of life and death that Yggdrasil represents. At once a 'tree of life', but also of death, the gallows on which Odin hung himself to gain greater wisdom and insight. The rune-scored roots feeding the trunk, feeding the branches, feeding the leaves, before returning to the soil, to that which exists "beneath the roots of a tree."[288]

If there was such a thing as a 'locked in' deterministic fate in the Nordic realm, then the Valkyries' role of choosing the slain would be a total illusion. Rather, what we're presented with better resembles a future and near future in flux that changes through our collective actions. Yet, we all must end, and in the literature, that also extends to the Gods themselves. Death is the force that upset that perfect, timeless world the Gods created, brought about at that first creation of mortality – Askr and Embla, who were 'fateless'[289] before the arrival of the *Nornir*. But mortality is ephemeral by nature, and Skuld's arrival, last among her sisters, became a matter of inevitability, unavoidable. Something that must happen, the force that the Gods try their hardest to delay.

What happens up to that point appears to be open to manipulation using magic or magical means. In period literature, that manipulation most often appears through the practice of *seiðr*, and as such we should dedicate some space to discuss the importance of the relationship between textiles, weaving, fate, and this oft-misunderstood tool.

In the *Saga of King Hrolf Kraki*, we encounter another character by the name of Skuld who is described as a powerful sorceress. Like many of her literary contemporaries, Skuld initially incites her husband, King Hjorvard, into declaring war on King Hrolf through questioning his manliness. "What a weakling you are," she said, "to accept whatever shame is handed to you."[290]

---

288 To use a phrase found in Hervararkviða [commonly referred to as The Waking of Angantyr] to describe the realm of the dead.

289 Völuspá 18. Bellows, The Poetic Edda: The Mythological Poems, 8. "two without fate"

290 The Saga of King Hrolf Kraki, trans. Jesse Byock (London, England, UK: Penguin Group, 1998), 70.

While orchestrating this opposition as an unwillingness to pay tribute to Hrolf, Skuld explains that she would win if war was to break out between them, despite Hrolf's seemingly undefeatable reputation up to that point. Hrolf agrees for the tribute payment to be delayed by three years, with the understanding that the payment would be made in full once those three years passed. Meanwhile, "Skuld assembled a troop of the best fighters as well as the worst rabble from neighbouring provinces. This treachery was concealed so that King Hrolf was completely unaware of it...it was done with the most skilful magic and sorcery. Skuld, to overpower her brother King Hrolf...summoned elves, norns and countless other vile creatures."[291]

On the battlefield, Skuld sits in a "black tent on the witch's scaffold"[292] and once she enters the fray herself, she conjures a "storm of enchantments"[293] which causes Hrolf's champions to fall around him. Her power on the battlefield is potent, and it's only once she kills Hrolf Kraki and takes power from him that she is killed herself, taken by surprise and tortured after only a short time on the throne of Denmark. Like her namesake, Queen Skuld represents a debt that must be paid, here, revenge for the rape of her elven mother by Hrolf's father, Helgi.[294]

---

291 Ibid, 70-1. It should also be noted that this is also an example of the 'old ways' being demonised. Here elves and Norns are thrown into the overall descriptor of "vile creature", which is not a characteristic that manifests in their other appearances. Byock suggests such examples may have been additions of a later Christian scribe.

292 Ibid, 76. The witch's scaffold may be understood to be the 'high seat' of seiðr, seiðhjallr which is sometimes translated to 'magic/incantation scaffold'. Hlidskjalf, Odin's high-seat, allows him to watch over all the realms. See Andres Siegfried Dobat, "Viking Age functional culture as a reflection of the belief in divine intervention", in Old Norse Religion in Long-Term Perspectives: Origins, Changes & Interactions, ed. Anders Andrén, Kristina Jennbert, and Catharina Raudvere (Lund, Sweden: Nordic Academic Press, 2006), 185-7 & Rudolf Simek, "The use and abuse of Old Norse religion: Its beginnings in high medieval Iceland", in Old Norse Religion in Long-Term Perspectives: Origins, Changes & Interactions, ed. Anders Andrén, Kristina Jennbert, and Catharina Raudvere (Lund, Sweden: Nordic Academic Press, 2006), 378.
Heide suggests that the seiðworker may want elevation so that the spindle can drop further before the individual has to stop their working to wind the spun yarn back in. Heide, Spinning Seiðr, 166.

293 Ibid, 78.

294 The language used within these chapters of the saga don't paint Skuld in an entirely negative light, and even could be said to be a heroic figure despite her unceremonious demise. This is discussed by Amanda Platz, Autonomous Power and Profound Agency: Women and Magic in the Icelandic Legendary Sagas (Ma thesis: Clemson University, 2021), 38-9.

It is weregeld she seeks, and weregeld she receives. She is the inevitable 'payback' for wrongs committed, and she thrives on the battlefield, raising the dead to fight where her army falls. "As many limbs as we cleave, shields as we split, helmets and mail costs as we hew apart...the encounters with the dead are the grimmest. We lack the strength to combat such opponents."[295] While these events are suggestive of the resurrective power of *seiðr* – and indeed, it certainly seems that Skuld can be accurately described as a *seiðkonur* [seiðwoman][296] - there's also a hint of a mockery here to the Norn Skuld.

As much as Queen Skuld takes, as many debts come due, she also takes from the Norn and the Valkyries equally, all while using a power that is so crucial to their duties. They are the 'Inheritors of Divine *Seiðr*', and it is that power which grants them mastery over the battlefield, as it served Queen Skuld in turn.

Death is the great necessity,
Hung on the great gallows weave,
Plucked from the world, a warrior's due
the debt that must be paid, the inevitable end.

---

295 Byock, The Saga of King Hrolf Kraki, 76.
296 Shaun B Kelly, An Examination of The Representations of Magic in The Saga of Hrolf Kraki (2012), 8

Inheritors of Divine Seidr, Magic in the Nordic World

"She saw Valkyries coming from far and wide,
ready to ride to the gods' realm;
Skuld[297] shouldered one shield, Skogul another,
Gunn, Hild, Gondul and Geir-skogul-
now the General's ladies are counted up,
Valkyries ready to ride over the earth."[298]

Before we explore the rationalisation of how and why the Valkyries potentially utilised *seiðr* throughout a host of their depictions, I should add crucial context and delve into the world of inference and the hypothetical. While we can conclude very little about the practical application of historical *seiðr*, that shouldn't stop us from collectively discussing its possibilities or otherwise discussing how it could have worked.

Academia has worked hard to illuminate this specific area of interest over the last two decades,[299] with momentum only building. It's the perfect moment to generate conversations on how *seiðr* may have played a crucial role in many Eddic events. I stand firm in the belief that, despite the centuries of academic discourse, we've only just started to break below the surface of the Eddas, armed as we are with new perspectives and information that shatter previous conventions and schools of thought.

---

297 Another attestation of Skuld being among the Valkyries.

298 Larrington, The Poetic Edda (Revised Edition), 8.

299 Neil Price, The Viking Way: Religion and War in Late Iron Age Scandinavia (Revised Edition), (Uppsala, Sweden: Uppsala University, 2019); Leszek Gardeła, Sophie Bønding and Peter Pentz, eds. The Norse Sorceress: Mind and Materiality in the Viking World (UK: Oxbow Books, 2023). https://doi.org/10.2307/jj.5699282.

There are things we've accepted as fact or common knowledge that have been revaluated, with promising paradigms emerging considering new information. The Valkyries, naturally, are very much included here, alongside further insight into *seiðr*. These are elements that were most at the mercy of Christian opposition, as archetypal as they were of Heathen beliefs and practices. The wild that must be tamed.

THE 'FIRST WAR OF THE WORLD'

Despite its apparent importance, we are offered scarce detail on the events of the 'Great War' between the Aesir and Vanir. In the mythological space it created a new dynamic, shifting the cosmic landscape, and allowed the divine to move forward in a new alliance. But it also leaves many questions unanswered. Why were seemingly the most prominent of Vanir gods selected to live among the Aesir? How did Freyja find herself among the Aesir once the dust was settled? She is not named among the Vanir hostages - her brother and father - and only two Aesir gods were apparently sent to live among the Vanir, Hoenir and Mimir.

If Nordic fate is malleable, then Odin's motivations throughout much of the Eddas can be seen as a preparation for what is to come. At a certain point, one may also see Odin's actions as preparing for what comes after *Ragnarök,* putting the pieces in place to try and navigate towards victory, or – if all else fails – an enduring legacy. This opens an opportunity to frame Loki's actions in a new light. Consider that by 'killing' Baldr, Loki may have secured his ultimate survival.

His daughter extends her hospitality and shelter during *Ragnarök* so Baldr may once more return when the destructive fires have burned out. There's a continual theme of Loki acting in ways that may seem antagonistic, but ultimately lead to greater power for the community or more beneficial circumstances, which contrasts quite dramatically with the sort of negative language often used to describe him.

Consider also **Caroylne Larrington's** position, that the magic of the runes lies in their ability to transcend time. To capture what was once believed ephemeral and intangible: words, stories, memories. As a writing system, the runes supplement "human memory and oral storytelling with a technology that would endure long beyond the human lifespan."[300]

Imagine the potency of this tool, the shift that a writing system would present to a people who had no ability to write down their thoughts and deeds. It would be a sort of magic, and that, as Larrington posits, is the core of Odin's sacrifice and discovery. Something that would 'continue' and travel through time. If we see Odin as the euhemerised human that Saxo presents him as, then Odin has truly beaten death and continued through 'magical' means, achieving immortality. Quite the feat for a simple Byzantine wizard!

Equally, time and time again we see the Jotnar try to interrupt Aesir efforts to avoid the prospective 'inevitable end' that *Ragnarök* represents. It's a war of attrition, but also one of unequal power. Through Idunn, the Aesir have access to eternal youth, remaining ever young and full of vitality. Her theft at the hands of Thjazi, Skadi's father, represents a dramatic shift in power in favour of the giants. It's a direct threat to the Gods' enduring nature, taking from them a tool which is vital for the maintenance of their ruling position.

While seen as antagonistic, it is easy to see how the Jotnar can be perceived as the 'underdogs', acting against a newer, seemingly eternal, force that views them as entirely other. My position stems from this power dynamic. I suggest that much of what we see happening in the Eddas comes down to the 'first war of the world', the 'great war' between the Aesir and Vanir, and the acquisition of a power that is fundamental to the relationship between the Jotnar and Gods from that point on.

This power is *seiðr*, and more specifically, the way *seiðr* is utilised by divine powers. Let's follow this prospective path further. We understand that, courtesy of Snorri in *Heimskringla*, the Vanir had *seiðworkers* among their ranks with Freyja being particularly proficient. "It was she who first taught the Aesir magic such as was practised by the Vanir."[301]

---

300 Carolyne Larrington, The Norse Myths That Shape the Way We Think (London: Thames & Hudson Ltd, 2023), 94.

301 Hollander, Heimskringla: History of the Kings of Norway, 8.

If the practice of *seiðr* was indeed capable of resurrection, as has been suggested by numerous academics,[302] it would be easy to see how a war between the Vanir and Aesir could reach a stalemate. The latter's talent for warfare perhaps found themselves against an undying Vanir army, with their dead coming back after the day's battle. Considering that the Vanir faction is so often seen as connected to vitality and fertility – vibrant and rich life – there is a clash here of enduring life with relentless death. An unstoppable force against an immovable object.

A seemingly endless battle against resurrected forces is a familiar recurring motif in the Nordic Eddas and sagas, and potentially here we see a seed being planted, a seed that would eventually sprout into Valhalla.[303] Perhaps Odin, with the thought of *Ragnarök* very much present in his mind from the Seeress' prophecy, saw potential in this magic. He remembered Gullveig, she who died and was given life again three times. This might explain Odin's actions that followed the great war between the Aesir and Vanir.

A truce and an exchange of hostages followed to reinforce the renewed peace, with Odin specifically seeking Freyja's *seiðwork* – impressive even among the incredible magical talents of the other Vanir. Again, there's very much the feeling in the literature that explanations have been washed away with time, the lines connecting Gullveig, Freyja, Odin and *seiðr* made almost incoherent. But connections remain, tentative though they may be a millennia later. Nonetheless, we have some evidence that Odin, among the other Aesir, learns *seiðr* through Freyja.

From there, we could suggest that some sort of bargain was struck, a bargain that would eventually lead to a distribution of the Valkyrie's yield. Perhaps, Odin offers Freyja half of the chosen dead for her hall, Sessrumnir, in exchange for teaching him *seiðr*, that coveted tool he saw the Vanir utilise in numerous ways during the war. He is a seeker of knowledge and power, so how fantastic a prize would something like *seiðr* seem to him? A prize that would forever shift the scales of power in favour of the Aesir.

---

302 Price, The Viking Way, 300-1; Ursula Dronke, 'The War of the Æsir and Vanir in Völuspá', in Myth and Fiction in Early Norse Lands (London: Routledge, 1996), 230-1; North, Heathen Gods in Old English Literature, (Cambridge and New York: Cambridge University Press, 1997), 85 & 108.

303 See North, Heathen Gods in Old English Literature, 108. North frames seiðr as the crucial tool that Odin uses to resurrect fallen kings to serve him in Valhalla. This is, generally, a view I would agree with.

The Jotnar frequently attempt to steal Freyja. She is wanted by the 'Builder' as payment for building an immense fortification around Asgard (the Vanir penetrated their walls during the war after all) is threatened of kidnap by Hrungnir alongside Sif, and is coveted as a bride by Thrym, a bargaining chip for the return of Mjolnir. Mjolnir isn't the treasure here, not the ultimate prize but a stepping stone to the Goddess herself. We are told of her beauty, she who is the "most glorious" of the Goddesses, but perhaps it's not her beauty that the Jotnar cherish, but her power.

> "What the giants threaten is not only the destruction of the gods and their world – that fate is expected – but the annihilation of the divine power to live again. Are they not continually trying to capture the magical goddess who has the secret of that divine power? And was this not the goddess that the Aesir tried vainly to kill in their war against her?"[304]

Writing here, **Ursula Dronke** argues from the position also held by **Maria Kvilhaug**: that Freyja is Gullveig, the 'witch' with the power of resurrection. The Vanir prove themselves relentless, newborn again with the new dawn, to attack and overpower the Aesir defences.

Once the Aesir walls are breached, the war appears to conclude without further bloodshed with the exchange of hostages, with prominent Vanir being invited to stay within Asgard's walls as Aesir. Freyja joins the rest of her family, and Odin acquires that most coveted of powers to bring about eternal life through undeath – stopping Skuld from continuing the natural cycle with the ultimate end. At least, for some time, Odin has circumnavigated the *Nornir* and the law of the cosmos.

---

304 Dronke, The War of the Æsir and Vanir in Völuspá, 223.

"Othin had the skill which gives great power and which he practised himself. It is called seith [sorcery], and by means of it he could know the fate of men and predict events that had not yet come to pass; and by it he could also inflict death or misfortune or sickness, or also deprive people of their wits or strength, and give them to others. But this sorcery is attended by such wickedness that manly men considered it shameful to practice it, and it was taught to priestesses."[305]

If Odin wants an undying army to fight against the perceived inevitability of *Ragnarök,* he wants the very best and most capable of Midgard's warriors[306] at his side when the time comes to fight for Asgard's very survival. Perhaps, Freyja and Odin then teach those that would become the Valkyries *seiðr* in turn, thereby connecting her to them. This not only establishes a connection between Freyja and the Valkyries, but also explains why the Valkyries are all women: *seiðr*, as we've established, was seen as a particularly feminine practice.

From their earliest incarnation, the Valkyries were strongly associated with taking life, but with this new tool under their belt, they could shape the battlefield to their whim and will, giving life, giving injury, withholding death, and dealing out wholesale slaughter. *Seiðr* allowed for control over fate, and it is that which was so treasured by Odin. From there, the associations with protection, a singularly Nordic dressing, grew. No longer were the Valkyries agents of carnage and gore, but gradually, something that could be better shaped towards civilisation, even the supposed pinnacle of it, nobility.

---

305 Hollander, Heimskringla: History of the Kings of Norway, 11. [in Saga of the Ynglings].

306 There's no mention of Odin collecting warriors from other realms/ worlds, so the inferred conclusion is that Odin presumably only collects fallen warriors from Midgard. A natural follow up question is, why is that the case? Was there ever an understanding that Odin collected from other 'worlds' too?

While I don't hold much weight at all in Freyja justifying the title of 'Queen of the Valkyries', as is common modern understanding,[307] I do see her as the archetype on which the Valkyries would eventually form, at least in the shape of their Nordic appearances. They are beings possessing magic, flying "into the strife", choosing the slain, serving as mead bearers, and exhibiting agency.

They evolved or adapted to be removed somewhat from their more blood-thirsty histories, though still potent forces and at home on their favoured environment, the battlefield, among the dead, dying and victorious. These monstrous origins, pagan, other, demonised, were not palatable to the ever-converting world and had to be diminished or completely vanquished from the cultural zeitgeist. Between that choice, the former prevailed, resilient in the face of ever-increasing antagonism to their original and earlier manifestations.

Snorri makes one specification in *Heimskringla* that I want to touch on considering a theory I will be outlining in later chapters. "'By these powers he [Odin] became very famous - his enemies feared him, but his friends trusted him, and believed in him and his power. Most of these skills he taught to those in charge of the sacrifices; they were next to him in all magic knowledge and sorcery.'" [308]

The theory relates to the Valkyries' role as battlefield priestesses, operating in a space with deeply ritualistic and religious undertones. Here, then, we may find further evidence for the Valkyries being taught Odin's powers to aid them in their task. They are, I would argue, in charge of the sacrifices on the battlefield.

Today, there's little room for argument when it comes to concluding that magic, witchcraft or sorcery was connected to spinning, weaving and general textile works within Scandinavia in the late Iron Age.

---

307 "Freya Norse Goddess | The Queen of Valkyries", Odin's Cave, accessed June 18, 2024. https://www.odinscave.com/blogs/norse-mythology-gods/introducing-freya-the-queen-of-valkyries

308 Translation by Neil Price. Price, The Viking Way, 39.

In the Viking Age, we have evidence that fate and the giving of life could be perceived as a thread, lending to the further image that the manipulation of that life through the manipulation of that thread was possible within the belief system, such as during the act of spinning or weaving.[309] Of course, this is all relatively recent, rarely were such conclusions drawn in the twentieth century, with much discourse on the topic of Nordic fate taking classical inspirations on the academic landscape.

Over the last couple of decades, this paradigm has dramatically shifted – in large part due to the work of **Eldar Heide**,[310] **Leszek Gardeła**,[311] and **Neil Price**,[312] among others – to give a greater significance to distaffs, and the act of spinning or weaving in connection to the practice of *seiðr*. Ultimately, I argue it is no coincidence that the Valkyries are associated so strongly with the two Gods who are called or inferred to be, at various times, the masters of this magic.

There's no doubt that the whole story has had crucial details omitted, and the form we have available to us in the modern day is what remains, partial remnants united in a vague arrangement. Further muddying the waters is that the verses remain ambiguous when it comes to establishing the chronology of the events, and whether they could be seen as wholly sequential changes from scholar to scholar. The order of the lines and stanzas across the entire poem are not totally uniform across translations.[313]

---

309 Michèle Hayeur Smith, The Valkyries' Loom: The Archaeology of Cloth Production and Female Power in the North Atlantic (USA: University Press of Florida, 2020), 18.

310 Eldar Heide, "Spinning Seiðr", in Old Norse Religion in Long-Term Perspectives: Origins, Changes, and Interactions, ed. Anders Andrén, Kristina Jennbert, and Catharina Raudvere (Lund, Sweden: Nordic Academic Press, 2004).

311 Leszek Gardeła, "A Biography of the Seiðr-Staffs. Towards an Archaeology of Emotions", in Between Paganism and Christianity in the North, ed. L. P. Słupecki, J. Morawiec (Rzeszów: Rzeszów University, 2009), 190-219.

312 Neil Price, The Viking Way: Religion and War in Late Iron Age Scandinavia (Revised Edition), (Uppsala, Sweden: Uppsala University, 2019)

313 Bellows, The Poetic Edda, 7.

Perhaps the most prominent example of the connection between manipulating fate and weaving comes to us by way of the Valkyries in *Darraðarljóð*,[314] in chapter 157 of *Njáls saga*. We are told of a man named Dorrud who witnessed the arrival of twelve individuals "riding together to a woman's room" [a *dyngja*, a room used for weaving], before disappearing inside. Intrigued, Dorrud approached the window of the *dyngja* and saw that there were women inside and that they had set up a loom. This loom, however, was made of human body parts and weaponry, drenched in blood and covered in gore and viscera.

"Men's heads were the weights, but men's entrails were the warp and weft, a sword was the shuttle, and the reels were arrows."

The Valkyries then sing their war-song gleefully.[315]

"See! warp is stretched
For warriors' fall,
Lo! weft in loom
'Tis wet with blood;
Now fight foreboding,
'Neath friends' swift fingers,
Our gray woof waxeth
With war's alarms,
Our warp bloodred,
Our weft corpseblue.

This woof is y-woven
With entrails of men,
This warp is hardweighted
With heads of the slain,
Spears blood-besprinkled
For spindles we use,
Our loom ironbound,
And arrows our reels;

314 There's some disagreement on the literal translation of this name, some refer to 'Song of the Spear', from the Anglo-Saxon 'daroþ', others say 'Song of Darraðar/Darrad or Dorrud from the character. But also, potentially, 'banner' so becoming 'The Lay of the Banner'. As such, I will be referring to Darraðarljóð as Darraðarljóð throughout this book to avoid potential confusion.

315 The full song deserves to be read in its entirety, but for brevity here I've chosen the most relevant stanzas.

With swords for our shuttles
This war-woof we work;
So weave we, weird sisters,
Our warwinning woof.

Now War-winner walketh
To weave in her turn.
Now Swordswinger steppeth,
Now Swiftstroke, now Storm;
When they speed the shuttle
How spear-heads shall flash!
Shields crash, and helmgnawerö [helmet hound]
On harness bite hard!

Wind we, wind swiftly
Our warwinning woof,
After that let us steadfastly
Stand by the brave king;
Then men shall mark mournful
Their shields red with gore,
How Swordstroke and Spearthrust
Stood stout by the prince.
Wind we, wind swiftly
Our warwinning woof;
When sword-bearing rovers
To banners rush on,
Mind, maidens, we spare not
One life in the fray!
We corpse-choosing sisters
Have charge of the slain.

Now surely 'tis gruesome
To gaze all around,
When bloodred through heaven
Drives cloudrack o'er head;
Air soon shall be deep hued
With dying men's blood
When this our spaedom
Comes speedy to pass.

So cheerily chant we
Charms for the young king,
Come maidens lift loudly
His warwinning lay;
Let him who now listens
Learn well with his ears,
And gladden brave swordsmen
With bursts of war's song".[316]

For comparison, I'll also include sections of Robert Cook's translation below, originally from 1997. DaSent's 1861 translation keeps some of the 'energy' of the original verse, alongside the literal translation of the Valkyries' names, while Cook leaves them unchanged for easier recognition.

"A wide warp
Warns of slaughter;
Blood rains
From the beam's cloud

A spear-grey fabric
Is being spun,
Which the friends
Of Randver's slayer
Will fill out
With a red weft

The warp is woven
With warrior's guts
And heavily weighted
With the heads of men.
Spears serve as heddle rods,
Spattered with blood;
Iron-bound is the shed rod,
And arrows are the pin beaters;
We will beat with swords
Our battle web

---

316 Translation is by George W. DaSent, The Story of Burnt Njal (1861), accessed November 21, 2023. https://sagadb.org/brennu-njals_saga.en#156

Hild sets to weaving,
And Hjorthrimul[317]
And Sanngrid[r][318] and Svipul,
With swords drawn.
Shafts will splinter,
Shields will shatter;
The dog of helmets
Devour shields.

-

We wind and wind
The web of spears,
And then stand by
Our stalwart king.
Gunn[r] and Gondul,
Who guarded the king,
Saw the bloody shields
Of the brave men.

We wind and wind
The web of spears,
There where the banners
Of bold men go forth;
We must not let
His life be lost –
Valkyries decide
Who dies or lives
Now it is gruesome
To gaze around,
As blood-red clouds
Cover the sky;
The heavens will be garish
With the gore of men
While the slaughter-wardens
Sing their song

---

317 Old Norse, Hjörþrimul
318 Old Norse, Sanngriðr

Our pronouncement was good
For the young prince;
Sound of mind
We sing victory songs.
May he who listens
Learn from this
The tones of spear-women
And tell them to men."[319]

There's much of note about this piece, not least because it offers the clearest presentation of the Valkyries' role on the battlefield within the breadth of the literature.

With every motion and verse, every pull or winding of the thread and loom, we have action on the battlefield, making it clear that the Valkyries are the cause of that action.

The verse below perhaps highlights this most clearly:

"Hild sets to weaving,
And Hjorthrimul
And Sanngrid[r] and Svipul,
With swords drawn.
Shafts will splinter,
Shields will shatter;
The dog of helmets
Devour shields".

The Valkyries are confident that their decisions in this *dyngja* will shatter spear shafts, and swords will cut through shields.

That is their intent and will, and there's no question of the result. Here too we have a juxtaposition of the weaving, a highly feminine activity, with the Valkyries holding swords in their hands. There's a purposeful clash of iconography in this image that accentuates the otherworldly aspects of the poem.

The entire song is punctuated with reminders that they are literally weaving with the lives and lifeblood of the men on the battlefield.

---

319 Cook, Njal's Saga, 303-6.

The stakes couldn't be higher, and the *dyngja* becomes a liminal space: part of the battlefield through the actions of those inside, but outside of it, almost in its own realm that Darrud experiences and witnesses by peering through a window.

He glimpses into the liminal to see the machinations behind the reality he is witnessing. A significant boundary is crossed. There is a long literary tradition of windows, doors and gates being considered the threshold between liminal spaces. This is just another example within that tradition, though with the common gender roles reversed.[320] The Valkyries thrive through subversion.

As mentioned above, we have the crucial phrase "Valkyries decide who dies or lives / We corpse-choosing sisters / Have charge of the slain."

Bek-Pedersen makes it even clearer, "The Valkyries have their choice of the slain."[321] There is no inference or suggestion at all to Odin having a say in what is occurring, it is not his will at play.

Equally, there's something very different to the *seiðwork* (I firmly maintain that is what we're witnessing in these verses) we're seeing here that is, as much as we can conclude, absent from Vanir practice.

They are not associated with macabre images of death, but Odin is. Here, then, we may see Odin's influence on the Valkyries and their specific brand of magical manipulation.

This weaving encapsulates all the madness and violence of battle, fitting for the frenzy God himself. We see, in the right hands, that *seiðr* is a potent tool. A pull here, a twist there, weaving endless possibilities.

Resurrection in Odin's hands, think of preserving Mimir's head, something not made completely whole again, has a grim undertone. Where Freyja and the Vanir are defined by life and rebirth- distinctly feminine attributes in the literature - Odin's influence perhaps brings a darker edge.

---

320 Iman Sheeha, 'Mistress, look out at window': Women, Servants and Liminal Domestic Spaces on the Early Modern Stage (London: Brunel University, 2020), 1.
321 Bek-Pedersen, The Norns in Old Norse Mythology, 137.

An overtly necromantic side to *seiðr*. Putting aside that, considering the elements of resurrection and communal with otherworldly spirits, *seiðr* seems innately connected to necromantic practices.

This manipulation allows them to alter the battle to ensure those chosen actually perish – whether that be making shields fail, driving a sword through to flesh, or guiding an arrow to its mark.

We see sources evoke the imagery associated with *seiðr* on numerous occasions, but mostly notably in *Darraðarljoð* ("men's entrails were the warp and weft") and *Vǫlundarkviða* [the Song of Volund], where the Valkyries spin flax. To note, Freyja also has a connection to flax through a heiti, Horn.

Göndul, who appears within *Sörla þáttr*,[322] *Heimskringla*, *Darraðarljóð* and the *Völuspá* [Voluspa, Seeress' Prophecy] among others, is a figure of particular interest in this conversation. Her name is often translated to "wand-wielder' or "staff/staffbearer", derived from 'gandr' - the staff that is strongly associated with *seiðr*.

As discussed by **Rudolf Simek**, Göndul could also mean "magical animal" or "werewolf", stating that this is no doubt connected to the Valkyries' core function over human fate.[323] **Neil Price** makes the connection between this and the 'gandir' spirit, with explicit overtones of sorcery connected with the battlefield.[324] 'Gandr' is also used as a word for 'wolf' in several kennings, including *hallar gandr* [hall wolf] and *storðar gandr* [coppice wolf].[325] The 'gandir' spirit is a sorcerer spirit, a helping spirit, who is sent out or summoned to provide information. This spirit may take on an animal form[326] commonly that of wolves.[327]

---

322 Though this appearance is identified with Freyja. I do not conclude that Freyja is Göndul in every instance, but rather a heiti appealing to her associations with seiðr and, therefore, being a staff bearer/gandir summoner. I'll address this in 'The Power of the Valkyrie" chapter.

323 Simek, Dictionary of Northern Mythology, 115.

324 Price, The Viking Way, 283.

325 Rudolf Meissner, Die Kenningar der Skalden: ein Beitrag zur skaldischen Poetik (Bonn and Leipzig: Kurt Schroeder, 1921), 101.

326 Clive Tolley, "Vǫrðr and Gandr: Helping Spirits in Norse Magic", Arkiv For Nordisk Filologi (1995), 67.

327 Aleks Pluskowski, "Conjuring Canids: Wolves and Dogs in Viking Age

While many academics have suggested that Göndul is the helpful spirit in this scenario, controlled by Odin,[328] I would argue that Göndul is the controller due to her name's etymology - that is to say, she wields the staff. It's also no coincidence that the Valkyries are strongly associated with wolves across their various appearances, both in utilising wolves and being among wolves in their duties, especially within the realm of kennings.

Reinforcing this conclusion is the fourteenth century curse made by Ragnhild Tregagås during her trial for witchcraft:

"Ritt ek i fra mer gondols ondu.
æin þer i bak biti
annar i briost þer biti
þridi snui uppa þik
hæimt oc ofund"

"I hurl the spirits of Gandul;
One bites you in your back
Another one bites your chest
And the third afflicts you
With hatred and envy."[329]

These spirits, presumably lupine in form, are described as being "of" Gondul. These *gandir* spirits were the tools of witches, summoned by way of this Valkyrie and her mastery over such entities.

Sorcery", in The Norse Sorceress: Mind and Materiality in the Viking World, ed. by Leszek Gardeła, Sophie Bønding, and Peter Pentz (Oxford: Oxbow Books, 2023), 229.

328 One of his names is Gǫndlir, which may mean 'user of [a] Göndul', again I suggest this is referring to Odin's position as 'Master of Seiðr', as in "User of Seiðr staff", rather than any implied mastery of Göndul herself. Ibid, 71.

329 Rune Blix Hagen, "'I Hurl the Spirits of Gandul'. Pleasure, Jealousy, and Magic: The Witchcraft Trial of Ragnhild Tregagaas in 1325", in Myths and Magic in the Medieval Far North: Realities and Representations of a Region on the Edge of Europe (Norway: The Arctic University of Norway, 2020), 144.

The Names and Behaviours of Valkyries

Much can be gleaned from a name within the Nordic world, and much too is expressed through the names of Valkyries. At first glance, it is easy to conclude that they embody the chaotic noise and horror of battle. The clashing of shields, spears meeting flesh, arrows raining from above, but there are outliers that paint a very different picture. For example, Eir can be translated to mean "heal", "help" or "mercy"[330] depending on the interpretation. There's also Ráðgríðr, meaning, possibly, "council-truce",[331] Nipt [Female relative, commonly "sister"] and Ölrún ["ale-rune"].

These names, while admittedly fewer in number than those explicitly associated with war and battle, strongly reinforce that, within contemporary literature, there was an awareness that Valkyries had a duty or duties outside that of choosing the dead on the battlefield and ferrying their souls to the afterlife. We understand that to be the case today, but this helps illuminate how they were perceived within the period, and that there was an understanding of their multifaceted nature during the time of writing.

Take Herja, whose name means 'devastate' or 'devastator', or Hjalmþrimul 'helmet clatterer', and compare that with Hervör Alvitr ["all-wise"]. These 'evolutions' happened within the period and were not additions of a much later time made in retrospect – this was how the Valkyrie was perceived to be and act. Regarding naming conventions and implied behaviour, we have a pattern of Valkyries evoking the image of *seiðr* – at least as it presents within the battlefield environment- whether through their names, or showcased abilities. We have human *seiðworkers* being capable of placing war fetters, that is to say, creating single seconds of fatal hesitation, a slow reaction, a moment of confusion, as if the individuals' limbs were bound by string.

---

330 Orchard, Dictionary of Norse Myth and Legend, 36.
331 Ibid, 194.

While the etymology of *seiðr* has been disputed across the last century, Heide concludes that etymological equivalents from Old High German and Old English mean "cord, string and snare, cord, halter", the important aspect being that these words reflect the utility of *seiðr* in terms of binding and attraction.[332] Fetters are the most evident example of this binding imagery, and the Valkyries revel in these fetters. As they weave the result of the battle, you can almost imagine these subtle manipulations happening across the field.

A second delay before a shield is raised, a person stepping to the side just as an arrow crests into the sky. A slip in concentration. It's a place where fates can change in an instance. And we have the Valkyrie Herfjötur, whose name means 'war-fetter', or 'fetter of the army'. The manipulation of weather, such as we see with storms and blizzards, is mirrored through the names Rota and Mist, and tied to battlefield imagery, as has been discussed in relation to kennings. Lightning, rain, thunder and fierce winds frequently accompany the Valkyries as they fly.

Hrist and Skogul represent the shaking, quaking imagery that conjures similarities with *Gísla saga Súrssonar* [Gisla Saga] and the actions of Audbjorg summoning an avalanche. Heide also emphasises that two sources, *Eyrbyggja saga* [The Saga of the People of Eyri] and *Fóstbrœðra saga* [The Saga of the Sworn Brothers], contain examples of invisibility being caused by spinning.[333] The Valkyries often fly invisibly above the battlefield. While Göndul bears the image of the Volva [Völva], wielding a staff and summoning spirits, with all the Valkyries knowledgeable in matters of fate, and its manipulation. Invulnerability, prophecy – see Sváva and her knowledge of Helgi – healing, empowering individuals: these are all behaviours and characteristics shared across *seiðr* and the Valkyries.

Equally, we see across the literature that to practice magic was to distance yourself from social norms and expectations.[334] It was of the wild, and couldn't exist peacefully in settlements, villages and towns which operated under strict rules and laws. To practice magic was to defy those laws and conventions, to move beyond human restrictions. Those that practiced magic belonged to a liminal space between human reality and the wild, the unknown, the other.

---

332 Heide, Spinning Seiðr, 164.
333 Ibid, 166.
334 I'll be breaking this idea down further in an upcoming chapter on liminality in the Nordic world.

What is magic if not working to manipulate fate? Acting in ways to interfere in what was planned, what was put in place, what would have happened. To have a say on the world around you. Your will and intention versus the flow of reality. Take Odin and Freyja. As aforementioned, I see the Valkyries as a sort of protégé of both Gods, a combined effort cultivated through a need to have a hand on the wheel, so to speak. I'm going to break that idea down further.

Odin and Freyja are very alike in many ways. They are magic users, they are wanderers, they are defined by passion and ecstatic, frenzied states. They are both associated with war and death. They have an ability to transform into birds, either through the possession of coats/cloaks or magical ability. The Valkyries too fulfil all those criteria.

We have the Valkyries display a knowledge of runes, they travel across realms, they are described as wearing swan coats and thus transform their *hamr*, they are the friends of the raven and the wolf, they have connections with the afterlife and necromantic practices, and they frequently exhibit behaviours that invokes the image of historical *seiðr*.

As will be discussed in more detail in the next chapter, certain Valkyries are described as possessing swan coats, most apparently Brynhildr and the *Völundarkviða* [The Lay of Volund] Valkyries. The ability to transform into birds, through the use of a coat or otherwise, is shared with Freyja and Odin. Like Odin, they have an ability to be hidden from the eyes of mortals, most exhibited during the manipulation of the battlefield, though this is not fully consistent across all such examples.

As part of their core duty, they could pass into the world of the dead as easily as they do the world of the living, travelling across realms seemingly as easily as we would travel across county or state lines. They are mead-bearers, evoking Freyja's role in the *Prose Edda* when she acts as hostess to the Jotunn Hrungnir in *Skáldskaparmál*.[335]

---

335 Faulkes, *Edda*, 77.

The Valkyries' knowledge of runes is showcased within *Sigrdrífumál:*

"Beer I give you, apple-tree of battle,
Mixed with magical power and mighty glory;
it is full of spells and favourable letters,
Good charms and runes of pleasure.

Victory-runes you must cut if you want to have victory,
And cut them on the sword-hilt;
Some on the blade-guards, some on the handle,
And invoke Tyr twice....."[336]

These words are closely echoed by Brynhildr in *Völsunga saga,* when she speaks to Sigurd about her knowledge of runes.

"Beer I give you,
Battlefield ruler,
With strength blended
And with much glory.

It is full of charmed verse
And runes of healing
Of seemly spells
And of pleasing speech.

Victory runes shall you know
If you want to secure wisdom,
And cut them on the sword hilt,
On the center ridge of the blade,
And the parts of the brand,
And name Tyr twice...."[337]

---

336 Larrington, The Poetic Edda (Revised Edition), 163.
337 The Saga of the Volsungs. The Norse Epic of Sigurd the Dragon Slayer, trans. Jesse Byock (Penguin Classics, 1999), 67-8.

These sections of the respective poems are strongly reminiscent of the *Hávamál* [Sayings of the High One] in which Odin lists the various runes he knows too. It seems Odin passed down his sacred knowledge to the Valkyries to aid them in their work. I call the Valkyries the 'Inheritors of Divine *Seiðr*', due to these tethers that exist between their behaviours and duty with the two masters of *seiðr*, Freyja and Odin.

As I've evidenced there are numerous instances of the Valkyries exhibiting tools and knowledge that are archetypal of these two Gods, lending to the conclusion that they are, in all ways, the inheritors of their collective mastery, and the most prized and potent of these tools would be *seiðr* itself.

To summarise, *seiðr* manifests in a multitude of ways in the sagas, from controlling the weather,[338] causing an avalanche,[339] transferring intellect,[340] and divination,[341] to cursing,[342] killing,[343] and offering invulnerability in battle[344] – alongside so many other uses. *Seiðr* has ties too to textiles, to weaving, bindings, threads, distaffs and spinning.[345]

It is a uniquely feminine power, and while we do have masculine practitioners historically, to be a man and practice *seiðr* was to sacrifice societal status. As such, a masculine practitioner of *seiðr* could be referred to with words such as argr, ragr and most prominently as a noun, *ergi*, all denoting behaviours or a nature that could be described as unmanly, passive, fragile or cowardly.[346] Cultural expectations being as they are, such terms were considered a grave insult at the time of the Viking Age.

---

338 Laxdæla saga: "Kotkel then prepared a high platform for witchcraft....a high blizzard came up." Keneva Kunz, The Saga of the People of Laxardal and Bolli Bollason's Tale (Penguin Group, 2008), 73.

339 Gísla saga Súrssonar [commonly referred to as Gisla Saga] chapter 18, courtesy of Audbjorg.

340 Saga of Hakon the Good, chapter 13. A dog is gifted with three men's wisdom.

341 Eirik the Red's Saga, chapter 4.

342 Gisla Saga, chapter 18: Thorgrimr places a curse that none shall help Gisli after he kills Thordis' husband, Thorgrim (not to be confused with the sorcerer himself).

343 Hrut's son Kari is "struck dead immediately". Kunz, The Saga of the People of Laxardal and Bolli Bollason's Tale, 79.

344 In the form of a woven shirt, "you've a shirt to protect you from harm". Herman Pálsson and Paul Edwards, Seven Viking Romances (Penguin Classics, 1986), 59.

345 Heide, "Spinning Seiðr."

346 Coultas, Perceptions of Male Queerness in Early Medieval Scandinavia, 5-6.

To exhibit unmanly behaviours was to be a *níðingr*, and worthy of universal contempt,[347] though such behaviours were not illegal. While far from common practice, *ergi* could also be used to describe women, though was used to denote sexual promiscuity[348] rather than the qualities discussed above. Women, considered unmanly by categorisation, were not seen as acting in a transgressive manner by adopting the characteristics men would be criticised for.

"Whereas a man who took on the "passive" role in a sexual act between two men was shunned for acting in a feminine way, it appears that there was no such stigma attached to either party in a sexual act between two women."[349] As touched on above, there was little recognition at all for sexual acts between women: sex was perceived to involve penetration only, and therefore defined entirely by male participation.

There is notable nuance made apparent within the examples we have, suggesting a complicated social contract of gender roles, expectations and behaviours. Within *Helgakviða Hundingsbana I* [The First Lay of Helgi Hundingsbane] a flyting occurs between Sinfjolti and Godmund, with each proclaiming they have penetrated the other. While various translations showcase a confusion as to the speaker of specific stanzas, many follow Bellows' decision to assign the verses as follows.

[Sinfjotli spake]:
"Nine did we | in Sogunes
Of wolf-cubs have;[350] | I their father was."[351]

In verse 44, Godmund responds:
"In Bravoll wast thou | Grani's bride,
Golden-bitted | and ready to gallop;
I rode thee many | a mile, and down
Didst sink, thou giantess, | under the saddle."[352]

---

347 Folke Ström, Níð, Ergi and Old Norse Moral Attitudes (London: University College London, 1974), 3-4.

348 Ibid, 4.

349 Coultas, 8.

350 Context here: within the Saga of the Volsungs, Sinfjolti and Sigmund kill a group of men in cursed wolf skins before donning the skins themselves, after that point they spend some time in 'wolf shape'.

351 Bellows, The Poetic Edda: The Heroic Poems, 50.

352 Ibid, 51.

There are accusations of being a 'mare', drawing comparisons to *Lokasenna* [Loki's Quarrel] where Odin uses the circumstances of Sleipnir's birth as a tool to effeminate and criticise Loki.

Note also should be given to the negative image of the Valkyrie within the exchanges between Sinfjolti and Godmund despite Sigrún being described in a positive manner just a few verses earlier.[353]

"You were a harmful creature,
A witch, a valkyrie, horrible, unnatural, with All-Father;
All the Einheriar had to fight,
headstrong woman, on your account."[354]

We may assume that a Valkyrie could be seen as something beautiful and terrible, mortal and supernatural, seemingly at the same time. This could be an attempt at reconciling these beings at a time of transition, with the older image remaining prominent within the cultural zeitgeist of the time. With the act of flyting being as it is - a performance to humiliate and exaggerate in equal measure - we must take such examples with some degree of suspicion.

Nonetheless, it is an interesting point that they adopt a stance that seems to revel in the boast of the act of penetration, at once emphasising the masculinity of the speaker and effeminising the target. The key here, then, is that it was considered important to not be the penetrated, only the dominator.[355] By being penetrated, the person would be acting 'as a woman would'. Practising *seiðr*, acting as a woman, would also be seen as adopting similar behaviours as to be criticised as effeminate and submissive.

"But this sorcery is attended by such wickedness that manly men considered is shameful to practice it, and so it was taught to priestesses."[356]

---

353 And Sigrun above, brave in battle." Larrington, The Poetic Edda (Revised Edition), 114. Another example of a Valkyrie being actively involved in a battle, rather than passively observing, as is often ascribed to them.

354 Larrington, The Poetic Edda (Revised Edition), 115.

355 Coultas, 17.

356 Hollander, Heimskringla: History of the Kings of Norway, 11.

As discussed above, we encounter some difficulty in delineating the exact behaviours that would cause *seiðr* to be considered an unmanly act, beyond suggestions that the act itself involved simulated sexual activity, or perhaps that the use of magic was seen as a sort of underhanded tactic. You need not face your enemy eye to eye with a sword in your hand if you are skilled in *seiðr*. You could, potentially, kill your foe from miles away, unexpectedly and on a whim.

That's also not to say that women practising *seiðr* were fully incorporated and accepted into society, with even the women considered other, living nomadic lives of apparent isolation, though still treated with respect when called upon, as we see in *Eiríks saga rauða* [Saga of Eirik the Red].

"Thorkel invited the seeress to visit and preparations were made to entertain her well, as was the custom of the time when a woman of this type was received. A high sear was set for he, complete with cushion. This was to be stuffed with chicken feathers."

"When she entered, everyone was supposed to offer her respectful greetings, and she responded according to how the person appealed to her."[357]

I ask again: what is the use of magic if not acting to intervene in the course of fate? I hold that *seiðr* is a tool that the Valkyries use, one tool among many given to them by Odin and Freyja. The Valkyries have been created or cultivated for a specific purpose, and they have thrived in that purpose. Within the literature, the Valkyries were seen as potent magic-wielders and used magic across many of their literary appearances. From resurrecting the dead, and placing war-fetters, to granting invulnerability in battle, changing shape, and conjuring storms, alongside a multitude of other uses besides.

---

357 "Erik the Red's Saga", trans. Keneva Kunz, in The Sagas of the Icelanders (USA: Penguin Group, Penguin Classics Deluxe Edition, 2005), 658.

The Swan Maiden and Waelcyrge

In rebuttal to **H. Munro Chadwick's** conclusion that "wælcyrge can hardly mean anything else than 'chooser of the slain'",[358] **Philip Purser** states, "While ...."wælcyrge" literally means "chooser of the slain," and while this name is the exact etymological parallel of the word Valkyrja.... the Old English wælcyrge cannot be satisfactorily defined in terms suitable for the Old Norse valkyrja. The two are not the same being."[359]

As I've highlighted above, I would disagree here in turn, in that the Nordic Valkyries cannot be solely defined by their role as 'Choosers of the Slain'. Among their widely agreed attestations, they exhibit behaviours that move far beyond that supposedly core role within the greater mythological landscape. In my view, this all lends to the perspective that the *Wælcyrge*, for much of her literary lifetime, is representative of an earlier incarnation of the Valkyrie.

A Valkyrie prior to efforts of domestication, a Valkyrie at her most slaughter eager. Here then, the *Wælcyrge* offers a potential presentation of the Valkyrie in their earliest oral form as we follow the timeline through the Anglo-Saxon poetic tradition to the Nordic tradition. In this, I find myself in agreement with Purser in his ultimate conclusion: "if any relationship may be found between the two war-women of the Germanic North, it is one of influence from the *Wælcyrge* to the Valkyrja."[360]

Like her Nordic counterpart, the *Wælcyrge* too undergoes a parallel journey towards euhemerism, starting in a form of primordial malevolence, then localised horror, to "corporeal and very real woman who walks the streets of England and incurs the very real-world wrath of God in the form of Danish-Viking invasions."[361] Finally, the Anglo-Saxon *Wælcyrge* is reduced to a sort of folkloric echo of the country's Pagan past, appearing here and there in unnamed appearances, scattered throughout charms and riddles. This figure is a persistent ghost of the Pagan old enduring in the sanctified, new world of Christian England.

358 H. Munro Chadwick, The Heroic Age (Cambridge: Cambridge University Press, 1926), 412.

359 Philip A. Purser, Her Syndan Wælcyrian: Illuminating the Form and Function of the Valkyrie-Figure in the Literature, Mythology, and Social Consciousness of Anglo-Saxon England (PhD Diss., Georgia State University, 2013), 181. I recommend this work for more information on the Wælcyrge.

360 Ibid, 174.

361 Ibid, 175-6.

Much of the scholarly work on the *Wælcyrge* relies less on named mentions, of which there is a notable scarcity, and more on analysis of potential *Wælcyrge*-like figures in period applicable literature, such as those proposed in *Beowulf*, with Grendel's mother representing the more malicious 'death-bringer' aspect in comparison to Wealhtheow, a more domestic 'mead-bringer' who weaves peace.

"The Scylding lady spoke: "Take this cup, my noble lord, gold-friend of men, and to the Geats speak kind words as is only right." [362]

Purser frames Grendel's Mother and Wealhtheow as a "Valkyrie-Diptych...one evil and one benevolent"[363] who "vie for the fate of the narrative's hero."[364] **Nora Chadwick** argues that Grendel's mother showcases notable similarities with the earliest conception of the Valkyrie,[365] in being a figure defined by malicious intent and vengeance.[366]

This finds consensus with **Helen Damico**, who writes: "As Chadwick has argued, Grendel's Mother, that *wælgæst wæfre* 'roaming slaughter-spirit' epitomizes the earlier concept of the valkyrie...she delights in carnage – she is a 'horror, glorying in the carrion'-"[367]

---

362 Beowulf: Translation and Commentary (Expanded Edition), trans. Tom Shippey, ed. Leonard Neidorf (London, England: Uppsala Books, 2023), 119.

363 Purser, Her Syndan Wælcyrian, 12. Consider the frequency we see a similar image being created in later works – the evil Valkyrie figure vs the good Valkyrie figure.

364 Ibid.

365 Nora K. Chadwick. "The Monsters and Beowulf", in The Anglo-Saxons: Studies in Some Aspects of Their History (London, UK: Bowes & Bowes, 1959), 175.

366 Alternative readings suggest that Grendel's mother is a heroic figure who seeks rightful vengeance for the death of her son. Kevin Kiernan, "Grendel's Heroic Mother", in Geardagum 6 (1984), 13-33.

367 Damico, The Valkyrie Reflex in Old English Literature, 178.

It may seem difficult to reconcile these two, on the face, disparate presentations. Instead, we should focus on the concept of an evolution towards more agreeable behaviours, an attitude that extended even to Goddesses and supernatural entities in the light of an ever-converting world. Indeed, while it was common for the malevolent and benevolent aspects of these proto-Valkyries to be separate and in apparent conflict with each other, within the fragmented Old English Epic *Judith*, we're potentially presented with a figure that embodies both manifestations within one body.

Like the noble-born Valkyries, Judith is often described as wearing metallic adornments, crossing into the nebulous nature of jewellery, wealth and armour. Damico argues convincingly that the examples presented here are less ambiguous than her Nordic counterparts. "Dress of metallic brightness is also attributed to Judith. Both she and the war-trappings of the soldiers are *golde gefrœtwod* (171b – 328b)...appear to be a formulaic system that expresses...adornment with gold of military equipment".[368]

Bēahhroden[369] is also used to describe Judith,[370] referring to being 'ring-adorned', a quality that Sigrun also possess, which I have posited would denote martial prowess, commonly the act of holding a shield or wearing chainmaille.

Akin to the earlier slaughter-eager Valkyrie, Judith seeks blood, beheading Holofernes while he is incapacitated in a drunken state. The language used in these lines strongly evokes the image of war fetters, binding an enemy in place.[371] By killing the Heathen Holofernes in this manner, the Christian Judith has 'chosen death' for him. However, unlike her Nordic sisters, she has barred his entry into Valhalla and sent him to Hell.[372]

---

368 Ibid, 183.

369 Albert S Cook translates "Bēahhrodene" as 'bracelet-decked ones' rather than ring-adorned. The term is ambiguous in meaning but is used to describe circular objects, necklaces, rings, bracelets etc. Albert S. Cook, Judith, An Old English Epic Fragment (Boston, USA: D.C. Heath & Co, 1889), 13. (Line 138).

370 Damico, The Valkyrie Reflex in Old English Literature, 183.

371 Judith Caywood, Rædende Iudithðe: The Heroic, Mythological and Christian Elements in the Old English Poem Judith (Undergrad thesis., University of San Diego, 2015), 33.

372 Ibid, 35.

With these examples, it's hard not to draw comparisons to even later thematic ideas such as the 'Madonna-Whore dichotomy'.[373] The Valkyries are either the seemingly chaste and pure protectors, or they are the blood-thirsty, vengeful, demonic and cruel Choosers of the Slain. While this dichotomy is not restricted solely to Christian ideals, it can be seen in antiquity too, it certainly seems to have been propagated by its theology, gaining popularity and momentum.

As it stands, I have and will attempt to remove the discussion of the Valkyrie from such reductive criteria, and into one of nuance, as reflected in the material we are analysing. Indeed, away from surface analysis they defy any characterisation as simple as 'Death-Bringer' and 'Mead-Bringer', as useful as those definitions may be when conducting overarching comparisons in the literature.

Moreover, within the corpus of scholarly work, I've seen various academics struggle to reconcile the two distinct images of the Valkyrie presented throughout the eleventh to the fourteenth century into a cohesive, unifying whole. I would say the answer, or at least part of it, lies in a simple observation: that within the greater sphere of Nordic cosmology, dichotomies and apparent juxtapositions are common, and I would argue, that not possessing such apparent contradictions is the exception, not the rule.

For instance, Odin being a cross-dressing, gender-bending God of magic, death, and frenzy, as well as the 'high one', a Chieftain God of wisdom, poetry and order. Freyja is a Goddess of beauty, love and sex, as well as magic, war and death, in addition to the associations brought about by being one of the Vanir; a God of wealth, fertility and life. The Valkyries, then, sit right at home with their tutors, creating a family of contradictions. All of this is also a unique by-product of being captured at a time of immense cultural change, moving from an oral Heathen tradition to a written Christian one, with the distancing of the 'primitive' before in favour of the 'civilised' after.

---

373 This term originates in psychoanalytic theory in the twentieth century, but manifests across literature, art and media. Sigmund Freud, On Sexuality: Three Essays on the Theory of Sexuality and Other Works, trans. James Strachey, ed. Angela Richards (Middlesex, England: Penguin Books, 1977), 231-42.

THE SWAN MAIDEN

"[Brynhildr] answered gravely from her seat, like a swan on a wave, in her mail coat, with her sword in her hand and her helmet on her head."[374]

The image of the 'Swan Maiden' is prominent across a plethora of world religions and mythologies, with repeating themes that are evocative and complex in equal measure. For the sake of brevity, we will be looking exclusively at the Swan Maiden in Germanic literature and folklore and explore how this figure ties into the presentation of the slaughter maidens over the course of their historical attestations.

It may be somewhat bewildering to discover that the swan is so strongly associated with the image of the Valkyrie. After all, swans don't normally conjure images of blood-thirsty, demonic warriors, but it is a description that remains persistent, nonetheless. The most prominent example of this type is found in *Völundarkviða* [The Lay of Volund] in the *Poetic Edda*.

"Early one morning they found on the shore of the lake three women, who were spinning flax.[375] Near them were their swan garments, for they were Valkyries. Two of them were daughters of King Hlothver, Hlathguth the Swan-White and Hervor the All-Wise, and the third was Olrun, daughter of Kjar from Valland...."[376]

---

374 Byock, The Saga of the Volsungs. The Norse Epic of Sigurd the Dragon Slayer, 81.

375 Fáfnismál 43 refers to Sigrdrifa as a "Goddess of Flax", though Larrington states this is a kenning for 'woman'. I suggest this is referring to the Valkyries as weavers/seiðworkers/ fate workers as exhibited here. Larrington, The Poetic Edda (Revised Edition), 161 & 303.

376 Henry Adams Bellows, The Poetic Edda: The Heroic Poems (Mineola, New York: Dover Publications Inc., 2007), 2.

The following image is painted: three Valkyries, Hlaðguðr Svanhvít, Ölrún, Hervör Alvitr, spin by a lake, watched by three brothers, Slagfith, Egil, and the titular Volund.

> "Girls flew from the south across Myrkwood,
> Strange young creatures, to fulfil fate;
> There on a lake shore they sat to rest,
> The southern ladies spun precious linen.
> One of them began to enclose Egil in her arms,
> The fair living girl in bright embrace;
> Another was Swanwhite [Svanhvit], she wore swan feathers;
> And the third, their sister,
> Wound her arms around Volund's white neck."[377]

This example is notable for several reasons, not least because it offers another instance of the Valkyries being depicted as engaging in textiles, but also because it's explicit in addressing their purpose for being there and engaging in those acts, in this case, "to fulfil fate".

It is also a point of intrigue that Larrington translates the name of this lake as 'Wolf-Lake", which further aids in entwining the Valkyries with these wild animals of the battlefield, the Jotnar, and Odin. In *Helreið Byrnhildar* [Brynhildr's Hel-Ride] we have the following:

> "A courageous king had our skin-garments,
> [those of] eight sisters,[378] borne beneath an oak
> I was twelve years old, if you wish to know
> When I gave oaths to the young prince."[379]

---

377 Larrington, The Poetic Edda. (Revised Edition), 98-9.

378 Presumably we can infer eight plus Brynhildr makes nine, common for gatherings of Valkyries. However, it can also be read to mean eight sisters total, which would be an unusual number considering Valkyries appear in pairs or in groups of three almost exclusively (or otherwise solo).

379 Pettit, The Poetic Edda. A Dual-Language Edition, 599. https://doi.org/10.11647/OBP.0308

The skin-garments are widely agreed to be referring to 'swan-cloaks', with the translator in this case making a note; "probably magical clothes that transformed the wearers into swans"[380] **Carolyne Larrington** makes the same connection in her translation notes: "Brynhild and her sisters were able to change their shape by means of magic garments, probably some king of bird, in connection with their life as Valkyries."[381]

Presumably cut off from realm travel, Brynhildr and her sisters are captured by the unnamed king. Donning animal forms,[382] *Therianthropy*, is used to attain freedom, embodying the lack of social expectations put upon an individual due to their role, perceived or otherwise, within society. The same language that is associated with animals is also used to describe those living outside of society and culture.

A prominent example lies in the Old Norse word *vargr* which can be used to mean a wolf or an outlaw equally.[383] The image of the *Berserkir*[384] is also one that straddles the line between the wild and the domestic, though there is also a strong association with madness and frenzy with these examples that is not used to describe outlawry.

There is something innately uncontrollable about these *Berserkir*, something that descends further into animalistic behaviour, something that makes their connection to civilisation even more tenuous. So absolute was their animalistic tendencies, that these beings were often not able to be reincorporated back into normal society,[385] in part due to the echoes of supernaturality that permeate their various appearances. They break beyond human behaviours and natural behaviours equally.

---

380 Ibid, 603.

381 Larrington, The Poetic Edda (Revised Edition), 307.

382 Often by wearing their skin, their hamr. Such beings are described as hamrammr, shape-shifters.

383 Timothy J.S. Bourns, Between Nature and Culture: Animals and Humans in Old Norse Literature (PhD.diss., Oxford: Oxford University, 2017), 213-4.

384 See Roderick Dale, The Myths and Realities of the Viking Berserkr (London and New York: Routledge, 2022) for more information on the Berserkr figure.

385 Ibid, 223.

These *Berserkir*,[386] like the Valkyries, are often described as wearing animal skins, with the assumption being that the skins aid or incite the act of 'shape-shifting'.[387] There's much within folklore that evokes this motif, with the Selkie being an obvious point of comparison.[388] It would also be remiss to overlook that shape-shifting appears to have ties to *seiðr*.[389]

Considering that the *Berserkir* had strong ties to the cult of Odin, this connection seems sensible. There's also an example of a woman, presumed to be the Valkyrie Kára, flying in swan form in *Hrómundar saga Gripssonar* [Saga of Hromund Gripsson] to protect her lover Helgi Haddingjaskati. I've not gone into detail about that here, as its far more fragmentary than the other examples given.

It should be considered significant that attestations of swan-cloak wearing Valkyries occurs only alongside mentions of human heritage,[390] suggesting that this was not originally part of the earlier 'Valkyrie mythos', but something that was incorporated in at a later date, aligning with the understanding of the Swan Maiden as a pan-continental tradition. This incorporation arrived at a time when the Valkyries were given more mortal roots and origins and conflating them with similar figures that appear in Germanic mythology and folklore at large.

This then serves as another marker of the changing face of the Valkyrie, snowballing to gradually collect other traits and behaviours of similar figures. Nonetheless, these traits shouldn't be considered alien in the characterisation of the Nordic Valkyrie, but a defining contribution that helped shape them within the corpus. After all, this propensity for wearing swan coats also aligns them with Freyja, and her possession of a falcon cloak that enables the wearer to change shape too, as discussed above. It's a seamless incorporation.

---

386 The name 'Berserkr' is also commonly translated to 'bear shirt'.

387 Stephan Grundy, "Shapeshifting and Berserkergang", Disuptatio, 3 (1998), 115.

388 Dan Coultas, Heathenry & The Sea (2021), 117-9.

389 Samantha J. Cairo, The Significance of Shape-Shifting and Transformation in Medieval Welsh and Icelandic Literature: The Ingenuity of Medieval Writers (MA thesis, Western Michigan University, 1999), 29. & Jenny Blain, Nine Worlds of Seid-Magic, Ecstasy and Neo-Shamanism in North European Paganism (London and New York: Routledge, 2002), 91.

390 It should be said here that I follow the Saga of the Volsungs in Brynhildr being the daughter of Buðli [Budli].

The three Valkyries here are all the daughters of Kings, or otherwise people of note. Kjar (alternatively, *Kjárr* or *Kíarr*) is specified to be "from Valland", which Snorri equates to Gaul in *Heimskringla*. Carl Edlund Anderson wrote, "There also seems to be a trace of Caesar in ON [Old Norse], preserved in the name of Kiarr or Kjárr..."[391] Though that conclusion is certainly up for debate, what may be concluded is that Ölrún's lineage was perhaps not Scandinavian, and would have been recognised as foreign in origin.

It is noteworthy that the Valkyries were not isolated to Scandinavian heritage, but that there was an awareness that they could be incorporated from individuals outside of the region. This, perhaps, hints of persevering pockets of Valkyrie-like figures across the greater Germanic region, maybe of the *Wælcyrge* or akin to it. Finally, there exists an interesting interaction between swans and ravens, with swans often being utilised in kennings for their carrion-seeking counterparts.

In *Sigurðardrápa I* [Sigurd's Poem] a raven is called the "Black

---

[391] Carl Edlund Anderson, Formation and Resolution of Ideological Contrast in the Early History of Scandinavia, (PhD diss., University of Cambridge, 1999), 44.

Swan of Battle".[392] In *Hákonardrápa* [Lay of Hakon] there's "Swan of the Raven-Wine".[393] In *Austrfararvísur* ['Verse of an Eastern Journey'], there's "Swan of the Wound".[394] In *Hǫfuðlausn* ['Head Ransom'], "of the Swan of the Battle-Serpent",[395] and so on. This image may have been informed by their association with the Valkyries or could be explained by the juxtaposition of the swan, typically an animal connected to grace and poise, with the imagery of battle.

Within *Beowulf*, swans were utilised in kennings for the sea, despite not being an animal of the sea. There's some debate as to whether the use of 'Swan-Road' is indeed a kenning, *kend heiti*,[396] or double kenning, a kenning within a kenning. **Robert Woodward** made the observation that the shape of the swan was strongly reminiscent of the curved prow of the *drakkar*, the famous Viking longship, offering a possible answer to this word play.[397] Often the meanings behind word choice are not immediately obvious, frequently enigmatic, and may lie in the abstract, or cultural context we're not privy to.[398]

---

392 Sigurðardrápa I, 2. Kari Ellen Gade, "Einarr Skúlason, Sigurðardrápa I 2", in Poetry from the Kings' Sagas 2: From c. 1035 to c. 1300. Skaldic Poetry of the Scandinavian Middle Ages 2, ed. Kari Ellen Gade (Turnhout, Belgium: Brepols, 2009), 539.

393 Hákonardrápa 1. Russell Poole, "Guthormr sindri, Hákonardrápa", in Poetry from the Kings' Sagas 1: From Mythical Times to c. 1035. Skaldic Poetry of the Scandinavian Middle Ages 1, ed. Diana Whaley (Turnhout, Belgium: Brepols, 2012), 156. "Hákonardrápa — Gsind Hákdr," The Skaldic Project, accessed June 17, 2024. https://skaldic.org/m.php?p=text&i=1216

394 Austrfararvísur 16. R. D. Fulk, "Sigvatr Þórðarson, Austrfararvísur" in Poetry from the Kings' Sagas 1: From Mythical Times to c. 1035. Skaldic Poetry of the Scandinavian Middle Ages 1, ed. Diana Whaley (Turnhout, Belgium: Brepols, 2012), 578. "Austrfararvísur — Sigv Austv", The Skaldic Project, accessed June 17, 2024. https://skaldic.org/m.php?p=text&i=1351

395 Hǫfuðlausn 6. Matthew Townend, "Óttarr svarti, Hǫfuðlausn," in Poetry from the Kings' Sagas 1: From Mythical Times to c. 1035. Skaldic Poetry of the Scandinavian Middle Ages 1, ed. Diana Whaley (Turnhout, Belgium: Brepols, 2012), 739. "Hǫfuðlausn — Ótt Hfl", The Skaldic Project, accessed June 17, 2024. https://skaldic.org/m.php?p=text&i=1340

396 As distinguished by Zeinab Gvarishvili: a kenning is based on metaphor, while a kend heiti is based on metonymy. Zeinab Gvarishvili, Kenning and Kend Heiti as the base model of the modern cognitive metaphor (2018), 2.

397 Robert H. Woodward, "Swanrad in Beowulf", Modern Language Notes 69,8 (1954), 544-6.

398 See Vlatko Broz, "Kennings as blends and prisms", Jezikoslovlje 12.2 (2011), 165-86. Broz tackles the semantics of kennings within Beowulf from a

Early vs Later Depictions of the Valkyries
A Comparison and Evolution

It will be a useful exercise to demarcate the depictions of the Valkyrie and their changes over the timeline of their attestations. There are common themes over the course of the appearances of the Valkyrie over several centuries, some with more prevalence over a certain period, others less so.

The Feral Valkyrie

While I tend towards individuality when it comes to equating various deities of different cultures with each other, an exception is made when analysing the similarities between the Valkyries and their earlier counterparts. This is a practice that is common too in scholarly works, seeing as the definition of a Valkyrie extends beyond the literal translation of their name and into broader behaviours that can be seen readily when looking at similar figures.

This perspective is reaffirmed by work around the aforementioned *Wælcyrge*, with that term being used historically, on occasion, to be the Old English equivalent for the classical 'Furies' or Erinyes.[399] However, the Furies or their Roman cousins, the *Dirae*, remain few in number (three by most counts), and are also defined by wrath, anger, punishment and vengeance, which would not accurately define either the actions or the characterisation of the *Waelcyrge* or the Valkyrie.

cognitive linguistic approach.

399 Hilda Roderick Ellis Davidson, Gods and Myths of Northern Europe (Harmondsworth: Pelican, 1964), 62.

There's something, for lack of a better word, more personal with the Erinyes and their targets, while the Valkyrie remain notably distant among many of their appearances. It's less of a sort of judicial punishment, as archetypal of the Erinyes, and more of a sacrificial offering determined by location and circumstance. If you are on the battlefield, you are fair game. As **Carolyne Larrington** succinctly phrases it, "Valkyries tend not to have any particular emotional or erotic interest in their prey."[400]

The same could not be said for the Erinyes, who were often invoked on an individual for a wrongdoing or crime, a reaction to a specific action, a call for justice on an individual who had escaped it. As mentioned in a previous chapter, we do have one fourteenth century example of a Valkyrie being invoked by Ragnhild Tregagås during her trial for witchcraft. This is notably the only example of the type. This example also highlights the image of the 'Supernatural Valkyrie' archetype. Something diminished and stripped of the divine importance of her earlier attestations.

"I hurl the spirits of Gandul;
One bites you in your back
Another one bites your chest
And the third afflicts you
With hatred and envy."[401]

It would also be remiss to gloss over the similarities between the literal definition of the most attested Erinyes, Alecto, Megaera and Tisiphone – meaning endless anger, jealous rage and vengeful destruction, respectively – and some of the Valkyries, the most obvious comparison being Sanngridr [very violent].[402] But that, I would say, is where the similarities end.

In the Old English poem *Exodus*, found in the Junius manuscript, a raven is described as *wælceasega* in line 161, literally meaning 'choosing/picking/picker of the slain.'[403] The themes and relations between battlefield animals, such as the wolf and raven, and the Valkyries or like beings remain consistent over time and geography.

400 Carolyne Larrington, The Norse Myths That Shape the Way We Think (London: Thames & Hudson Ltd, 2023), 67.
401 Hagen, I Hurl the Spirits of Gandul, 144.
402 Simek, Dictionary of Northern Mythology, 275.
403 Ibid, 65.

There is a continual theme of supernatural, often feminine, figures dealing death, flying unseen across battlefields and 'choosing the slain'.

"þufas þunian, þeod mearc tredan,
on hwæl
Hreopon herefugolas, hilde grædige,
deawigfeðere ofer drihtneum,
wonn wælceasega. Wulfas sungon."

"Brandishing banners on the borderland march.
The horn-billed raven hailed
the skiesover doomed men,
dark picker of the slain; wolves chanted." [404]

I agree with the conclusion made by **Hilda Roderick Ellis Davidson**, "there is little doubt that the figure of the Valkyrie has developed in Norse literature into something more dignified and less blood thirsty as a result of the work of the poets over a considerable period. The alarming and terrible creatures who have survived in the literature in spite of this seem likely....to be closer in character to the choosers of the slain as they were visualized in heathen times."[405]

This earlier depiction of the Valkyrie lies in stark contrast to their later developments, while the former is a feminine force dominant on the battlefield, the later Valkyrie is so often defined by their masculine partners. "The tamed Valkyrie represents, therefore, the triumph of a man who has overcome death itself through his masculine prowess and desirability."[406]

This timeline then presents the Valkyries undergoing a transformation over the course of their literary appearances. Their earliest depictions tend towards behaviours defined by animalistic behaviour, bloodthirsty war songs, and things of that ilk. As we move through the Viking Age, they become more noble in their presentation, becoming more human, and losing their more supernatural duties. The sacrificial, ritualistic language practically vanishes, and they become defined by their protective nature more than anything else.

---

404 Translation is from S.B Greenfield, "Exodus (Lines 1–275)", Old English Newsletter 21 (1987), 15–20.

405 Davidson, Gods and Myths of Northern Europe, 66.

406 Varley, The whirling wheel, 246.

So, let's take a closer look at the later literary depictions of these beings, and what qualities they possess. Because, while they are very much more noble in their presentation, they still often present themselves in blood-spattered armour, just minus the 'feralness' and 'untameability' of their older depictions. One trait that remains fairly consistent throughout this timeline, is that the Valkyries remain liminal in nature. In the later literary tradition, they possess abilities that mark them as distinct from the everyday humans around them.

They have, apparently, an innate greatness that makes their nature obvious, with those that encounter them able to immediately identify them as something 'other'. In the earlier traditions, they move around and across the battlefield clouded from human observation, and they can traverse our world and the world of the Gods with few challenges. They can fly, have mounts that can fly, they can change their shape, and they can manipulate the battlefield in line with their choices. They deal in death, or protect individuals from death, or otherwise heal those who they decide are not to die.

THE PSYCHOPOMP

Though often used as the defining element of Valkyries, their role as Psychopomp is also one of the most inferred, at least when it comes to dedicated word space to that duty. *Hákonarmál* may be the most obvious source for this element of choosing the slain, but it's interesting in that the Valkyries seem to depart before Hakon to inform Odin of his imminent arrival, seeing as they are not present when he arrives in Valhalla.

The Valkyries in *Njal's* Saga can be seen, albeit in a rather ambiguous manner, as taking the dead when they depart through the form of a weave torn into several pieces and distributed among their number. As it is, despite being commonly labelled as a Psychopomp, the emphasis on choosing who dies overshadows that descriptor, leading to my conclusion that the Valkyrie cannot be accurately encapsulated by the title of Psychopomp alone. Not to mention that this descriptor also ignores their various other roles and manifestations.

The word *Psychopomp* comes from the Greek *psychopompós* meaning "Guide/ Conductor of Souls" and is a common role across numerous world religions and mythologies.[407] These guides show the path to the afterlife, accompanying the departed soul on that journey. They are an innately liminal being, existing right on the line between the world of the living and the world of the dead.

There may be an argument that the Valkyrie dons the role of 'Guide' in several ways, including in her heroic image as the guide to heroes, and in travelling between our world and the world of the Gods. Within Jungian theory, the Psychopomp manifests in dreams, helping the individual in the form of a wise man or woman, or helpful animal.

These Psychopomps navigate the space between the subconscious and unconscious mind, 'the Lower World', which is "the domain of animal spirits, spirit guides and the ancestors: the place to which human spirits travel upon physical death."[408] While I don't prescribe to a Jungian worldview, it does highlight that there is a consistent association between our world, and others that are populated by humanoid figures and animalistic forms that possess knowledge or understanding outside of our own. The Psychopomp travels these world and is defined by them.

The Heroic Valkyrie

How do the later Heroic Valkyries differ? Well, they are often tied to human relationships, whether that be through marriage, or through birth, frequently identified as the daughters of kings. They don't seem to ferry people to the halls of the afterlife, and they seem to almost exclusively be based in 'our world', though with abilities that make them removed from normal humans. I mentioned it earlier, but they are at least easily recognisable as being a Valkyrie to those around them, through what specific criteria we can only really guess at. Perhaps something that makes them seem to have an innate greatness, they're often described, after all, as shining on horseback, bright and beautiful.

---

407 "No scholar can claim that he knows all the paradises, hells, underworlds....though he may be certain that there will be a river and a bridge; a sea and a boat; a tree, a cave...a demonic or angelic psychopomp." Mircea Eliade, Occultism, Witchcraft and Cultural Fashions: Essays in Comparative Religions (Chicago and London: The University of Chicago Press, 1976), 42-3.

408 Michael Drake, The Great Shift and How to Navigate It (USA: Talking Drum Publications, 2018), 82.

"Three times nine girls, but one girl rode ahead,
white skinned under her helmet;
the horses shook themselves, from their manes
dew fell into the deep valleys...."[409]

There's a larger literary trope playing into all of this as well,
the idea of our heroes quite literally courting death. Heroes
are considered extraordinary due to their ability to perform
extraordinary feats. The people and beings around them are mythic,
they are favourites of those that protect them, and give them a
potent advantage over others. The heroic lays are, in many ways,
the stories of humans being elevated to almost godlike status, while
on the other side of the coin, the Gods in turn are being gradually
stripped of their power.

The Valkyries, I suggest, are the natural middle ground
here, considering that they have always been liminal and of both
worlds throughout the timeline of their depictions. They are made
human by nature, but not by duty, albeit their power is reduced to
protection over a handful of individuals, apparently. One of the key
examples of this presents itself in *Helgakviða Hjörvarðssonar* [Lay
of Helgi Hjörvarðsson] with Sváva and the titular Helgi. Here we
have a Valkyrie, Sváva, creating an identity and purpose for Helgi.

He is taken from being utterly unknown to having a name
and a duty of his own, a life-defining mission. Sváva then acts to
protect Helgi during battle and build this reputation of being a keen
warrior. He only dies when Sváva is absent, and a troll-woman
curses him during a *holmgang*.[410] But even then, the pieces are in
place for an extraordinary resurrection of seemingly both Helgi and
Sváva into Helgi Hundingsbane and Sigrún respectively, with Helgi
solidifying his position as a Nordic literary hero.

---

409 Larrington, The Poetic Edda (Revised Edition), 124.
410 Helgakviða Hjörvarðssonar 34-43. Ibid, 125-6.

THE MEAD BEARER

"Hrist and Mist, I wish would bear a horn to me,
Skeggiold and Skogul,
Hild and Thrud, Hlokk and Herfiotur,
Goll and Geirolul,
Randgrid and Radgrid, and Reginleif;
they bear ale to the Einheriar."[411]

Aside from choosing the slain, the other aspect of the Valkyries that is often seen as archetypal of that title is to serve mead in Valhalla, but even here there is a lack of consistency when it comes to the sources. Ultimately, the Valkyries are not mentioned in every instance that we have of mead being served in the hall of the slain. Perhaps most damning is that we don't have a single textual account of any chosen dead being greeted by a Valkyrie with mead in Valhalla.[412]

As it stands, it's not a controversial statement to conclude that this prominent image of a Valkyrie mead-bearer comes from the rather comic *Eiríksmál* [The Lay of Eirik] which paints this image of a bumbling Odin being awoken and caught unaware at a new important arrival into his hall, and the Valkyries, these blood-thirsty battle Goddesses, are painted, in turn, as mead-bearers.

"What kind of dream is this, that I thought that a little before daybreak I was preparing Valhǫll for a slain army? I awakened the einherjar, I asked them to get up to strew the benches, to rinse the drinking cups, [I asked] valkyries to bring wine, as if a leader should come."[413]

---

411 Ibid, 53.
412 Murphy, Herjans Dísir, 132.
413 Eiríksmál 1. R. D. Fulk, "Anonymous, Eiríksmál', in Poetry from the Kings' Sagas 1: From Mythical Times to c. 1035. Skaldic Poetry of the Scandinavian Middle Ages 1, ed. Diana Whaley. (Turnhout, Belgium: Brepols, 2012), 1003.

There's a satirical edge to it, someone having fun with the imagery, enjoying the juxtapositions. As this piece is often dated to around 954, I see it as a key turning point in the transformation of the Valkyrie from one nature to another. We don't have mead-bearing Valkyries, literarily speaking, prior to *Eiriksmal*, with *Hrafnsmal* [The Lay of the Raven] being the only agreed appearance of a Valkyrie prior to this date, roughly fifty years earlier.

Here, the parallels with Odin are hard to ignore, with the unnamed Valkyrie speaking to a raven to source information after a battle, in much the same way it is inferred Odin does with Huginn and Muninn. There is an implication that this Valkyrie is sourcing information on the location of the recently deceased, potentially to fulfil her duty to ferry the slain to their afterlives. She notes his blood-spattered appearance, the carrion in his claws, with interest.

"What is the matter with you, ravens?
From where have you come with gory beaks at break of day?
Flesh hangs from your claws;
the stench of carrion comes from your mouths;
I think you lodged last night near where you knew corpses were lying."[414]

Hrafnsmal presents itself as an intriguing comparison point for Valkyric scholars, as it includes a Valkyrie upon the battlefield, but without the aggressive, proactive action she would normally be associated with in such a setting. The ability to speak to birds was seen as a uniquely royal gift, at least when we see similar powers manifest in the heroic sagas. Considering that, we can perhaps better conclude here that this Valkyrie is essentially acting *as Odin*, denoting her mythological station, rather than a suggestion of a royal, human lineage.

---

414 Hrafnsmál 3. R. D. Fulk, "Þorbjǫrn hornklofi, Haraldskvæði (Hrafnsmál)", in Poetry from the Kings' Sagas 1: From Mythical Times to c. 1035. Skaldic Poetry of the Scandinavian Middle Ages 1, ed. Diana Whaley (Turnhout, Belgium: Brepols, 2012), 91.

I conclude this due to the time it was composed and the framing of the conversation as one happening in a supernatural space – the deathly quiet after a battle's conclusion. While *Eiriksmal* presents itself as the first instance of a Valkyrie mead-bearer this image is far from consistent afterwards. In *Hákonarmál* we noticeably have the Aesir serving alcohol[415] despite two Valkyries, Skögul and Göndul, being on the battlefield upon Hakon's death.[416]

No Valkyries are present when he arrives in Valhalla. We're then faced with the idea that *Eiriksmal* itself led to influencing much of the later depictions of this image,[417] eventually tying into the domestication of the Valkyrie into the shape of wives and daughters. This served to compliment and continue the Christianised ideals of the role of women in society and thus the role of the Valkyrie. **Luke John Murphy** agrees with that sentiment and adds, "it seems likely that those valkyrjur who are relegated to carrying cups or horns of alcohol do so as a result of an idealised vision of female behaviour in a hall as seen from the point of view of masculine warrior culture". [418]

I do not fundamentally disagree with the Valkyries being described as mead-bearers, as it's a characterisation that raises questions and further associations. Paramount is that, within the early medieval period, the act of serving and imbibing alcohol was of considerable societal importance and highly ritualised,[419] with the feasting hall being a crucial part of the political and cultural landscape. It was a crucible in which allies were created, and ties reinforced.

---

415 Hákonarmál 16.

416 Hákonarmál 8 – 13.

417 Indeed, Snorri directly references Eiriksmal in Skáldskaparmál in the Prose Edda, allowing us to ascertain that he was at least familiar with the piece and its specific contents, if not directly influenced by that content in his depiction of the Valkyries.

418 Murphy, 121.

419 Charles Riseley, Ceremonial Drinking in the Viking Age (Diss., University of Oslo, 2014), 2.

The act of hosting was a delicate balance between fulfilling all the requirements of guest rites, while navigating subtle social nuances. Involvement within such spaces was indicative of belonging to the community. As **Stephen Pollington** emphasises, these "public demonstrations of solidarity with kindred and political leadership were of immense importance"[420] amid a greater environment otherwise seen as hostile. The mead hall was the royal court of the Viking Age, the centre of local politics and power.

Aside from being a hall of the warrior slain, Valhalla is, more than anything else, a mead hall with Odin acting as sacral host and king. The framing of this afterlife as a place of order, culture and political power is compelling when you consider that it is also a place of disorder and slaughter.

Earlier in this work, I suggested that the Valkyries use of rune magic, especially the use of carving runes on drinking horns, and Ölrún, a Valkyrie whose name translates to 'ale rune', has the potential for further discussion. Not least of which is in offering an exploration outside of *seiðr* for Valhalla's propensity towards endlessly resurrecting the 'dead'.

It is a hall of constant rejuvenation, both with the *Einherjar* and also in Saehrimnir, Adhrimnir's boar which is slaughtered each day only to be made whole once more, to be eaten again and again.[421] Mead accompanies this endless supply of boar meat, apparently served by the Valkyries who are versed in rune magic, who know the power of carving runes on cups or horns to achieve various results. When looking at the power of magic alcoholic drinks on physical health when consumed, we have examples of curing wounds as well as inflicting injury or fatigue.[422]

---

420 Stephen Pollington, "The mead-hall community", Journal of Medieval History 37 (2011), 21.

421 Grímnismál 18 and Gylfaginning, chapter 38. Faulkes, Edda, 32.

422 Jesus Fernando Guerrero Rodriguez, Old Norse Drinking Culture (Ph.D thesis, University of York, 2007), 317.

Within *Göngu-Hrólfs saga* we have the following section that highlights this concept:

'The larger of the two vessels is for the entire army; the other, smaller one, is only for Hrolf and Stefner, and in the case of the latter two there is to be the additional effect that there will never be discord between them. Accordingly, when the men have partaken of the wonderful beverage, they forget about their wounds: those that have been most anxious to flee, now become most eager for the fray, even egging on the others.'[423]

Outside of the realms of Gods, these magical drinks possessed qualities that one would expect of alcoholic beverages but magnified and made special. There's a potency to these examples that move beyond what many would expect to achieve from a sip or cupful of alcohol. Within the realms of Gods, these beverages hold a power that cannot be seen to be born from exaggerations or creative allegory. **Maria Kvilhaug** suggests that the Godly mead itself may contain the power of immortality, continuing the theme of mead being a powerful and sacred drink.

"What makes them resurrect eternally? A drink. The drink that the Valkyriur served these einheri [Lone Rulers] – a precious mead, milked from the she-goat Heiðrun [Heath-Rune / Bright Open Space Symbol]....the "goat" who produces this mead takes her nourishment directly from the world tree, the universe tree..."[424]

Gotland runestone
G 268 Stenkyrka,
Lillbjärs III.

Close up sketch

---

423 Jacob Wittmer Hartmann, The Göngu-Hrólfssaga: A Study in Old Norse Philology (New York: Columbia University Press, 1912), 40.

424 Maria Kvilhaug, The Great Knowledge (USA: The Three Little Sisters LLC, 2023), 213.

We also have archaeological examples of feminine figures appearing to carry drinking horns. These figures, among other armoured examples, are often "reflexively labelled as Valkyries."[425] We are relying on ambiguous gender identifiers to make conclusions, which as has been discussed, is built on shaky ground and remains in constant shift. Simply, then, we can't absolutely conclude these figures to be Valkyries outright, as they often aren't depicted with any typical iconography that one would expect to see, such as armour and weaponry. It's a point of ongoing debate in academic circles,[426] and an area I lean in the direction of scepticism.

"The Dises" (1909) by Dorothy Hardy[2]

___

2 Featured in Guerber, The Myths of the Norsemen: From the Eddas and Sagas, 144. The image was included in later reprints of the book.

___

425 Leszek Gardeła , Peter Pentz and Neil Price, "Revisiting the 'Valkyries'. Armed Females in the Viking Age Figurative Metalwork", Current Swedish Archaeology, 30 (2022), 96; Julia Wihlborg, "Last Ride of the Valkyries: To (re) interpret Viking Age Female Figurines according to Gender and Queer Theory", Kyngervi 2 (2020), 22-39; Andrea Pintar, Valkyries or Valiant Women: The World of Women, Weapons and War in Viking Age Scandinavia (University of Amsterdam/VU University, 2016).

426 Ibid.

The Supernatural Valkyrie

There is one more form in which we can ascribe to the Valkyrie, and that is as a supernatural echo, carried through folk tales and stories into the modern day. This Supernatural Valkyrie frequently manifests within dreams, a space that could masquerade as mere superstition, a remnant of the beliefs of the past. These Valkyries tend to embody their most violent aspects and are strongly associated with blood. Otherwise, we have them appear alongside figures who would seem to be representative of their more noble aspects.

This juxtaposition presents a jarring image, but I would state that it is an effort to try to reconcile the two apparently disparate images of the Valkyries over the course of their timelines. We also have considerable semantic weakening over this period, with the Valkyries slipping further into the apparent 'catch-all' term of *Disir*, at least in how it was used in the thirteenth century and beyond to mean supernatural female.

Within this form, the Valkyrie also became incorporated into the pan-Germanic 'Wild Hunt', which will be discussed in more detail below. Together, these historical manifestations present an ability to manipulate hundreds, if not thousands of lives on a battlefield while also nurturing and guiding those individuals who have the potential to change many lives in turn.

Post-Conversion Folkloric Interpretations
- The Wild Hunt-

"When they ride forth on their errand, their armor sheds a strange flickering light, which flashes up over the northern skies, making what men call the "Aurora Borealis," or "Northern Lights."[427]

As addressed, there is a common trend of later works retroactively influencing the perception of the past. This quote by **Thomas Bulfinch** claims ancient origins in the time of the Viking Age, but I can find no other mention of it prior to Bulfinch's own work. If this is an invention by Bulfinch, we're faced with another example of a misconception being born and propagated.

Indeed, this fact is included on the 'Visit Norway' website,[428] among numerous other places. Despite its origins, it's also something that resonates with practitioners today, seamlessly incorporated into their belief structure. This presents another consideration in how the myths of the past continue to 'live on' in the people, becoming folk tales and stories. There's a sort of shelter in that medium, distanced from religious confrontation. It's an effort that stems from the Eddas and sagas, with euhemerism offering sanctuary, even if that wasn't the goal, to these beings and deities.

"What happens to gods when their cults die? Someone once said that the gods of the old regime become the demons of the new, but there is an alternative: sometimes they shrink, retire to the country and sink comfortably into some borrowed local story."[429]

---

427 Bulfinch, Bulfinch's Mythology: The Age of Fable or Stories of Gods and Heroes, 180.

428 "Facts about the Northern Lights", Visit Norway, accessed March 19, 2024. https://www.visitnorway.com/things-to-do/nature-attractions/northern-lights/facts-about-the-northern-lights/ This article even uses the phrase "strange flickering light" direct from Bulfinch's work.

429 Ingrid Barton, "The Giant of Pen Hill", in The Anthology of English Folk Tales (Gloucestershire, UK: The History Press, 2019), 176.

This is how our Gods endure in a world that became antagonistic to their existence. They continue in one form or another in the minds and hearts of people the world over. The ember of the post-conversion Valkyrie, surviving, though floating disembodied and detached through time, found itself ignited through Nordic romanticism, morphing once more into an inferno, even if the Valkyrie of this time was largely distinct from her earlier forms.

This inferno is best represented by Wagner's work when it comes to the Valkyries themselves, considering his influence on modern interpretations, and the subsequent effort towards reclamation of a period that, by all concerns, never existed. The image of the Wild Hunt exists alongside the romanticist movement, though rather than embodying the noble, dignified, mortal Valkyrie lover, tried to capture the supernatural echo of ferality. The perception of the Nordicist and supremacist movements was two-fold: a careful balance of espousing the strength and dignity of the past, while also presenting a wild, untameable thing that did not fit into the mould of civility.

What we see is a clash of a thoroughly converted Christian world wanting to incorporate qualities of the Heathen past, a past it had so thoroughly rejected and tried to erase. When it comes to persevering elements of folklore, the Wild Hunt remains one of the most evocative. As a creation of the later medieval period, it is important to emphasise that the Wild Hunt can best be described as a frequently recurring motif within Germanic cultures which doesn't appear in its most recognisable form during the Viking Age.

Where it does manifest is in the appearance of a more ambiguous spectral rider, either appearing individually or in groups.[430] *Njal's Saga* contains one such rider, appearing in Hildiglumr's vision. Hildiglumr's father proclaims it the 'witch-ride' [*gandreið*], which Price associates with *gandir* spirits.[431] These terrible figures create an ambiguous category of supernaturality that stem from tenth, eleventh and twelfth century literature but have appeared throughout numerous works in the millennia since.

---

430 Price, The Viking Way, 291.
431 Ibid.

Asgårdsreien [The Wild Hunt of Odin] (1872) by Peter Nicolai Arbo

Today, the Wild Hunt is seen as a much larger and complete concept than its original incarnation, devoid of its highly localised origins. But this localisation is important, with each manifestation of the Hunt, their qualities, behaviours and associations differing slightly to incorporate cultural touchstones. Within Welsh mythology, for example, the leader of the Wild Hunt is Gwynn ap Nudd, King of the 'Otherworld' [*Annwn*] and the *Tylwyth Teg*, the Welsh 'Fair Family' or 'Fair Folk'. He rides alongside the *Cwn Annwn*, his hunting dogs, and acts as a psychopomp figure, taking the souls of the dead to the world beyond. Within English mythology, the leader of the hunt is most referred to as Herla,[432] and the Wild Hunt becomes 'Herlaþing' [Herla's Gathering].

---

432 At other times, it's Woden (Anglo-Saxon name or counterpart of the Nordic Odin). A recent novel, Song of the Huntress by Lucy Holland reimagined Herla as a woman and lover to Boudicca. Here, she also leads the Wild Hunt but is assigned her position by Gwynn ap Nudd. Annwn retains its liminal nature, with one day in the otherworld equalling a hundred on the mortal plain. It's an interesting take that captures the fluidity of the Wild Hunt as an enduring literary concept.

The hunt takes on different masks across the European continent too, called the Dead Hunt, the Host, Bokkenrijders, and the Old Army, among other titles. Within Scandinavia, Odin often takes the mantle of leadership, and the Wild Hunt becomes 'Odin's Hunters',[433] or the *Oskoreidi* ["wish-ride"], which some surmise relates them directly to the Valkyries, who are occasionally described as 'Wish-Maidens'.[434]

In light of the Hunt's connection with the dead, storms, violence, choosing potential victims and their description as a horde of screaming spirits, it's little surprise that the Valkyries have been incorporated over time. To a lesser degree, the Nordic tradition is also said to incorporate Sigurd and Gudrun (of *Völsunga saga* fame), but this is worthy of significant note due to Gudrun's potential to be labelled as one of the honoured *Disir*.

"[Sigurd] then met the Wild Hunt led by Gudrun Horsetail, who asked him if he would prefer being the first in her troop or the last in heaven. Sigurd chose to follow her."[435]

This Gudrun would align with the guise she adopts in *Sturlunga Saga*.

"Eyolf Thoesteinsson dreamed that a woman visited him riding a gray horse. She came from Nástrǫnd, "Shore of Corpses", the empire of the dead. She appeared to him several times, eventually revealing that she was Gudrun Gjukedotter."[436]

---

433 Priscilla K. Kershaw, 'The One-eyed God: Odin and the (Indo-)Germanic Männerbünde', Journal of Indo-European Studies, 36, (1997), 29.

434 Price, The Viking Way, 291.

435 Lecouteux, Phantom Armies of the Night, The Wild Hunt and the Ghostly Processions of the Undead, 191.

436 Translation from Lecouteux, Phantom Armies of the Night, The Wild Hunt and the Ghostly Processions of the Undead, 191.

Claude Lecouteux reasons that this creates a bridge between the Wild Hunt and the *Dísir*, the *Nornir* and the *Fylgjur*.[437] Gudrun's attestation within *Sturlunga Saga* and her association with the Wild Hunt would enforce this perspective.

Saxo's *Gesta Danorum* certainly leans in that direction, if not aligning her entirely with the Valkyries, with his character of Guthruna [Gudrun] appearing as a sorceress who enchants an opposing army to fight each other.[438] Saxo never uses the term 'Valkyrie', or an equivalent, throughout his work, but frequently alludes to their behaviours.

Within each regional incarnation of the Hunt, the details also change dramatically. The overall historical image is one of constant flux, adopting to new beliefs and retellings. From hordes of fairies to the lone huntsman, to a horde of vengeful spirits.[439]

These figures bounce between mythological otherworld type beings, to mortal kings made other through enduring superstition. In the case of the Scandinavian variants, it moved from the former to the latter tagging onto the euhemerising efforts of post-conversion writers. The greater Germanic landscape offered a useful environment on which to secure the image of Odin as a mortal king made into an echo of superstition. Not just that, but a king turned violent spectre defined by violence and frenzy, used as a tool to emphasise the 'primitivism' of old Heathen beliefs.

> "Another class of spectres will prove more fruitful for our investigation: they, like the ignes fatui, include unchristened babes, but instead of straggling singly on the earth as fires, they sweep through forest and air in whole companies with a horrible din. This is the widely spread legend of the furious host, the furious hunt, which is of high antiquity, and interweaves itself, now with gods, and now with heroes. Look where you will, it betrays its connexion with heathenism."[440]

---

437 Ibid, 191-2.

438 Fisher, History of the Danes, 258.

439 Ronald Hutton dedicates time to distinguish the various versions in Ronald Hutton, "The Wild Hunt and the Witches' Sabbath", Folklore, 125 (2014), 161–78.

440 Jakob Grimm, Teutonic Mythology, trans. James Steven Stallybrass (London: Routledge, 1999), 918.

As Pollington states, "Relegation of ancient gods and supernatural figures to the margins of tradition – to folklore and fable – is a commonplace of cultural studies."[441] This approach has defined the Nordic gods throughout time, separated from their worship and histories. Look too towards the fable-esque framing that Saxo presents the Shield-Maiden figures in his works. There is a conscious effort to diminish the past as superstitious eccentricities. They're merely lessons to be learned from, silly stories of the old ways.

The defining characteristics of the Wild Hunt strongly resemble the behaviours of the early Valkyries. They ride through the air on steeds, screaming into the night, blood-lusted and hungry for human souls. They are furious and rage-filled and otherworldly by all definitions. Something so alien from human-born civilisation as to be unable to be integrated at all, defiant in its face.

They represent death, and the fear of death, which could be swift and sudden and sometimes entirely at the whims of natural powers seemingly far beyond human imagination. It's possible, maybe even likely, that the Hunt and the Valkyries stemmed from similar origins – a primordial nightmare before the time of "formal mythology".[442]

Through their incorporation, albeit fragmentary, the Valkyries experienced a reinforced narrative of their earlier incarnation, touching once more on the wild aspects of their nature which would come to persevere, haunting the landscape that they once rode victoriously upon. Initiated once more "into the wild, untamed forces of nature in its dark and chthonic aspects".[443]

Beware the screaming silence,
of misty wood, and open field,
in the dead of night, they come.

---

441 Pollington, Woden: A Historical Companion, 391.
442 Ibid.
443 Susan Greenwood, "The wild hunt: A mythological language of magic", in Handbook of Contemporary Paganism (2008), 195.

THE VALKYRIES AS LIMINAL BEINGS

Crossing boundaries, whether that be of the physical, metaphysical, or social variety, often leads an individual into a place of supernatural power, though often at the cost of cultural and societal reputation within the Nordic corpus. As mentioned above, a notable example of boundary-breaking behaviour appears in *Ljósvetninga saga*, with a magic practitioner named Thorhildr [Þórhildur], who was dressed in breeches with a helmet on her head and an axe in her hand. "Þórhildur úti og gyrð í brækur og hafði hjálm á höfði og öx í hendi."[444]

While dressed in this way, she performs magic:

"She headed down to the fjord and seemed to grow in stature.[445] She waded out into the shallows and struck her axe into the water, and Guthmundr could observe no change.... she then waded out into the shallows and struck a blow into the water. There was a loud crash, and the water turned all bloody."[446]

Liminality manifests in fascinating ways within the late Iron Age, offering a crucial glimpse into the 'logic' of religious practices, and more insight into archaeological discoveries. Being between two worlds, crossing boundaries, breaking social conventions, or being between two states of being was a place that often resulted in the attainment of power, wisdom, or knowledge.

---

444 The Saga of the People of Ljosavatn, in The Complete Sagas of Icelanders Including 49 Tales Volume IV, trans. T.M Andersson and W.I. Miller, ed. Viðar Hreinsson (Reykjavik: Leif Eriksson Publishing, 1997), 230.

445 There is also a thematic relationship between growing in size, or of being of great size, and acts of magic that appear frequently in the sagas and Eddas. The association with 'Risar' with largeness and their apparent magical 'otherness' falls in line with conclusions made within this book. Here though, it may be more relevant to refer back to "high-towering" Skögul, creating this image of a colossal, innately magical being.

446 Translation by T.M. Andersson and W.I. Miller, The Saga of the People of Ljosavatn, 230-1. Again, blood seems to be a signifier of liminality, or heralding something otherworldly.

As psychopomps, as travellers between Asgard and Midgard, as feminine beings engaging in bloodthirsty acts in the culturally perceived masculine realm of battle and war, as magic users, as (on occasion) empowered humans, as death deities that walk the living earth, the Valkyries I would argue, are exemplars of this phenomenon. They are the guardians of two distinct worlds: life and death, and they act in ways that accelerate a person's journey over that threshold, or bar them from entry.

In an earlier chapter I used **Judith Jesch** as an anchoring point to frame my opinion that women could, potentially, be warriors in the Viking Age. But, let's now take that quote at face value, "..that the very few women buried with weapons were warrior women in life seems the least likely explanation of all."[447] Then women shown wielding weapons in a warrior capacity would be considered a significant boundary transgression, highly unusual, controversial and against societal convention.

The Valkyries are paragons within this perspective, at once combining the apparent strict masculine paradigm of being warriors, with the feminine realm of weaving and textiles, only reinforcing the Valkyries' connection with *seiðwork*. Much the same can be said of Odin and Freyja too, internalising both masculine and feminine qualities. If we turn back to *Darraðarljoð*, we have the Valkyries utilising weaving, being present in the *dyngja*, creating a loom out of weapons and gore-splattered body parts, and manipulating the battlefield.

In my view, this is the most explicit form of liminality in the literature. A perfect equilibrium between what would have been seen at the time as absolute masculine and absolute feminine behaviours. Brynhildr herself, the most famous Valkyrie in the literature,[448] is seen as both a highly capable warrior, and "more skilled in handicraft than other women."[449] Almost as though, by being the latter, she is given freedom to explore the former within the expectations of the greater society and societal norms. Either way, she too embodies this image of perfect liminality.

---

447 Jesch, The Viking Diaspora, 107.

448 Perhaps ironically, seeing as she is probably not Nordic in origin, but a Germanic figure that was engineered into Nordic dressings, considering the various manifestations of Brynhildr across continental literature. From the Icelandic queen who loses her supernatural strength, to Valkyrie who loses her supernatural powers – becoming ordinary and mortal, a fall from extraordinary heights.

449 Byock, The Saga of the Volsungs, 73.

There's power in moving beyond boundaries, an understanding that if one can withstand the repercussions of crossing boundaries, to pay the cost for such power, that something incredible lies in wait. The space between boundaries is a place of unknowable potential. It's a potential that Odin understood, moving beyond death and the veil between life and death to learn the secrets of the runes, as well as moving across the perceived gender boundary to learn *seiðr* from Freyja.

This also touches back on the idea that great power must also come at a great cost. Often, more specifically, seen in the notion that there is a great personal cost for communal gain. Nothing is given freely. Whether that be Odin offering an eye to attain greater wisdom or 'giving himself to himself' upon Yggdrasil,[450] Heimdall offering his ear to attain greater awareness for the betterment of the community,[451] or arguably, Gullveig undergoing torture and murder to emerge as someone else,[452] there are several such examples.

With Gullveig's torture and Odin's act upon Yggdrasil especially, there is an interpretation that we are witnessing a rite of passage, an initiation into greater power born from sacrifice,[453] and from temporarily being exposed to the threshold between life and death, the liminal space between those worlds. Gullveig's identity as a Volva [Völva] and *seiðworker* are widely discussed, with her ability to resurrect herself and to defy death being hallmarks of *seiðr*, a tool through which, as **Maria Kvilhaug** specifies, one could change the ultimate fate: death.[454]

---

450 Hávamál 138. While Yggdrasil is not mentioned by name here, it's common consensus that this verse is referring to the world tree. Lindow, Norse Mythology: A Guide to Gods, Heroes, Rituals, and Beliefs, 321.

451 If we're to follow Larrington's reasoning in her translation of Völuspá 28 – "She knows that Heimdall's hearing is hidden / under the bright-grown sacred tree" – Heimdall has sacrificed an ear in much the same way as Odin sacrificed his eye to Mimir's well. As Heimdall is known for his exceptional senses, we can perhaps infer that this sacrificial act was the cause. Larrington, The Poetic Edda (Revised Edition), 7.

452 "three times she was reborn....Bright One they called her...the seer with pleasing prophecies." Völuspá 22 & 23. Larington, The Poetic Edda (Revised Edition), 6.

453 Clunies-Ross first detailed how Gullveig's torture was highly reminiscent of a sacrifice orchestrated by the Aesir. Margaret Clunies-Ross, Prolonged Echoes -Old Norse Myths in Medieval Northern Society, Volume I: The Myths (Odense, Denmark: Odense University Press, 1994), 204.

454 Kvilhaug, The Maiden with the Mead, 138.

It is Odin, after all, that initiates the war between the Aesir and Vanir, and with it an opportunity to acquire the talent that Gullveig and the Vanir possessed.[455] **Ursula Dronke** notices a reflection in Gullveig's torment via spear and her inability to die, with Odin's spear-throw over the Vanir host, and their proposed continuous resurrection on the battlefield. "-we could suppose that the Vanir -like Gullveig- have revived 'reborn' from Odinn's spear-cast-perhaps frequently repeated, opt, ósialdan -and the Aesir find to their dismay that their victims are--as she was-'still living."[456]

Through *seiðr*, both Freyja and Odin are representative of liminality, with their halls being a natural reflection of this space they inhabit. It would be easy to conclude that Valhalla, like its master, does not entirely belong to a single 'world', but instead exists in the space between boundaries. Here, the boundary between life and death. I would argue that Valhalla isn't a 'true' afterlife, not by the classical definition of being a final resting place, as its inhabitants can experience 'death', only to be brought to 'life' once more. Like being in a limbo, or a state between life and death, not truly part of either.[457]

Hail to the warrior women,
To the Gate-Guardians of the great threshold,
Keepers of sacred knowledge,
By your decree, we may pass beyond
and learn life's secrets.

---

455 Ibid, 139.

456 Ursula, Dronke, The Poetic Edda: Volume II: Mythological Poems (Oxford: Oxford University Press, 1997), 43.

457 This is an image repeated by Hildr and her exploits in resurrecting two eternally warring armies. Which will be addressed below.

THE POWER OF THE VALKYRIE

The dressings of a Valkyrie have been discussed at length by academics, used as a guiding light when demarcating their numerous appearances from similar figures. While I have put forward an argument that these often don't go far enough in terms of behaviours and associations, there are consistencies: armour, weaponry, comfortable in environments of conflict, an otherworldly essence that marks them as different from the people around them, the use of magic, and a control over fate.

Regardless of whether given mortal origins or divine, the Valkyries showcase abilities that certainly mark them as supernaturally powerful, even outside of their ability to change the course of battle through their actions. These instances of incredible supernatural power are seen as outliers, used to fuel the argument that these figures certainly couldn't be Valkyries, who are restricted to the role of servant as maids of Odin. They must be someone else, perhaps Freyja in an adopted guise or an unknown Goddess figure, defying easy classification of spirit, Vanir, *Disir*, or Aesir.

This isn't solely at the feet of modern writers and scholars either; in actions that evoke God-like power, there is a rise in rhetoric that replace the Valkyrie with a known Goddess. In the latter, the most common example is in replacing the Valkyrie with Freyja, who naturally exhibits similar behaviours anyway, and is, as such, a natural fit. With that tendency in place, we have a vicious cycle of any outlying behaviours being attributed to other figures, which keeps the Valkyries at an agreed 'power level' of their perceived role in the literature.

A key example of this is Þorgerðr Hölgabrúðr, who I state is a Valkyrie for reasons I will discuss below. While she exhibits all the iconography and 'dressings' of a Valkyrie, she is not seen choosing the slain or serving mead in Valhalla, and as such is often dismissed from being counted among their number. This is despite our very first literary appearance of a Valkyrie in *Hrafnsmal* not abiding by those very same definitory behaviours.

This has created a misalignment in the corpus, with the definition of Valkyrie being altogether too limited, whilst the existence of like figures such as the *Disir*, and elements of the pluralistic soul, almost necessitating such restrictive criteria as a scaffold for discussing the material as it is presented.

Below then, I will highlight two figures, one who is explicitly stated as a Valkyrie across several sources[458] yet is often equated to Freyja by later sources, and another who is not explicitly stated as a Valkyrie but exhibits all the behaviours and characteristics of one. As far as I could see, there is no academic commentary on the latter being labelled as a Valkyrie in available modern study.

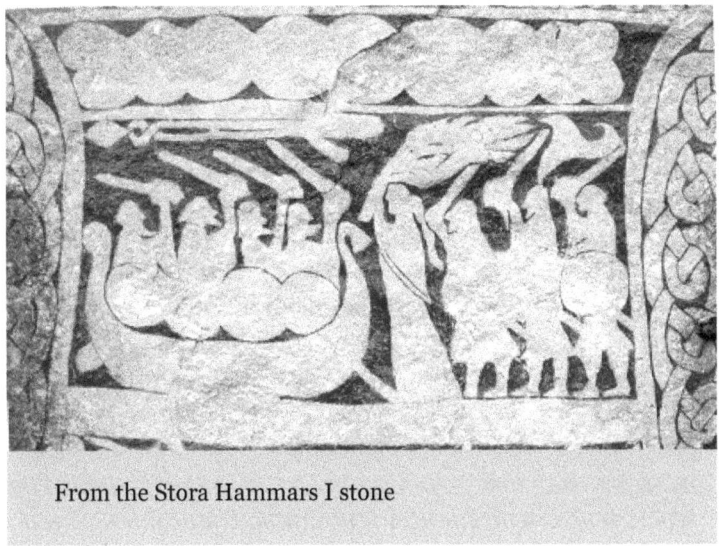

From the Stora Hammars I stone

HILDR HǪGNADÓTTIR

Hildr is an evocative Valkyrie, in that she displays one of the most extraordinary instances of sheer power in the sagas even with consideration of the divine actions of the Aesir, Vanir and Jotnar. Hildr's most prominent appearance occurs in *Hjaðningavíg* [Battle of the Heodenings], which is documented fragmentedly within *Ragnarsdrápa*, Snorri's *Skáldskaparmál*, Saxo's *Gesta Danorum*, and *Sörla þáttr*.

458 Hildr appears in Hjaðningavíg [The Battle of the Heodenings], Darraðarljóð and Völuspá. There is some disagreement whether the Hildr in the former is truly the same as the explicit Valkyrie presented in the latter two sources, but I will outline my reasoning to say they are below.

The image of this never-ending battle is a popular one in Germanic literature, finding reference across several other works, including the Old English *Deor*[459] and the Middle High German *Kudrun*.[460] While the story was evidently known in one form or another throughout the Germanic world, I will be focusing here on the Scandinavian versions of the legend.

Within *Sörla þáttr*, dated to the fourteenth century, Hildr, like many of her fellow Valkyries, is presented as the daughter of a king, and is described as excelling "all other women in beauty and understanding."[461] However, here Hildr is not made the instigator of the eternal battle, instead it is Göndul, who is widely believed to be Freyja[462] within this retelling.

This is with the consideration that an earlier chapter describes how Freyja is forced by Odin to engineer the eternal battle between the two kings:

"Othin replied that considering how she had come by it she should never get it back: "—Unless you bring about a quarrel between two kings, each of whom has twenty kings subject to him; so that they shall fight under the influence of such spells and charms that as fast as they fall they shall start up again and fight on—unless there be some Christian man so brave and so much favoured by the great good fortune of his liege lord that he shall dare to take arms and enter among the combatants and slay them. Then and not till then shall the labours of those princes be brought to an end—whoever may be the chief who is destined to free them from the oppression and toil of their disastrous lot."

Freyja agreed to this and recovered the necklace."[463]

---

459 Kemp Malone, "An Anglo-Latin Version of the Hjaðningavíg', Speculum, 39: 1, (1964), 35-44.

460 Gudrun, a mediaeval epic, trans. Mary Pickering Nichols (Boston and New York: Houghton, Mifflin and company, 1889), 102-17.

461 Chapter six. The Tháttur of Sörli. The Complete Fornaldarsögur Norðurlanda: Legendary Sagas of the Northland, trans. Nora Kershaw (1921). "Sörla þáttr", Germanic Mythology, accessed March 27, 2024. https://www. germanicmythology.com/FORNALDARSAGAS/SORLATHATTURKERSHAW. html

462 Britt-Mari Näsström, Freyja, the Great Goddess of the North (Harwich Port, USA: Clock & Rose Press, 2003), 20.

463 Chapter two, Kershaw, The Tháttur of Sörli. The Complete Fornaldarsögur Norðurlanda: Legendary Sagas of the Northland. It's interesting that Odin is acting through Freyja here, suggesting he is unable to achieve this result through his own power, which is also reflected in examples discussed

There is a reference contained within *Sörla þáttr* to ales that have been enchanted by Göndul with magical properties that contained both "wickedness and forgetfulness", with a later drink offering an antidote to those conditions. This draws back to the earlier discussion around the Valkyrie Ölrún, and in the use of runes that Brynhildr taught to Sigurdr. Evidently, there was an understanding that ale or ale horns could possess magical qualities, and also be used as a vehicle to enchant someone else.

As a result of drinking this ale, Hedinn becomes enraged, seeking to take Hildr by force, rather than asking her father for her hand. Hildr mentions that she has "had a warning in dreams"[464] that her father and would-be husband would fight to the death. She expresses sadness at potentially having to use magic to avoid what is to come, especially in having to expose her father to the "ruinous effects of magic spells".[465] This may be an artefact of the earlier version of the story, seeing as Hildr does not perform any magic herself over the course of this telling.

"And when he came into the glade, there he saw Göndul seated on her throne. They greeted one another cordially. Hethin [Hedinn/Heðinn] told her what he had done and she expressed her approval.

She had with her the horn which she had carried before, and she offered him a drink from it. He took it and drank; and when he had drunk, sleep fell upon him, and he let his head sink into her lap. And when he had fallen asleep, she slipped away from under his head, saying:

"Now I devote both you and Högni and all your followers, and lay you under all the spells imposed by Othin."
Then Hethin awoke and saw the fleeting shadow of Göndul, but she appeared to him now to be big and black;[466]and he recalled everything and realised how much mischief he had done."[467]

throughout this book.

464 Chapter six, Ibid.

465 Ibid.

466 Certainly reminiscent of something terrible and terrifying, such as the Valkyries are often stated.

467 Chapter six. Kershaw, The Tháttur of Sörli. The Complete Fornaldarsögur Norðurlanda: Legendary Sagas of the Northland.

With regards to the Christian elements incorporated into this piece, the Gods are depicted in a rather poor light. Odin blackmails Freyja to act according to his will here, while Göndul/Freyja resorts to trickery by giving Hedinn enchanted ale. At the end of the story, Göndul /Freyja becomes something large and terrifying, something 'other'. It's all rather unflattering to the morality and power of the old Nordic Gods.

As it isn't explicitly stated within the text itself, and the conclusion is ultimately based on a resistance to assign any power and agency to the Valkyries, I lean more towards this being Göndul or a one-off occurrence of Freyja using the name Göndul to disguise herself. The dedication made to Odin[468] alongside the terrible image that she presents herself as once the guise has been dropped, certainly leans towards this being a Valkyrie and not Freyja, even considering the mead-bearing, Valkyrie-esque roles that Freyja is associated with too.

If this is understood to indeed be Freyja using the name Göndul[469] I would state that this was certainly not a consistent understanding across the literature. It is important to consider that this work is dated some four hundred years after *Ragnarsdrápa* at a time when the Valkyries were more recognisable as the mortal-born noble-women of the heroic lays. Here, then, was a time where the power of the Valkyries was attributed more to Freyja and like Goddesses than the Valkyries themselves, who were straying further and further into the realms of mortal and human associations in the literature.

Indeed, at the time of the composition of *Sörla þáttr*, 'Göndul' could easily be seen as an alternative heiti for Freyja given the associations of staffs with the practice of *seiðr*. The association of *seiðr* staffs that comes with the potential etymology of the name Göndul also acts as a barrier here, with that being seen as emblematic of Freyja herself, rather than informing us of the Valkyries greater connections to *seiðr*, as I consider to be the case.

---

468 Even with the additional context of Freyja being coerced into action in chapter two, Näsström calls it a consecration to Odin, which I would agree with. "...she chooses death for him". As has been discussed, this would fall more in line with the first and most consistent role of the Valkyrie, to choose the slain. Näsström, Freyja, the Great Goddess of the North, 20.

469 The connection between Freyja and the Valkyries has been established above, and the nature of that connection would suggest she could ask a Valkyrie to do this task in her stead. Saying that, this is a later work – made obvious by its more explicit Christian insertions – which often includes such inconsistencies.

Within Bragi Boddason's *Ragnarsdrápa*, believed to be composed in the ninth century, we have a telling of the battle between Hedinn and Hogni that paints an image of Hildr delighting in the bloodshed and inciting the violence. This example also highlights the understanding that the Valkyrie could heal as well as wound and kill, depending on what they wanted to achieve on the battlefield. Hildr is healing on mass through the act of resurrection, acting in defiance of natural progression.

"That curing-Þrúðr[470] of bloody wounds [Valkyrie, Hildr] did not offer the splendid ruler the neck-ring for the sake of cowardice at the assembly of weapons. Thus she continually behaved as if she was hindering the battle, although she was inciting the princes to accompany the sister of the complete monster of a wolf [Hel].
And the booty-destroying evil-doer among women [Hildr] took control on the island on behalf of the Viðrir [Odin]..."[471]

Here, then, we see a Valkyrie figure who more closely assembles the gore-splattered carnage demons of the earlier sort. **Elizabeth Ashman Rowe** agrees, stating that Hildr seems most like those "fierce elemental spirits who delight in slaughter and bloodshed,"[472] rather than the 'noble mortal born Valkyrie' who is prone to protective acts, or the mead-serving Valhalla-based Valkyrie archetype.

To note, the use of kennings in the appropriate verses do not mention that the dead would go to Odin, but rather there is purposeful specification of 'Hel', which raises some questions. Not least of which, is that if we're to believe that Hildr is in fact a Valkyrie, then this is a significant outlying behaviour, and only finds tentative evidence in Saxo's description of warring armies in his depiction of Hel within *Gesta Danorum*. We can only really guess at the reasoning here. Maybe, this outlying behaviour is supposed to be seen as a corruption, something unnatural and against the 'natural order' of Valkyries delivering their dead to Odin.

---

470 A good example of the rules presented in Skáldskaparmál of the name of a Goddess being used as a shorthand for other feminine figures. Though here, Þrúðr is also the name of a Valkyrie

471 Margaret Clunies Ross, "Bragi inn gamli Boddason, Ragnarsdrápa", in Poetry from Treatises on Poetics, Skaldic Poetry of the Scandinavian Middle Ages 3, ed. by Kari Ellen Gade and Edith Marold (2017), 27.

472 Elizabeth Ashman Rowe, "Sǫrla þáttr: The Literary Adaptation of Myth and Legend", Saga-Book 26 (2002), 43.

Almost like Hildr is playing with the lives of these people, holding them in a space that is beyond and outside the Gods' remit. Perhaps there was some consensus that the battle takes place in the fields outside Hel's halls or a place equally of the otherworld? A place not quite of the world of the dead or the world of the living? Perhaps by breaking the natural progression of life and death repeatedly, Hildr has created a sort of 'Valhalla' of her own.

A place of death made into a place of undeath, the battle uninterrupted until the end of all things. Those that are victorious from the day's fighting notably do not, and cannot, leave, creating a space that exists outside of time. Maybe there was an understanding that someone wasn't well and truly dead until they had finished their 'journey' into the respective halls of the dead? We can only make guesses, and likely there is no logical and 'tidy' answer to this question.

Snorri includes a prose section prior to quoting Bragi's work directly:

> "But during the night Hild went to the slain and woke up by magic all those that were dead. And the next day the kings went onto the battle-field and fought, and so did all those who had fallen the previous day. This battle continued day after day, with all those who fell, and all the weapons that lay on the battle-field, as well as shields, turning to stone. And when day came, all the dead got up and fought, and all the weapons were usable. It says in poems that the Hiadnings must thus await Ragnarok."[473]

All this frames Hildr as a master of fate on this fated battlefield, all while epitomising the liminal nature of it. It's an incredibly impressive feat, even considering the feats of Gods and giants. *Sörla þáttr* remains a significant anomaly in fully replacing Hildr from being the instigator of the eternal battle where that motif appears, though all versions reference the names of Valkyries, or behaviours and roles typical of Valkyries. As discussed, resurrection was arguably understood to be possible through the practice and mastery of *seiðr*.

---

473 Faulkes, Edda, 123.

ÞORGERÐR HÖLGABRÚÐR

There has been much discourse on the nature of Þorgerðr Hölgabrúðr [Thorgerdr Holgabrudr] and her common characterisation of being a Goddess, a giantess or one of the honoured *Dísir*. [474] Much of the argument seems to lie in the perception of Þorgerðr as being beyond the normal representation of the Valkyries, yet, with what I have posited over the course of the book and will continue to discuss, I am not certain that can be soundly concluded. Rather here, in Þorgerðr, we have a Valkyrie who was worshipped individually as a Goddess in her own right.

It's surprising, considering the nature of the Valkyries, that we don't have more examples of this emerging in the literature. If the role of the Valkyrie was understood to reflect the perspective I have discussed above, that they chose who lives and who dies on the battlefield, you may expect more instances of explicit worship, which is not the case. Again, this may be due to the criteria with which we have judged the Valkyries in the past, resistant to assigning any sort of independence away from Odin. However, we can say much the same about many of the Gods outside of Odin, Thor and Freyr, who enjoy a bounty of such examples in comparison to many of their peers.

The most prominent appearance of Þorgerðr Hölgabrúðr lies in *Jómsvíkinga saga* [Saga of the Jomsvikings].

---

474 Davidson argues that Þorgerðr is another guise adopted by Freyja. Hilda Ellis Davidson, Roles of the Northern Goddess (London and New York: Routledge, 1998), 177-8. McKinnell follows that line of reasoning, suggesting that the cult of Þorgerðr falls in line with the Vanir worship. John McKinnell, "Þórgerðr Hölgabrúðr and Hyndluljóð", in Mythological Women. Studies in Memory of Lotte Motz 1922-1997, ed. Rudolf Simek and Wilhelm Heizmann (Wien: Fassbaender, 2002), 265-90. See also Gunnhild Røthe, "The Fictitious Figure of Þorgerðr Hölgabrúðr in the Saga Tradition", in The Fantastic in Old Norse/Icelandic Literature: Preprint Papers of the 13th International Saga Conference, Durham and York 6th-12th August 2006, I-II, ed. John McKinnell, David Ashurst and Donata Kick (Durham: Centre for Medieval and Renaissance Studies, 2006), 836-45.

"And in his prayer he called upon his patron goddess, Thorgerd[r] Holgabrud[r]. But she would not hear his prayer and was wroth.... At last he offered his own seven-year-old-son; and that she accepted."[475]

It must be said that this exchange evokes the story of Isaac and Abraham in Christian lore,[476] though the positions are almost reversed, in that Hakon offers his son to Þorgerðr without her requesting such an action. We also see a similar situation play out in classical myth, with a wrathful Artemis retaliating against Agamemnon when he kills one of her sacred stags. This retaliation is in the form of commanding the winds to make sailing to Troy impossible. Agamemnon sought to rectify the situation by offering his daughter, Iphigenia, to Artemis as a human sacrifice.[477]

"And right soon the weather began to thicken in the north and clouds covered the sky and the daylight waned. Next came flashes of lightning and thunder, and with them a violent shower.....although the Jomsvikings hurled stones and other missiles and threw their spears, the wind turned all of their weapons back upon them..."[478]

As above, the Valkyries often appear alongside thunder, lightning and storm imagery. The ability to conjure storms quickly seems within their remit, creating a sort of pathetic fallacy to their various literary appearances. Here, in an echo of the classical myth above, the winds impede progress and force the Jomsvikings' weapons to be turned back against them.

---

475 The Saga of the Jomsvikings, trans. Lee M. Hollander (USA: University of Texas Press, 1988), 100.

476 Genesis 22:1-10 (King James Version).

477 "When the expedition [for Troy] had mustered a second time at Aulis, Agamemnon, while at the chase, shot a stag and boasted that he surpassed even Artemis. At this the goddess was so angry that she sent stormy winds and prevented them from sailing. Kalkhas then told them of the anger of the goddess and bade them sacrifice Iphigeneia to Artemis." Stasinus of Cyprus, Homerica: The Cypria Fragment 1, trans. Hugh G. Evelyn-White (1914), accessed June 24, 2024. https://www.theoi.com/Olympios/ArtemisWrath2.html#Agamemnon

478 Ibid, 101.

"Havard the Hewing was the first to see Thorgerd[r] Holgabrud[r] in the fleet of Earl Hakon,...and when the squall abated a little they saw that an arrow flew from every finger of the ogress..."[479]

This is noteworthy by itself: Valkyries are one of the few categories of entity who are described as Goddesses and ogresses almost interchangeably. Not even Jotnar turned Goddesses, such as Gerdr and Skadi, are described in such a manner. We are told that Þorgerðr is Hakon's patron Goddess, yet she is later described as an ogress - a troll, a giant, a being of the wilds.

Other translations call her a "monstrous woman",[480] certainly not befitting of the title of Goddess, but one that absolutely falls in line with the description of the Valkyries. Something beautiful, noble, refined, and bloodthirsty, feral, unrestrained. Perhaps most tellingly is that Þorgerðr, in *Skáldskaparmál*, is described as the daughter of a king, King Hölgi[481]. Within *Skáldskaparmál* too she is listed among the troll-wives, alongside Gryla, Jarnsaxa, Hyrrokin and many others, making it clear that she is considered a Jotunn by Snorri.[482]

Published in "Ekermann, A. (1895). Från Nordens forntid : Fornnordiska sagor bearb. på svenska / Med orig. teckn:r af Jenny Nyström-Stoopendaal. Stockholm, P. A. Norstedt.

---

479 Ibid.
480 Davidson, Roles of the Northern Goddess, 177.
481 Faulkes, Edda, 112.
482 Ibid, 156.

Within *Harðar saga ok Hólmverja* [The Saga of Hord and the People of Holm], Þorgerðr Hölgabrúðr takes on another role more explicitly aligned with a being who operates in a role defined by fate and death.

"Grimkel went to Thorgerd Horgabrud's temple and was going to make a pronouncement about Thorbiorg's marriage, but when he came into the temple the gods were all in a great commotion and were getting ready to leave their pedestals. Grimkel said: 'What's the meaning of this and where are you off to, and where will you now direct good fortune?'

Thorgerd said, 'We shall not direct good fortune to Hord, since he has plundered my brother Soti of that fine gold ring of his and done much other disgrace to him. I will though instead direct good fortune towards Thorbiorg, and such a great light shines above her that I am afraid that it will cause a separation between us. But you will have only a short time to live.'

He then went away and was very angry with the gods. He went home for fire and burned up the temple and all the gods and said they should never again tell him grievous tidings. And in the evening when people were sitting at table, Grimkel Godi suddenly dropped dead and he was buried south of the farmyard."[483]

This is not unlike the behaviour of 'typical' Valkyries, knowledgeable as they are presented when it comes to imminent and foreseen death, or in ensuring death comes to pass. With all this in mind, we must consider that Þorgerðr is a Goddess who is associated with the appearance of storms, plays an important role in giving victory during battle, is described as the daughter of a king and sister, and is at once a Goddess, but also described as "monstrous", an "ogress" and a "troll-wife". These are all things that would reinforce a conclusion that Þorgerðr is nothing else but a Valkyrie. If Þorgerðr can indeed be classified as a Valkyrie, then she acts as a focal point in the greater argument against the Valkyrie's ongoing servant status.

---

483 Three Icelandic Outlaw Sagas: The Saga of Gisli, The Saga of Grettir, and The Saga of Hord, trans. George Johnston, ed. Anthony Faulkes (London: University College London, Viking Society for Northern Research, 2004), 297.

Fenja and Menja at
the mill. Illustration
by Carl Larsson

WILD VS CIVILISATION, THE POWER OF 'THE WILD'

*"Metamorphoses, cavalcades, ecstasies, followed by the
egress of the soul in the shape of an animal—these are
different paths to a single goal. Between animals and souls,
animals and the dead, animals and the beyond, there exists
a profound connection."*[484]

You can certainly read the Eddas as a story of the Gods taming
the wild to create society and civilisation.[485] Furthermore, as **Helga
Kress** suggests, it wouldn't be difficult to read further, to see a
repeated theme of the Gods overpowering and taming women,
frequently giantesses who are emblematic of this wildness that must
be quashed, controlled and, if at all possible, integrated.

---

484 Carlo Ginzburg, Ecstasies: Deciphering the Witches' Sabbath, trans.
Raymond Rosenthal (London: Hutchinson Radius, 1990), 263.
485 Helga Kress, "Taming the Shrew: The Rise of Patriarchy and the
Subordination of the Feminine in Old Norse Literature", in The Cold Counsel.
The Women in Old Norse Literature, ed. Sarah M. Anderson and Karen Swenson
(New York: Routledge, 2001), 83.

These attempts at domestication often come by way of threat of violence or servitude, with both approaches removing their agency. Like wild animals, these supposedly wild peoples, commonly giantesses, have an attribute to them that is desired: their wisdom, beauty or strength. These qualities represent a utility or quality that makes them 'useful' or desirable to the Gods and, in the heroic poems, mortal kings.

Take *Grottasöngr* [The Song of Grotti] and the "mountain-giant"[486] girls who are tasked with grinding the millstone without rest by King Frodi. This millstone, called Grotti, was said to be so large that no man was strong enough to move it,[487] yet was magical in nature, granting "riches and treasures, peace and happiness".[488] These giant girls appear, by all concerns, normal, despite their strength, and so Frodi assumed they were just human, without asking or questioning their heritage further. These giantesses are named Fenja and Menja, and they are revealed over the course of the poem to have created the magical millstone they are now tasked with relentlessly rotating.

"Nine winters we were playmates,
strong girls, brought up under the earth;
the girls were doers of mighty deeds,
we ourselves moved the mountain-seat from its place.

We rolled the boulder over the giant's dwelling
so that the earth in front of it began shaking;[489]
We swung the fast-turning stone,
the heavy boulder, so that mean seized it."[490]

---

486 Larrington, The Poetic Edda (Revised Edition), 253. In relation to the argument presented at the very beginning of this book, the word specifically used here is bergrisa ["mountain-risi"], which suggests that these giantesses may have been recognised as non-Scandinavian and particularly large by the writer's contemporaries. If that assumption is correct, you have to question why Frodi thought they were ordinary human women!

487 A quality stated by Snorri in the Prose Edda: Faulkes, Edda, 107. Note parallels with Hyrrokin and her strength being unmatched in all of the realms.

488 Larrington, The Poetic Edda (Revised Edition), 252.

489 Regardless of size, the Jotnar are frequently associated with language that evokes earthquakes – whether that be Fenja and Menja here, but also Hyrrokin and Skrymir. Loki, the son of a Jotunn who is often given Jotunn status too, is said to cause earthquakes while he is imprisoned and tortured by serpent venom below the earth.

490 Larrington, The Poetic Edda (Revised Edition), 253.

Frodi is a king who enjoys prosperity and wealth through the magic and utility of the giantesses he has imprisoned. But, he doesn't understand the power he has tentatively contained, and is overcome by greed. On the other side, the giantesses represent the fall from grace that colours the depiction of the Jotnar throughout their appearances in the literature.

They were something great, they warred, they were made other, and then they were imprisoned, enslaved and made lesser. "Mud eats away at their feet"[491] – a far cry from the glory and honour they achieved on the battlefield. I must also focus on the language that accompanies these warring pursuits, which certainly echo the language surrounding the Valkyries themselves, who we know could be of Jotnar descent.

"And afterwards in Sweden,
we two fore-sighted ones advanced in the army;
we challenged bearlike warriors, we smashed shields,
we marched through the grey-corsleted army.
-
We overthrew one prince, we supported another one.....
-
there we scored with sharp spears
blood out of wounds and reddened the sword."[492]

As I will examine below, the imprisonment of these wild forces is a temporary situation and cannot be maintained indefinitely. Here, at the song's conclusion, Fenja and Menja embrace their war-like behaviour once more and take vengeance on Frodi by summoning an army through Grotti's magic. The millstone is then broken beyond repair by the giantesses: "Let's grasp the handle, girl, more tightly! We're not frozen stiff in slaughtered men's blood.... The wooden mill-shafts shuddered...the heavy grindstone broke in two."[493] The similarities here to descriptions of the Valkyries are difficult to ignore.

---

491 Ibid, 254.
492 Ibid, 253-4.
493 Larrington, The Poetic Edda (Revised Edition), 254-5.

Finally, Fenja and Menja are referenced within kennings for gold; "the grinding of Fróði's slave-girls", "Fenja's menial work", and "Fenja's grinding".[494] As mentioned previously, I maintain that gold was seen as a nebulous quantity that reflected violence and war as much as it reflected wealth. After all, the exhibition of power so often goes hand in hand with violence.

Another example of this sort exists within *Skírnismál* [The Lay of Skirnir] regarding the giantess, Gerdr. Freyr looks upon Jotunheim and sees Gerdr as she departs her father's house. He immediately becomes "lovesick"[495] by her appearance, and asks his servant, Skirnir, to find the giantess and convince her to go with him. Skirnir's initial attempts consist of bribing Gerdr with golden apples and jewellery; essentially, youth and wealth. When she refuses those, Skirnir switches tact, and proceeds to threaten her with violence.

Skirnir spake:
"Seest thou, maiden, | this keen, bright sword
That I hold here in my hand?
Thy head from thy neck | shall I straightway hew,
If thou wilt not do my will."

Gerth spake:
"For no man's sake | will I ever suffer
To be thus moved by might;
But gladly, methinks, | will Gymir seek
To fight if he finds thee here."

Skirnir spake:
"Seest thou, maiden, | this keen, bright sword
That I hold here in my hand?
Before its blade the | old giant bends,--
Thy father is doomed to die.

---

494 All mentioned by Clive Tolley, Grottasõngr the Song of Grotti (London, UK: University College of London, Viking Society for Northern Research, 2008), 24. From Lausavísa 8, Bjarkamál 4/3, Lausavísa 24/Øxarflokkr 6/Háttatal 43.
495 Bellows, The Poetic Edda: The Mythological Poems, 108.

I strike thee, maid, | with my magic staff,
To tame thee to work my will;
There shalt thou go | where never again
The sons of men shall see thee."[496]

He goes further still, cursing her with rage, longing, wrath and sorrow. He calls her "most evil maid"[497] and claims that the Gods will become her enemy, opposing her at every turn. It is under this barrage, threatening physical, spiritual and mental torment, that Gerdr admits defeat, promising that Freyr will be granted "delight".[498] Outside of another potential reading of *Skírnismál* as a story of the wildness being tamed for agricultural endeavour,[499] this is a tale of a forced relationship.

It isn't difficult, considering Freyr's position as a fertility deity and his many 'well-endowed' depictions, to see the sword as a representation of the God's penis.[500] By giving Skirnir his sword, Freyr is potentially also "surrendering his sexual independence",[501] an acknowledgment that, in one small way, Gerdr has taken from him something which gives him power. Freyr is lovesick, utterly infatuated with the giantess, as **David Varley** points out, she has quite literally disarmed him.[502] This disarmament will prove costly come *Ragnarök*, with the once-fertile land being razed with fire as its utility and life cycle comes to an end, to be made fertile once more.

Yet, with that interpretation in mind, it's difficult to overlook the more explicit overtones, and the theme of sexual violence and domination through violent acts, threatened or otherwise.[503] Women, again often giantesses, within the Eddas and sagas are used to represent an old sort of power, a wildness and magic that means they must be conquered and made tame for masculine powers to thrive. This motif occurs frequently, with the language around feminine power becoming more villainous as we move further past the point of conversion.

---

496 Ibid, 114-5.
497 Ibid, 117.
498 Ibid, 119.
499 Varley, The Whirling Wheel, 167.
500 Sexual metaphor is a frequently utilised tool within the Eddas and sagas. See Lucy Anne Keens, Scenes of a sexual nature: theorising representations of sex and the sexual body in the sagas of the Icelanders (PhD thesis, University College London, 2016).
501 Varley, The Whirling Wheel, 170.
502 Ibid, 171.
503 Kress, Taming the Shrew, 82.

Of these examples of giantesses undergoing an attempt at domestication, only Skadi emerges as an example of an ability to return to the wild of her own free will. Her violent, vengeance seeking march on Asgard upon the death of her father, Thjazi, is quelled through diplomacy. Namely, a marriage with the Vanir-turned-Aesir, Njord, appropriate weregeld, with her father's eyes thrown into the sky in an act of remembrance, and a humbling action from Loki to make her laugh.[504]

Skadi is not met with aggression, which might be expected considering the language used to describe Jotnar opposition, alongside the numerous examples we have of murderous intent from the Aesir.[505] The marriage doesn't last, with both parties being discontent at the others' favoured home, namely being by the sea and being high in the mountains, which Skadi returns to after the marriage collapses.

There's probably a thematic story being told here of the incompatibility of a relationship between the earth and the sea,[506] but for our purposes, Skadi's power and wildness is only temporarily diluted through her incorporation into the Aesir, and she leaves, presumably, on good terms considering she is later[507] instrumental to Loki's binding. She, eventually, gets her vengeance, and utilises an emblem of the wild, a snake, as part of Loki's punishment.

Magical spaces often go hand in hand with the wild, and feminine figures are often framed within those spaces to emphasise their possession of magic. This very much includes the Valkyries. As one such example, **Stephen Pollington** highlights that Saxo describes Valkyrie-like figures as 'feminae sylvestres', 'women of the woods', pointing out that it's interesting that Saxo uses the word for woodland, *sylvestra*, rather than the word for timber, *lignum*, as it clashes with the common conclusion that Saxo was making a reference to these figures utilising spears and spindles as part of their magic.[508]

504 Told in Snorri's Skáldskaparmál. Faulkes, Edda, 61.

505 "Then he saw Thor in an As-rage, he was travelling at an enormous rate and swung his hammer and threw it from a great distance at Hrungnir." Faulkes, Edda, 79. Thor is also called the "enemy and slayer of giants and troll-wives", Faulkes, Edda, 72.

506 They are, after all, unable to ever be truly united. Greek Mythology includes a similar story with Ouranus (sky) and Gaia (earth), and Atlas' punishment to forever hold the celestial skies on his shoulders, keeping the two apart.

507 With the consideration that mythic time is amorphous.

508 Stephen Pollington, The Elder Gods: The Otherworld of Early England (UK: Anglo-Saxon Books, 2022), 348.

Using **Peter Fisher**'s translation of Saxo's *Gesta Danorum* [History of the Danes]:

"About that time Hother happened to be hunting when he wandered from his path in a mist and came upon a retreat of forest maidens.[509] As they saluted him by his own name he asked who they were, to which they replied that their special function was the control the fortune of wars by their guidance and blessings. They were often invisibly present on the battlefield and by their secret help afforded the desire outcome to their favourites, since, they informed him, they were able to award success or defeat at pleasure."[510]

These figures are undoubtedly, to my mind, Valkyries, given the description of their duties and abilities elaborated here. "Forest maidens" or "women of the woods" sits comfortably alongside their other kennings and attestations, at once almost deceptively vague, but also emphasising their innately wild nature. While the current paradigm of thought is that the word choice was referencing spears and spindles, I would argue this is also a continuation of the theme of the Valkyries, and like beings, being of 'the wild' in some aspects and of 'civilisation' in others. They are magical by their nature, with nature being uniquely magical. Hother experiences the magic of the Valkyries first hand at the conclusion of their conversation:

"No sooner has he heard these words than he found that the dwelling had vanished and that he was suddenly standing alone and unsheltered in the centre of a plain beneath the open sky. He was especially amazed at the rapid disappearance of the maidens, the false illusion of their home and the change of scenery, but was unaware that what had occurred to him was only a mockery, a meaningless deception contrived by magic."[511]

---

509 Fisher translates feminae sylvestres as forest maidens.

510 Fisher, History of the Danes, 69. The motif of meeting a Valkyrie in a forest also exists in Sörla þáttr, mentioned above. These are the 'noble women' existing in places outside of civilisation.

511 Fisher, History of the Danes, 70.

This excerpt highlights the tone in which Saxo presents much of his work, and the distance with which he frames the events within it. The mythological beings are presented as illusions, utilising trickery, enforcing the position he would himself hold; the old Gods and those associated with them are of the past, fading, ephemeral, temporary, clinging on to the world around them through fragmentary appearances. They operate through "deception" and delight in "mockery", playing with humans on a whim, to achieve paltry, though unknowable, goals.

Bede wrote in his *Historia ecclesiastica gentis Anglorum* [Ecclesiastical History of the English People] that missionaries should seek out rural, inhospitable places on which to establish ecclesiastical outposts.

> *Cedd chose a site for the monastery among some high*
> *and remote hills, which seemed more suitable for the*
> *dens of robbers and haunts of wild beasts than for human*
> *habitation. His purpose in this was to fulfil the prophecy of*
> *Isaiah: 'in the habitation of dragons, where each lay, shall*
> *be grass, with reeds and rushes', so that the fruits of good*
> *works might spring up where formerly lived only wild*
> *beasts, or men who lived like wild beasts.*[512]

He continues, writing that this site was then purified through prayer and fasting from the "taint of earlier crimes"[513] in preparation for the construction of the monastery. The language is particularly uncharitable, relating a sense of primitivism and criminal activity, and a distinct lack of civilisation. Paganism is equated to a dragon, something monstrous, old and dangerous to mankind's progression.

As **Michael D.J Bintley** summarises, the mindset of the early English Christians was one of reclamation and recovery. "In these locations, where the dragons of pagan ignorance once lay, the green shoots of Christian recovery might then spring forth."[514] You may go further and say that the goal for this pursuit was one of erasure, an elimination of sacred sites, beliefs and practices, starting from the space those beliefs originally existed.

512 Bede, Ecclesiastical History of the English People, trans. Leo Sherley-Price (England: Penguin Group, 1990), 181.

513 Ibid.

514 Michael D. J. Bintley, "Where the Wild Things Are in Old English Poetry", in Representing Beasts in Early Medieval England and Scandinavia, ed. by Michael D. J. Bintley and Thomas J. T. Williams (Boydell & Brewer, 2015), 205.

Pagan beliefs are of the wild, defined by being in wild spaces, propagating in those places, while the new Christian religion thrived in population centres. Pagan, as a label, refers to this, from the Latin *pāgus* meaning rural district or country. Similarly, consensus points to the origin of 'Heathen' being the Old English *hǣþen* or *hǣð*, meaning untilled or uncivilised land.[515] From the very beginning, then, the 'old ways' have been defined by these wild spaces, those away from the walls of hamlets, towns and cities.

Within the corpus, and in archaeological evidence, there is an overwhelming abundance of motifs that showcase and emphasise the wild and animalistic, often with reference to religious and ritualistic behaviour, and, more specifically, the veil between the sacred and the mundane. Animals have a long-established history of being perceived as mediators between the physical and supernatural worlds, especially within "shamanistic" religious systems.[516]

Academic models of Iron-Age worldviews place considerable weight on boundaries and barriers: the worldly and the otherworldly, the blurred lines in the act of ritual with the divine, bogs and bodies of water as places of sacred liminality, the hall as a place of hierarchy and order, with the grave as its unliving counterpart. All contrasting with the wild, 'the outfield', the violent, and the fragmented.[517] Animals, innately of the wild, can operate outside of the strict rigidity of society. They are emblematic of freedom, with many being defined by boundary crossing behaviour, especially those capable of flight or movement through water.

In *Gylfaginning* [Beguiling of Gylfi] 16, "Fuglar tveir fæðast í Urðarbrunni. Þeir heita svanir" - "Two birds feed at Urdrbrunnr, they're called swans."[518]

---

515 Stephen A Mitchell, Witchcraft and Magic in the Nordic Middle Ages (USA: University of Pennsylvania Press, 2011), 26.

516 A conclusion highlighted in M. Eliade, Shamanism: Archaic Techniques of Ecstasy (London: Arkana, 1989).

517 As visualised by plate 34, in In the Darkest of Days: Exploring Human Sacrifice and Value in Southern Scandinavian Prehistory, ed. Matthew J. Walsh, Sean O'Neill and Lasse Sørensen (Oxford: Oxbow Books, 2023).

518 My translation. Urdrbrunner is where the Nornir operate, so the swan being here is an interesting specification.

A swan can travel on land, air, and sea, representing significant boundary crossing behaviours, though it is predominantly associated with water. Historically, going back millennia, water has been regarded as a liminal environment that "bridges paradoxes, transcends the different human and divine realms, allows interactions with the gods, and enables the divinities to interfere with humanity."[519]

In the Nordic sphere, lakes, rivers and oceans are often places of power, wisdom and secret knowledge.[520] Three wells lie under three roots of Yggdrasil: *Mimisbrunnr*, *Hvergelmir* and *Urðarbrunnr* [Urdrbrunnr], where the *Nornir* are said to dwell. In her essay *At the Water's Edge*, **Julie Lund** explains that the word brunnr can also be translated as "a spring, stream or watering place,"[521] before concluding that the use of the word *sæ* alongside *brunnr* in the Voluspa is better conceived as a lake.

When viewed in partnership with the presence of swans at Urdrbrunnr, and the description presented in *Vǫlundarkviða* [the Song of Volund] of Valkyries "fulfilling fate" with their swan coats beside them, the imagery surely moves beyond pure coincidence. The Valkyries, at one point of their continual evolution, must have been seen to have a connection with the three named *Nornir* and in occupying a position alongside those beings when it comes to manipulating and forging fate in the Nordic cosmology.

It wouldn't be an unwieldy inference to suggest that the lake in *Vǫlundarkviða* may be seen as a representation of Urdrbrunnr. If we perceive this lakeshore as a liminal space, then we may see an instance here of a meeting of the mundane with the sacred, the divine and the mortal world at a moment of importance - a moment of crucial fate. There is evidence too of important rituals and sacrifices being held in wells ("Fons") by **Adam of Bremen** in his *Gesta Hammaburgensis Ecclesiae Pontificum* [Deeds of the Bishops of Hamburg], though Lund too says this word is potentially better translated to mean 'spring'.[522]

---

519 T. Oestigaard, "Water", in The Oxford Handbook of the Archaeology of Ritual and Religion, ed. T. Insoll (Oxford: Oxford University Press, 2011), 38.

520 See Dan Coultas, Heathenry & The Sea (2021) for a thorough breakdown of the importance of water/the sea in modern Heathen beliefs.

521 Julie Lund, "At the Water's Edge", in Signals of Belief in Early England: Anglo-Saxon Paganism Revisited, ed. Martin Carver, Alexandra Sanmark and Sarah Semple (Oxford and Philadelphia: Oxbow Books, 2010), 56.

522 Julie Lund, "Banks, Borders and Bodies of Water in a Viking Age Mentality", in Journal of Wetland Archaeology, vol 8 (2008), 58.

Undoubtedly, the Viking Age people placed a significance on these water sources in a ritualistic setting. **Carolyne Larrington** emphasises this significance when she associates the composition of the *Hávamál* [Sayings of the High One] with a ritualistic setting: "-when the speaker...begins to recite arcane knowledge – spells, runes and other kinds of wisdom – he claims to be seated by Urðr's well. This suggests that the well has a ritual purpose."[523] Specifically, it is a place where sacred knowledge and insight is shared. It is also interesting that, within the *Hávamál*, we are told that there is a "sage's high-seat" at "Urd's spring",[524] which once more connects the image and practice of *seiðr* with fate.

From my perspective, the participant[s] may be acting as a sort of avatar or representation of the *Nornir*, with the expected result being that their intent is made reality, akin to the *Nornir's* actions being made reality on the greater cosmological landscape. Otherwise, it almost seems like these areas are seen as particularly 'active' by the divine, where they are most present, or is an environment that draws their attention. Those performing the ritual want these acts to be witnessed, and for them to be considered significant. We may see similar situations in trees being considered a manifestation of Yggdrasil, with lakes and other water sources representing the three 'wells' beneath the three roots.

Yet, the comparisons continue beyond that imagery. In the *Ljósvetninga saga* excerpt mentioned above, we had water being the medium through which the magical ritual was conducted, almost as if compelling Thorhildr's will to be written into reality through her actions. Urdrbrunner itself is directly connected to the idea of fate through the *Nornir* attending it.

Heimdall, who guards the boundary between the realm of the Gods and the realm of the Jotnar, is potentially born of nine daughters:

> "Nine women bore him, the spear-magnificent man,
> Giant-girls, at the edge of the earth."[525]

---

523 Larrington, The Norse Myths That Shape the Way We Think, 35.

524 Larrington appears to agree with the translation of 'well' to mean 'spring'. Larrington, The Poetic Edda (Revised Edition), 27.

525 Larrington, The Poetic Edda. (Revised Edition), 250. It's also interesting that a God already associated with guarding and enforcing boundaries is born "at the edge of the Earth".

It is commonly inferred that these "nine giant-girls" are the daughters of Aegir and Ran, namely, the waves, as they exist on the "edge of the earth". That is to say, the place where the earth meets the sea, which would make Heimdall a God born of the sea. Moreover, he possesses the hall *Himinbjörg*, which stands at the point where the Bifröst meets 'heaven.'[526] He is a God of boundaries and thresholds,[527] acting as a guardian of the realm of the Gods from the potential of invading Jotnar. It's no wonder, then, that Heimdall and Loki appear antagonistic of each other, with one tasked with enforcing boundaries, while the other revels in crossing them.

Saga and Odin drink together in *Søkkvabekkr* [Sunken Bench] where "cool waves resound."[528] While Frigg's hall is *Fensalir* [Fen Halls], which reinforces the importance of such places as fens and springs to the Old Norse religion. Many scholars compare Frigg's Hall and its complimentary associations with the image of the Goddess Nerthus presented in **Tacitus's** *Germania*.

"There is nothing noteworthy about these peoples individually, but they are distinguished by a common worship of Nerthus, or Mother Earth. They believe that she interests herself with human affairs and rides among the peoples. In an island of the Ocean stands a sacred grove, and in the grove a consecrated cart, draped with a cloth, which none but the priest may touch. The priest perceives the presence of the goddess in this holy of holies and attends her, in deepest reverence, as her cart is drawn by heifers. Then follows days of rejoicing and merry-making in every place that she deigns to visit and be entertained....until the priest again restores the goddess to her temple, when she had her fill of human company. After that, the cart, the cloth and, if you care to believe it, the goddess herself are washed clean in a secluded lake."[529]

---

526 Faulkes, Edda, 20.

527 Lindow, Norse Mythology: A Guide to Gods, Heroes, Rituals, and Beliefs, 174.

528 Larrington, The Poetic Edda. (Revised Edition), 49.

529 Tacitus, Agricola and Germania, trans. Harold Mattingly and ed. James Rivers (Penguin Classics, 2010), 53-4.

One of these "peoples' is identified by Tacitus as the Langobardi, who I referenced earlier in this work when discussing Freyja's connection to the Valkyries. Within the *Historia Langobardorum* writer **Paulus Diaconus** calls the patron of the Langobardi 'Frea' [Frēa], who is most often equated with Frigg. Alternatively, there is also strong evidence to associate Nerthus with the Vanir,[530] with the etymological connection to Njordr, and the prevalence of wagons, water and cyclical rituals with that 'family' of Gods.

All these examples, partnered with a repeated behaviour of the depositions of weapons, valued goods, and human remains within bodies of water suggest that these were places believed to be inhabited or observed by the Gods. This is a hallmark of Germanic pre-Christian ritualistic behaviour. As mentioned at the beginning of this chapter, animals too were seen as liminal by their very nature. Horses were perhaps most prominent with their associations of being 'between worlds', powerfully represented with the image of Odin's eight-legged horse, Sleipnir.

Considering Odin's associations with violent death,[531] and his journeying to the world of the dead on the back of Sleipnir, it's perhaps little surprise that horses were common elements within burial rites of Scandinavia.[532] The horse is a wild animal made tame and domesticated, emblematic of Aesir, and to a lesser extent, Vanir worship and religious behaviour. The Valkyries are uniquely tied to wildness, either through their behaviour and characterisation, propensity for wolf-riding, their lineage and ancestry, or their connections to Freyja and Odin, who both have a capacity to assume animal forms too.

---

530 McKinnell, Meeting the other in Norse myth and legend, 50.

531 E. Turville-Petre, Myth and Religion of the North, 56.

532 Discussed within Maeve Sikora, 'Diversity in Viking Age Horse Burial: A comparative study of Norway, Iceland, Scotland and Ireland', The Journal of Irish Archaeology, 12 & 13 (2004).

While eagles tended to be Odin's preferred animal form for flight, and a common animal in terms of royalty and deity equally, Freyja's falcon form[533] is more obviously tied to this idea of the wild made domestic. There is evidence for falconry practices from the early Viking Age on the memorial stone at Klintebys in Gotland, which features a horseman accompanied by a dog with a bird sitting in his hand. This is far from the only rune stone that depicts such a scene.[534] These examples continue the image of the Aesir and Vanir Gods being associated with tamed animals, whether that be horses, dogs, falcons, goats, cats, cattle, or otherwise.

While the former is associated with order and civilisation, it must be pointed out that the wild boar is also strongly emblematic of the Vanir gods. Yet, the two wild boars most closely tied to the Vanir are not of natural creation. Freyr's Gullinbursti ["Golden-Bristles"] was created by the dwarves Sindri and Brokkr, while Freyja's Hildisvini ["Battle-Swine"] is the transformed Ottar, a human devotee of the Goddess.[535] These are animals created by divine hands, given wildness by their appearance, but not by their nature.

The metaphor may be expanded to highlight how the Vanir can be conceived as the 'middle ground' between the Aesir and Jotnar, embodying characteristics of both. There's a warning that perseveres throughout all of this, with many sagas touching on the wildness that still exists in all animals, domestic or otherwise. *Vatnsdœla saga* [Saga of the People of Vatnsdal] describes how a herd of domesticated pigs escape their bounds,[536] when they are found again, they have become wild once more.[537]

---

533 Which Loki dons too – he is commonly classified as a Jotunn, an external entity, bought into the fold of the Aesir.

534 Sigmund Oehrl, "I am Eagle" – Depictions of raptors and their meaning in the art of Late Iron Age and Viking Age Scandinavia (c. AD 400–1100)", Raptor on the fist – falconry, its imagery and similar motifs throughout the millennia on a global scale. (Wachholtz, 2020), 36.

535 From Hyndluljóð [Song/Lay of Hyndla]. Prior to the reveal of Hildisvini's identity, Freyja claims the boar is of Dwarven construction, likely referring to Gullinbursti's origin considering she directly refers to "golden bristles". Larrington, The Poetic Edda (Revised Edition), 246.

536 Vatnsdœla saga, in Íslenzk fornrit VII, ed. by Einar Ól. Sveinsson (Reykjavík: Hið íslenzka fornritafélag, 1939),43.

537 There's also a mention here of their leader, Beigaðr [Beigadr] refusing

Domesticity in the sagas is a temporary occurrence that must be reinforced and diligently maintained over time. The image is preserved, with only Odin himself among the Aesir and Vanir Gods (fittingly) being aligned with animals that can truly be called 'wild', those that were never tamed or domesticated to serve society: eagles, ravens, and wolves being the most obvious. He is most comfortable in moving into the unknown.

After all, Odin frames himself as the master of the wild. He tamed Geri and Freki.[538] The Aesir and Vanir both use animals to pull their chariots, or otherwise ride them.[539] They take on animal forms to achieve specific goals. Animals are made into a utility. The Jotnar are the wilds given form, butting heads with the Aesir and their focus on civilisation and order. Throughout these examples, there is a theme of domestication being categorised as something that only exists within the confines, boundaries, and walls of civilisation. Wildness, in some ways, is inevitable.

There's an uncertainty to this mastery, a sense that it is barely contained, even with the Gods' power acting to restrain it. There's no mistaking the larger ideas presented by Odin's greatest enemies being a monstrous wolf and a colossal snake. As Lindow points out, there's an irony too presented in Odin being considered the 'Feeder of the Wolf' with his associations of the battlefield and with Geri and Freki, while also being destined to 'feed' Fenrir at *Ragnarök*.[540]

---

to return and instead swims across a lake to make his escape. The presence of the lake may be seen as a representation of a permanent boundary crossing, with Beigadr unable to return to his previous life.

538 Grímnismál 19.

539 Thor and his chariot pulled by goats, Gylfaginning, chapter 21. Faulkes, Edda, 22. Freyja and her chariot pulled by cats, Gylfaginning, chapter 24. Faulkes, Edda, 24. Freyr rides a chariot pulled by Gullinbursti at Baldr's funeral. Gylfaginning, chapter 49. Faulkes, Edda, 50.

540 Lindow, Norse Mythology: A Guide to Gods, Heroes, Rituals, and Beliefs, 120.

The wild is ravenous, and even here there is a question posed: what happens when Odin no longer has the power to 'feed the wolf'? What would happen should he not feed Geri and Freki, his ever-consuming wolves, in his hall? As **David Varley** writes, "Symbolically, all three wolves represent the same force: that of a relentless appetite for destruction."[541] He continues, "Like Loki, Freyja and Skadi, the norns/valkyries are a dangerous externality that has been internalised with divine society."[542]

With all of this, there's a sense of finality and determinism in that Odin so frequently looks to control the uncontrollable, and even with the combined powers of the Aesir, he will ultimately fail and be consumed by those very same forces. Further, Loki, Freyja, Skadi, Gerdr, the three 'main' *Nornir* and the Valkyries are all of 'the outside' and the external, brought into the fold.

There are elements of danger that persevere, most notably in the former, who will seemingly prove to justify that edge of mistrust. If my theory about Sif being originally conceived as a Jotunn within her Nordic appearances was understood to be true, then she also represents this idea of externality being brought into the fold. There's an effort to sanitise within many of these examples, with many histories being unknown.

With the Valkyries so often exhibiting 'wildness', it's crucial too to discuss their nature as a "dangerous externality". I would go as far as to suggest that the Valkyries' nature is crucial to their development within the Norse corpus. That is to say that there was a need for explicit wildness that could be kept almost at a distance from the Gods themselves to act as they wished.

They are liminal, they are wild and civilised, they were or could be human, and their duty was of the human battlefield, a place born because of civilisation and organisation but defined by wildness. This was not a place that could, potentially, be navigated in the same way by those not of a dangerous externality. Most of the Gods, in one way or another, may be limited by not existing between worlds or having undergone such a transition.

---

541 Varley, The whirling wheel: the male construction of empowered female identities in Old Norse myth and legend, 241.

542 Ibid.

A similar justification could be drawn to Loki, who while seemingly assimilated into the Aesir, can be kept at a distance to act in ways they cannot within the confines of social expectation. As a trickster entity, Loki innately clashes against those very same expectations, representing the antitheses of civilisation, or things that can cause significant instability within its infrastructure.

"Civilization is born with the emergence of boundaries, physical as well as psychological: rules of decency and propriety, property borders, psychological boundaries.."[543] Writing from a Jungian perspective, **Helena Bassil-Morozow** sees Loki as the trickster archetype, forever cast into a role that puts him at odds with the Gods around him who yearn for maintenance of the status quo.

While not as dramatic as to cause the end of the world, the Valkyrie also represents a force in the same vein. Not quite tricksters, but a force that resists domesticity and endlessly crosses boundaries.

"Arise too, Ruta, and show your snow-pale head,
come forth from hiding and issue into battle.
The outdoor carnage beckons you; fighting now
shakes the court, harsh strife batters the gates."[544]

"a reference to the deathly pale head of the valkyrie, the spirit brooding over the battlefield personifying slaughter, who is summoned at the outset of battle".[545]

Ruta, presumably the Valkyrie Róta, is a supernatural spectre being summoned at the carnage unfolding outside the gates of this settlement. Drawn to the violence like a raven to carrion. Something wild, uncivilised, but necessary and needed. The speaker acknowledges her presence, deems it inevitable. Her head is snow-pale, deathly pale, possibly referencing the early, blonde, shining Valkyries we see in *Helgakviða Hjörvarðssonar* with Sváva.

---

543 Helena Bassil-Morozow, "Loki then and now: the trickster against civilization", International Journal of Jungian Studies vol 9, no 2. (Glasgow, UK: Glasgow Caledonian University, 2017), 88.

544 Fisher, The History of the Danes, 58-9.

545 Ibid, 47 (of the translation notes)

The world of the Valkyrie is a strife-filled, carnage-born and shaking world. Something inhuman, and 'outdoor', inherently of the wild and outside law and order. This Ruta is from this place of law and order but can pass to the outside world seamlessly. The Valkyrie is of both worlds, and arguably, neither, because of that liminality. In *Völsunga saga* [Saga of the Volsungs] when Sigrún arrives with her fellow Valkyries, we are told that looking at them is "like looking into a fire"[546] – calling on the idea of something primal and inhuman.

Too bright to look at, with their armour shining like a nova. These Valkyries are of the noble-born archetype, but still possess some of the defining qualities of the early Valkyrie and her otherworldly attributes. In *The Viking Way*, **Neil Price** calls them the "Female Demons of Carnage",[547] and I think that nicely summarises their depiction and appearance in their earliest attestations. Those elements certainly endured over the centuries too, most notably in *Njal's Saga*, which is believed to have been composed around 1270 to 1290,[548] though describing events from much earlier, in either the tenth century or early eleventh century.

We can rationalise this persevering, older image of the Valkyries is due, primarily, to the anonymous author likely referencing elements and themes from earlier sources if not incorporating sections whole piece. The latter is a common inference made in current academia, with the argument being based on inconsistencies between the poetic and prose sections regarding the battle it is said to be describing. Today, many conclude it is not describing the Battle of Clontarf, but a battle that occurred a century earlier, in 919.[549]

---

546 Byock, The Saga of the Volsungs. The Norse Epic of Sigurd the Dragon Slayer, 50.

547 Price, The Viking Way, 277.

548 Discussed in Thorsteinn Gylfason's introduction to Njál's Saga, trans. Lee M. Hollander (Wordsworth Classics, 1998).

549 Amanda. L. Green, Knocking on Death's Door. A Re-examination of the

As **John Hines** states, "the very inconsistencies between poem and saga …point to the poem being a text delivered to the saga author from antiquity and one which would not or could not be distorted to fit into its final known context.[550]" If this holds true, then *Darraðarljóð* reinforces the Valkyrie timeline I've presented here, rather than being an apparent anomaly within it.

Depending on the exact age of *Darraðarljóð* we're likely seeing a Valkyrie that seems little removed from the *Waelcyrge* before it.

"With our shields we must strike
this fabric of victory.
Hildr goes to weave
and Hjorþrimul,
Sanngriðr, Svipul,
with unsheathed swords:
the shaft will break,
the shield will shatter,
the sword will pierce armour."[551]

Later on, we have, "Gunnr [or Guðr[552]] and Göndul, who protected the king, saw men's shields covered in blood."[553] Here we have a depiction of the Valkyries' dual role on the battlefield; determining the fate of the battle on mass, while protecting key figures that have gained their favour or otherwise would perish should they not intervene. There's also a notable inference here of the weaving being imperfect, or haphazard; a sort of unrestrained action, with the Valkyries becoming lost in their blood lust and war-song.

So much so that Gunnr [or Guðr] and Göndul need to be physically near the king to ensure that their sisters don't cause a wayward arrow or spear to accidentally hit their mark. The witnessing of blood on the shields denotes that they have left the liminal space of the *dyngja* and are now in the midst of the action, bearing witness to the savagery of the battle. Again, there's absolutely a wildness to them and their greater realm.

Old Norse Worlds of Death (Háskóla Íslands, 2022), 205.

550 John Hines, Old-Norse Sources for Gaelic History (UK: University of Cambridge, 2002), 5

551 Bek-Pedersen, The Norns in Old Norse Mythology, 136.

552 Bek-Pedersen replaces Gunnr here with Guðr, all other translations the author could find state Gunnr, though they are interchangeable and likely refer to the same being.

553 Bek-Pedersen, 137.

The battlefield is a place of slaughter, with imagery calling to mind animals and animalistic behaviour: "the dog of helmets / Devour shields."[554] It is within these verses that we have the phrase "The Valkyries have their choice of the slain."[555] As mentioned above, there's certainly something almost sacrificial and ritualistic about that wording. The idea, perhaps, that they are unleashed on the battlefield to feast and delight in bloodshed before returning to the home of the Gods with their bounty.

If the battlefield is a place of slaughter and bloodshed, with the Valkyries being in control of that landscape, then we can perhaps rationalise that these beings are offered something akin to sacrifices, in much the same manner as we would understand to be given to a 'traditional' God or Goddess.

If Þorgerðr Hölgabrúðr can indeed be classified as a Valkyrie, at least in behaviour and context, then here we see an example of these beings being worshipped as Goddesses within their own power, removed from their association with Odin. I propose that Þorgerðr, and her companion Irpa, are Valkyries, thriving within a lingering understanding of their power as Goddesses, and worshipped as such. I also hold that they would not have been alone in such a station. Maybe time will validate that perspective.

I came, I saw, I conquered. Vig, Vigr, Vigi.

In this section I will discuss some Old Norse linguistics, and the possible connections we can make with word similarities. I'm still new to the art of linguistic analysis, but I'm nonetheless fascinated with what sort of potential clues linger still within language. Here, we will be looking closer at the words surrounding violent acts and their relation to words that describe hallowing, sacred rites, religious behaviour, and protection.

---

554 Cook, Njal's Saga, 304.
555 Ibid.

The Old Norse word *Vig* refers to fighting, battle and slaughter. We see this with the 'final battlefield' called Vígríðr, or 'battle-surge'. The Valkyries in turn are called *"Vígmóðar"* ['slaughter-furious' or 'slaughter-eager']556. The word *Vigr,* which we find reflected in the later English word 'Vigour', means 'able-bodied' or rather 'able-bodied-enough-to-fight'.557 Though it also, on occasion, refers to a spear or rod,558 with *Vigra* being the plural. Viga is the nickname given to the blood-thirsty Glum.

A more common word within a modern Heathen vocabulary is 'Vé', to mean a holy or sacred place, with etymological connections to contemporary Germanic words to mean consecrate, idol (Old English *wēoh*), and sanctification. It is thought too that the phrase 'Þor vigi', which appears on the Velanda Runestone559 among others, means '(may) Thor protect' or '(may) Thor hallow'. As a verb, *Vigja* is often taken to mean "to hallow or consecrate".

Though, as **Bernard Mees** reasons, the common interpretation today of hallowing and sanctification was probably not understood in the same manner to the Viking Age people. To bless something was not necessarily to remove evil forces or intent, but to curse "against violators or haunting by ghosts".560 It was a proclamation of intent towards normality, not necessarily a cleansing action.

---

556 From Víga-Glúms 6. "VGl Lv 6V (Glúm 6)/5 — ásynjur 'goddesses'", The Skaldic Project, accessed June 12, 2024. https://skaldic.org/m. php?p=wordtextlp&i=4407759

557 "Vigr", Old Icelandic Dictionary, accessed June 24. 2024. https://old-icelandic.vercel.app/word/vigr-2

558 Zoëga, A Concise Dictionary of Old Icelandic, 490.

559 Runic inscription Vg 150 in Scandinavian Runic-text Database latest, Department of Scandinavian Languages, Uppsala University, accessed Jan 15, 2024. http://kulturarvsdata.se/uu/srdb/82904281-014a-4698-8d96-be3d1bdddddo

560 Bernard Mees, "Þrymskviða, Vígja, and the Canterbury Charm." Viking and Medieval Scandinavia 9 (2013), 147.

These examples open the opportunity to connect the words meaning protection, sanctification and sacred to fighting, to spears, and to killing. After all, to protect can be to kill those who threaten safety. To hallow can be to banish those that would do harm. In the 'Nine Herbs Charm', *Nigon Wyrta Galdor*, there is a clear association made with healing and doing battle or otherwise depicting violent action against something that would do harm. This theme of healing, hallowing and protection with violent activity, in my view, helps reconcile Eir's position as a Valkyrie.

> "You're called Una, that most ancient plant.
> You defeat three, you defeat thirty,
> you defeat venom, you defeat air-illness;
> you defeat the horror who stalks the land
>
> ...
>
> Now! May the nine plants do battle against nine glory-fleers,"
> [561]

There's a prevalent thematic image here of healing and rejuvenation as being in battle with an ailment, disease and infection. There's a fight happening on a personal landscape, with the stakes being the loss of life, or the preservation of one. That's also putting aside the prevalence of such a situation on the battlefield, with hundreds if not thousands of lives hanging in such a balance.

Moreover, a reinforcement of this connection lies in the word *blót* and the verb, *blóta* which has etymological connections to Proto-Germanic and Old English words for sacrifice *(blótan)* and worship. The word 'sacrifice' naturally brings to mind the aspect of blood offerings, and it is here that **Jón Hnefill Aðalsteinsson** emphasises that the importance of the sacrificial blood was the original meaning behind the word *blót* rather than referring to the general act of sacrifice.[562]

---

561 Translation by Joseph S. Hopkins for Mimisbrunnr.info. "Nigon Wyrta Galdor", Mimisbrunner.info, accessed October 15, 2023, https://www.mimisbrunnr.info/nigon-wyrta-galdor

562 Jon Hnefill Aðalsteinsson, Blót í norrænum sið (Háskólaútgáfan

All in all, it is clear that blood undoubtedly had religious significance for the people of the Viking Age, as can be seen most readily from this excerpt from Snorri's *Heimskringla*:

"To this festival all the men brought ale with them; and all kinds of cattle, as well as horses, were slaughtered, and all the blood that came from them was called "hlaut", and the vessels in which it was collected were called hlaut-vessels. Hlaut-staves were made, like sprinkling brushes, with which the whole of the altars and the temple walls, both outside and inside, were sprinkled over, and also the people were sprinkled with the blood".[563]

We see a similar image presented within *Hyndluljóð* [Song/Lay of Hyndla], with Ottar, a devotee of Freyja, constructing an altar on which he made sacrifices.

"He's made a sanctuary for me, faced with stone,
Now that stone has turned to glass;
He's reddened it with fresh ox blood,
Ottar has always trusted in the goddesses."[564]

Before this all becomes misconstrued as some argument for mass sacrificial acts in modern Heathenry, I would posit that there was an innate connection between the battlefield as a place of slaughter and as a sacred place equally. To fight in that space, to be exposed to the Valkyries, and to Odin too, was to exist on a razor-thin knife's edge. To be in a blood-soaked space where the Valkyries would have their choice of the slain, to have their choice of sacrifices. It's a ritualistic space, embodying the liminality of the line between life and death. Victory or defeat. Those that enter the battlefield may once more return to the land of the living, or they could swiftly take their journey to whatever lies beyond.

Félagsvísindastofnun, 1997), 236.

563 "Hakon the Good's Saga", Sacred Texts, accessed June 23, 2024. https://sacred-texts.com/neu/heim/05hakon.htm See also Hollander, Heimskringla: History of the Kings of Norway, 107.

564 Larrington, The Poetic Edda (Revised Edition), 246.

It's also noteworthy that ritualistic spaces also blurred the lines between human and animal, aiding the overall image of the battlefield being of religious, ritualistic importance. "Pre-Christian archaeological contexts suggests that ritual practice brought humans and animals together so that differences between them were almost obliterated. Animals became mouthpieces for human communication and for human thought."[565] Note the frequency with which these lines blur in instances of the appearance of the Valkyries, from *Hrafnsmal*, to the animalistic imagery presented in *Darraðarljóð,* as discussed above.

There's something of a transactional agreement in these instances. An innate understanding that the debt of being on the battlefield and engaging in acts of violence opens one up to death and injury. It's a place of uncertainty, a place of death being reaved and created by those that are living. Indeed, the battlefield could be considered a place that only exists for the dead, and those that engage in that space can be labelled, for all intents and purposes, as dead until victory or defeat is secured. I'll call this idea *Schrödinger's Swan*, with all individuals being in a state of quantum limbo until the chaos subsides and the living can be counted and moved on from that life-wine-stained field.

This is an idea echoed by **Thomas J.T. Williams,** "[violent events]...were moments that saw the boundary between life and death crossed by multiple individuals in quick succession, accompanied by an uninhabited outpouring of aggression that went well beyond the norm of day-to-day social discourse.[566]" A battlefield is an extraordinary place, even when framed within the very different expectations of the Viking Age.

But even explicitly social and religious environments were also tinted in blood-red tones, with violent acts being interlaced with religious practice and legal discourse alike. None were more distinguished in these spaces than the *Goði* [Godi]. The image of the Godi we have, as previously described in *Heimskringla*, finds consensus in *Eyrbyggja saga* [The Saga of the People of Eyri] in terms of the environment and language exhibited.

---

565 Kristina Jennbert, Animals and Humans: Recurrent Symbiosis in archaeology and Old Norse Religion (Lund: Nordic Academic Press, 2011), 199.

566 Thomas J.T. Williams, "For the Sake of Bravado in the Wilderness': Confronting the Bestial in Anglo-Saxon Warfare", in Representing Beasts in Early Medieval England and Scandinavia, ed. Thomas J.T. Williams and Michael D.J. Bintley (Boydell & Brewer, 2015), 181.

"There was a sacrificial bowl on the platform too, with a sacrificial twig shaped like a priest's aspergillum for the blood of animals killed as offerings to the gods to be sprinkled from the bowl. Inside the choir-like part of the building the figures of the gods were arranged in a circle right round the platform."[567]

Other translations of this chapter mimic the language used in *Heimskringla,* especially around the word *hlaut* . "On the stall should also stand the blood-bowl, and therein the blood-rod was, like unto a sprinkler, and therewith should be sprinkled from the bowl that blood which is called "Hlaut", which was that kind of blood which flowed when those beasts were smitten who were sacrificed to the Gods. But round about the stall were the Gods arrayed in the Holy Place."[568]

This excerpt recalls descriptions of the Valkyries, perhaps most obviously in *Víga-Glúms saga*: "Me thought I was standing out of doors, and that I saw two women who had a trough between them, and they took their stations at Hrisateig and sprinkled the whole district with blood."[569]

The poetic verse that follows removes the ambiguity surrounding the maidens' identity:

"I saw the maids of carnage stand,
In grim and vengeful mood,
As the battle rag'd, and they drench'd the land
In slaughter'd warriors blood."[570]

567 Eyrbyggja Saga, trans. by Hermann Pálsson and Paul Edwards (Penguin Classics, 1989), 29.

568 William Morris and Eiríkr Magnússon, The Saga Library vol. II, The Story of the Ere-Dwellers with The Story of the Heath-Slayings (London: Bernard Quaritch Ltd, 1892), 8-9.

569 Chapter 21 Víga-Glúms saga. Edmund Walker Head. The Story of Viga-Glum (Illustrated Edition)(1866), 77.

570 Ibid, 78.

I posit that the Valkyries are seen, on numerous occasions, as acting in a manner which runs parallel with the sacred rites of human Godi, or otherwise paints their actions as deeply sacred and ritualistic in nature. The Valkyries often appear overseeing the human landscape acting as priestesses and establishing a vital connection between the mundane and the divine.

This takes on a more explicit turn when framed within their role as psychopomp, carrying the chosen to their afterlife halls, watched over by the divine. Consider this excerpt from **Aḥmad ibn Faḍlān's** seminal work *In the Land of Darkness* which introduces us to an 'Angel of Death', who acts as the religious, sacrificial leader over the community's burial rites.

> "Then came the 'Angel of Death' and she spread the bed with coverings... she is in charge of sewing and arranging all of these things, and it is she who kills the slave girls. I saw that she was a witch, thick-bodied and sinister."[571]

I would draw attention to this 'Angel of Death' having an important role when it comes to textiles within the community, once again reaffirming a seemingly innate relationship between religious rites, specifically sacrificial ones, with 'witchcraft' and textile work.

The following excerpt describes the sacrifice of a slave girl at the funeral of her master.

> "Next, six men entered the pavilion and [lay with] the girl, one after the other, after which they laid her beside her master. Two seized her feet and two others her hands. The old woman called the Angel of Death came and put a cord round her neck in such a way that the two ends went in opposite directions. She gave the ends to two of the men, so they could pull on them. Then she herself approached the girl holding in her hand a dagger with a broad blade and [plunged it again and again between the girl's ribs], while the two men strangled her with the cord until she was dead." [572]

---

571 Aḥmad ibn Faḍlān, Ibn Fadlan and the Land of Darkness: Arab Travellers in the Far North, trans. Paul Lunde and Caroline E.M. Stone (Penguin Classics, 2011), 51.

572 Ibid, 53.

While it is important to bear in mind the degrees of separation between ibn Faḍlān and those he is observing (he is unfamiliar with the culture and doesn't speak the language) that distance and unfamiliarity also offers an element of honesty, describing what he sees often without further commentary. However, there are also notable contradictions between passages, suggesting that embellishments and additions have been made alongside the original text,[573] carried through translations over the last millennia.[574]

Still, it would not be a large leap in inference to see how this 'Angel of Death' may be acting as akin to, or as, an avatar to the mortal Valkyrie figure, embodying her cultural position and described in words that ibn Faḍlān would be familiar with. The mortal Valkyries we encounter may be a euhemerised representation of the divine Valkyries, or perhaps there was an understanding that they possessed a similarly ritualistic role within the community.

The possibility of female cult leaders within the Nordic world is not a radical or new suggestion, finding reinforcement in the above excerpt through this 'Angel' figure and her briefly mentioned 'daughters'.[575] The most prominent example of ritualistic exhibitory behaviours would be in the form of the Volva [Völva], those famed staff-bearers, who, if we're to infer grave ownership through the presence of staffs, were given elaborate burials despite being described in a manner that emphasises 'otherness' in the sagas.[576] There's a misalignment here between the literary record and the archaeological record, but one that can best be explained by a changing social expectation around the practice of the old ways.

---

573 D. M. Dunlop, "Zeki Validi's Ibn Faḍlān," Die Welt des Orients, 1:4, (1950), 307.

574 Tonicha Mae Upham, Equal Rites: Parsing Rus' Gender Values Through an Arabic Lens (MA thesis, University of Iceland, 2019), 11.

575 Lunde and Stone, Ibn Fadlan and the Land of Darkness: Arab Travellers in the Far North, 53.

576 Leszek Gardeła, A Biography of the Seiðr-Staffs. Towards an Archaeology of Emotions, In L. P. Słupecki, J. Morawiec (eds.), Between Paganism and Christianity in the North (Rzeszów: Rzeszów University, 2009), 190-219.

Magic was a potent tool that gave Heathen women their power within the socio-cultural framework, something that balanced the scales in such a way that was seen as acceptable, even if the degree of that acceptance seems to wildly fluctuate across sources. This can be seen perhaps most potently (and surprisingly) within Saxo's *Gesta Danorum*, with **Birgit Sawyer** commenting that it's in the use of magic prior to the ninth book in that work that Heathen women find that connection to power, with that power fading with the introduction of Christianity and, by extension, the slow extinguishing of magical practice.[577]

Erin Caffey makes a similarly astute observation in relation to the manifestation of women's power with reference to verse 118 of the *Hávamál*.

"I saw a man who was wounded sore
By an evil woman's word;
A lying tongue his death-blow launched,
And no word of truth there was."[578]

Caffey suggests that this verse is taken from the Volva's point of view. The implication being that "a woman's tongue – her voice – is her weapon and, should that be taken from her, truth (wisdom) will no longer prevail, the völva reveals women's autonomy and influence as a major threat to men's power."[579] The action of Odin silencing this woman echoes a larger movement towards silencing women, as oral traditions, so defining the intangible Heathen past, were brought to an end.

Heathen practices empowered women in ways that would be gradually stripped away with the coming Christianity, and the subsequent move to the written record. The oral tradition allowed for more accessibility, while literacy could be controlled, and access restricted. This is saying nothing of the relationship between spoken, or sung, words and magical practice too, as can be seen with *Galdr*.

---

577 Birgit Strand Sawyer, "Women in Gesta Danorum," in Saxo Grammaticus: A Medieval Author between Norse and Latin Culture, Danish Medieval History and Saxo Grammaticus, 2, ed. K. Friis-Jensen (Copenhagen: Museum Tusculanum, 1981), 151.

578 Bellows, The Poetic Edda, The Mythological Poems, 54.

579 Caffey, Femininity in Medieval Scandinavia: How Paganism Forged Gender Equality, 23-4.

While early Christianity, during the period it was still considered a "radical underground movement", held greater rights for women in terms of spiritual leadership,[580] at least in comparison to other religions of the time, by the time Christianity starts to move across Northern Europe, the axis had dramatically shifted. Though women from royal lineages or noble blood were granted positions of authority and opportunities for education within the Christian Church in the early medieval period,[581] many experienced fewer opportunities and restricted rights.

To the degree that it isn't a controversial statement to say that Scandinavian Pagan women experienced greater social freedoms and autonomy than their continental Christian counterparts.[582] Though, consideration should be given on the limitations of our literary evidence, not least of which being an unavoidable lens that spotlights exalted positions over the lives of the 'common person'. When it comes to the lives of women, that obfuscation becomes doubly apparent.

THE DISIR AS PRIESTESSES

As **Stephen Pollington** posits, the term *'Disir'* may be better used as akin to 'priestess': "*Dis* apparently therefore means 'honoured woman' or perhaps the term 'priestess' captures the nature of the office more closely... a high-born female who is empowered to undertake sacrifice on behalf of the community."[583]

The *Disir* as a collective seem to embody a halfway point between the divine and the mundane, sometimes more of one, sometimes more of the other. This, ultimately, lends itself to the difficulty in defining the *Disir*. They are ephemeral and, by their nature, challenging to encompass through language. I want to touch on a quote by **Helen Damico** that I used near the beginning of this book that neatly summarises the conflation of the *Disir* with the Valkyries.

---

580 Isabella Double, "Women and their Roles in Early Christianity", Dies Legibiles II: vol 2 (Smith College, 2022). It is largely agreed that women were crucial drivers of Christianity's early growth.

581 Henrietta Leyser, Medieval Women: Social History of Women in England 450-1500 (UK:Palgrave Macmillan, 1995), 20.

582 F. Regina Psaki, "Women's Counsel in the Riddarasögur: The Case of Parcevals saga", in The Cold Counsel. The Women in Old Norse Literature and Myth, ed. Sarah M. Anderson and Karen Swenson (New York: Routledge, 2001), 201.

583 Stephen Pollington, The Elder Gods: The Otherworld of Early England (UK: Anglo-Saxon Books, 2022), 315.

"In both their benevolent and malevolent aspects, the Valkyries are related to a generic group of half-mortal, half-supernatural beings called *idisi* in Old High German, ides in Old English, and dis in Old Norse...they are armed, powerful, priestly. They function as arrangers of destinies and intermediaries between men and the deity."[584]

Considering the topic of discussion within this chapter, I want to focus on the choice of the word "priestly". Something crucial to ritualistic activity. This description of the *Disir* as a 'priestess' or divine *Gydja* may reconcile Freyja's kenning of *Vanadis* in Snorri's *Skáldskaparmál*, especially when we also look at further descriptions that paint an image of Freyja as a noted priestess of the Vanir, as seen in *Heimskringla*.

'Othin appointed Njorth and Frey to be priests for the sacrificial offerings, and they were the diar [Gods] among the Aesir. Freya was the daughter of Njorth. She was the priestess at the sacrifices [*Blót-gyðja/Blot-gydja*]. It was she who first taught the Aesir magic such as was practiced among the Vanir.'[585]
'Freya kept up the sacrifices for she was the only one among the godheads who survived.'[586]

Though these paint a euhemerised depiction of the Nordic deities, it is illuminating for its detail. Snorri was unlikely to have fabricated a narrative that positioned a Goddess in any lingering position of power, so we must conclude he was basing it on common knowledge or material that has been lost. As it stands, we could potentially draw an inference that Freyja here is encompassing the element of the mortal *Disir*, the original ancestral matriarchal figure that was tied so innately to blood offerings and ritual behaviour. With Freyja made mortal by Snorri's telling, she fulfils this image of the *Disir* as I have outlined from the outset.

---

584 Damico, The Valkyrie Reflex in Old English Literature, 176.
585 Hollander, Heimskringla: History of the Kings of Norway, 8.
586 Ibid, 14.

We can state that, at least in many contexts, the act of shedding blood within the Nordic sphere implies an innate sacredness to the action. In this, the Godi is a figure of religious importance, but also a crucial political one. As **Jon Hnefill Aðalsteinsson** writes, the role of the Godi was understood to be two-fold. "They kept control of the administration and at the same time, they took the lead in religious affairs. They controlled legal business at assemblies, and they presided over sacrifice in the temples and at assemblies."[587]

The unification of religious and legal affairs is made evident in the *Landnámabók* [Book of Settlements] with the detail offered on the Godi's oath ring:

"A ring weighing two ounces or more should lie on the stall in every chief Temple, and this ring should every chief or godi have upon his arm at all public law-motes (logthing) at which he should be at the head of affairs, having first reddened it in the blood of a neat [horned oxen] which he himself had sacrificed there. Every man who was there to transact any business, as by law provided by the Court, should first take an oath upon the ring and name for the purpose two or more witnesses..."[588]

This section is reminiscent of *Eyrbyggja saga* [The Saga of the People of Eyri], mentioned above. However, the characterisation of the Godi as both a political and religious figure emulates the characterisation of the Valkyrie. At once being a political mead-bearer in Odin's halls and participating in religious activity on a blood-stained battlefield. This is another area of similarity that lies more with Freyja in her role as *"blot-gydja"* alongside her mead-bearing attestations, than it reflects Odin.

---

587 Jon Hnefill Aðalsteinsson, A Piece of Horse Liver: Myth, Ritual and Folklore in Old Icelandic Sources (Haskolautgafan, 2012), 121.

588 The Book of the Settlement of Iceland, trans. T. Ellwood (Kendal. T.Wilson, 1898), 221.

The Valkyries may have been understood to fulfil a similar role of priestess too but working singularly in the context of the battlefield. It's not difficult to see that the language in skaldic poetry so often alludes to the killing of enemies being something of a sanctified, sacrificial act, a dedication to Odin.[589] While they are the choosers of the slain, Odin is framed as the receiver, the recipient. With the conception of Odin as the frenzied gallows God, the mad God of the battlefield, a warrior could offer a gift through violent acts. A gift of bloodshed and gore, who Odin will receive into his hall to prepare for the coming of *Ragnarök*.[590]

To carry this idea further still, the spilling of blood or the idea of an object being "reddened by blood" could imply sacredness and being 'of the Gods'. The Valkyries are often described in such terms, 'Their byrnies were drenched in blood[591]' and 'Spears blood-besprinkled / For spindles we use.'[592]

A similar occurrence can be found in *Sturlunga Saga*, with the Valkyries Gunnr and Göndul sitting in a blood-drenched house:

"Þat dreymði mann í Skagafirði, at hann þóttisk koma í hús eitt mikit; þar sátu inni konur tvær blóðgar ok réru áfram. Hónum þótti rigna blóði í ljórana. Önnur konan kvað:
Rouin vit ok róum vit,
rignir blóði,
Guðr [Gunnr] ok Gündul
fyrir gumna-falli:
Vit skulum ráðask
i Rapta-hlíð;
þar munum blótaðar
ok bölvaðar."[593]

---

589 Klas Wikström af Edholm, "Human sacrifice in Old Norse Skaldic Poetry", in In the Darkest of Days: Exploring Human Sacrifice and Value in Southern Scandinavian Prehistory, ed. Matthew J. Walsh, Sean O'Neill and Lasse Sørensen (Oxford, UK: Oxbow Books, 2023), 112.

590 Ibid, Wikström af Edholm details the skaldic evidence for this perspective in this work.

591 Helgakviða Hundingsbana I, Larrington, The Poetic Edda (Revised Edition), 112.

592 Translation is from George W. DaSent, The Story of Burnt Njal (1861). "The Story of Burnt Njal", Saga Database, accessed November 21, 2023. https://sagadb.org/brennu-njals_saga.en#156

593 Gudbrand Vigfusson, Sturlunga Saga including The Islendinga Saga of Lawman Sturla Thordsson and Other Works (Oxford Clarendon Press, 1878), 220.

"A man in Skagafjörður dreamed that he was coming to a large house. Two women were sitting there, covered in blood, rocking. He thought[594] it was raining blood from the ceiling.[595] The other woman chanted:

We're rocking and rocking
[said Gunnr and Gondul]
Blood rains down
Before men are slaughtered.[596]
We should go[597]
To Raptahlíð[598]
For their[599] curses and sacrifice."[600]

There is a suggestion here that the Valkyries may be summoned through the spilling of blood, with the manifestation of blood in this liminal dream state heralding a need for their presence in the town of Raptahlíð: "blood rains down before men are slaughtered". Of course, similar behaviours are attributed to carrion birds and scavengers, strongly evoking the earlier 'feral' Valkyrie and her associations.

The large house may be understood to be a longhouse, which has significant associations with culture, law and civilisation within the Scandinavian world, presenting a further juxtaposition with regards to the imagery of the wild clashing violently with an environment defined by order. This may be interpreted as a statement of the fragility of order, and how easily that environment can be tarnished and ruined.

---

594 "He thought" or "it seemed to him".

595 More specifically, the ventilation opening in the roof, coming from ljóri.

596 "man-fall", slaughter.

597 Or "resolve" – i.e. We should resolve Raptahlíð, which is in need of our presence/action.

598 Other sources say 'Raftahlíð' which is a place in Iceland, so this is likely a scribal error in Vigfusson's work.

599 Could also be that the Valkyries are going to be cursed and sworn at as a result of their imminent actions.

600 My translation, as I couldn't find a complete and accessible English translation. Thank you to Denise Vast for the additional help parsing the poetic verse!

Within this example, we likely see further evidence that the Valkyries are often seen conducting "ritualistic chants,"[601] further reinforcing their association with religious and ecstatic behaviours. A similar image is presented in *Gísla saga Súrssonar* [Gisla's Saga/ Gisli the Outlaw], with the presence of two dream-wives, one good and one evil.

> "Then in a second dream...this woman came to me and tied a blood-stained cap on my head, and before that she bathed my head in blood and poured it all over me, covering me in gore.
>
> And he spoke a verse:
> I dreamed a dream of her,
> woman of the serpent's lair.
> She washed my hair in Odin's fire
> spilled from the well of swords.
> And it seemed to me
> Those hands of the ring-goddess,[602]
> Blood-red, were bathed
> And drenched in gold-breaker's gore."[603]

Note that this figure drenches Gisli with blood, and is one half of a pair, the evil to the good. It's certainly possible, alongside the two groups present in the Story of Thidrand and Thorhall, that this was an attempt at reconciling the two distinct aspects of the Valkyrie as protector and guide, and blood-eager being calling for slaughter. Gisli continues, offering more detail on the possible identity of this entity beyond the hazy image of an 'evil woman'.

---

601 Terry Gunnell, The Origins of Drama in Scandinavia (D.S.Brewer, 1995), 338.

602 The translation notes indicate this is a kenning for woman, in other words, the woman who is appearing within the dream. I would say that this reinforces the Valkyrie nature of the mystery figure (goddess, and the language surrounding rings).

603 Translation by Martin S. Regal, "Gisli Sursson's Saga", in The Sagas of the Icelanders (World of the Sagas) (US: Penguin Group, Penguin Classics Deluxe Edition, 2005), 549.

"I thought I felt how
The valkyrie's hands,
Dripping with sword-rain,
Placed a bloody cap
Upon my thickly grown,
straight-cut locks of hair.
That is how the thread-goddess
Woke me from my dream."[604]

While we have a long tradition of interlacing terms from one group to another, and as such shouldn't take any description at face value, I have established that the use of the word 'Valkyrie' as a descriptor was a deliberate act. It was a title with significant cultural weight, with duties, behaviours and characteristics that were distinct from other similar figures, such as the *Disir*.

Valkyries could be *Disir,* but not all *Disir* could be Valkyries. At the very least, it helps solidify a connection between the Valkyries and the behaviours exhibited by this woman. Foremost, an association with blood, violence and liminal spaces. Moreover, **Judy Quinn** makes an observation when she states that the Valkyries moved to a "pluralistic dream tradition, in which figures of traditional authority could be accommodated within a Christian framework".[605]

Essentially, by placing the Valkyries, an element of the old religion, into a dream environment, the writers could preserve their cultural traditions without conflict with the incoming and developing conversion to the new religion. As such, it shouldn't be assumed that the Valkyries appearing in dreamscapes was archetypal of Pre-Christian views, but rather as a reaction to best preserve the traditions of old in an environment that was growing ever-more hostile towards them.

It's up for debate on the degree to which this effort was a conscious, deliberate effort, or if it was the result of an ever-developing scepticism. Quinn also adds that the "two bloodied Valkyries Guðr [or Gunnr] and Gondul rock and chant about their mission to Rafthlið where they will be worshipped by the sacrifice of warriors."[606]

---

604 Ibid, 550.
605 Judy Quinn, "The Use of Eddic Poetry in Contemporary Sagas", in The Australian-Icelandic Cultural Society (Melbourne), Volume 3 (1987), 60.
606 Ibid.

As has been discussed, there's notable academic pushback on the notion that the Valkyries were ever worshipped, or of a station that would merit such worship - but the imagery and language frequently lends itself to that conclusion. There is a purposeful word choice that reaffirms and emphasises the associations with blood, sacrifice, ritual behaviour and worship among the Valkyries many appearances.

Moreover, the rocking motion assigned to the Valkyries within *Sturlunga Saga* seems to tie into the portrayal of ecstatic trances within the literature, with Freyja and Odin possessing heiti that potentially echo that image too in *Skjálf* and *Skilfingr*, respectively. The ecstatic trance is a condition removed from constraint and restraint. There's a possibility that Skögul's name also refers to this 'shaking' uncontrollability, an ecstatic state of ritualistic activity.

The plentiful spilling of blood alongside Valkyrie appearances also emphasises the supernatural horror elements of the Valkyries as death deities. There's something inherently otherworldly and primal about their iconography and adornments. An almost dream-like or nightmare-like state, exaggerated and horrific in equal measure. Even when written by post-conversion writers, the Valkyries remain as evocative as ever.

When you combine this with the later heroic depiction of the Valkyries, you achieve a notable similarity between the Godi as a political figure with crucial religious duties, and the Valkyrie as a political and noble figure, born into privilege but elevated through duty into a place of religious, sacred and supernatural power. Over these excerpts, the blood of the sacrificed animal is a sanctifying element in the process of oath-making and law-speaking equally, with this tradition persevering into the conversion period.

Daniel Bray writes that the blood of the sacrifice could be understood to carry "something of the power of the gods",[607] with the act of making an oath on a blood-reddened ring potentially invoking "the power of the gods to oversee the keeping of those oaths."[608] Further, there is recurrent evidence that the blood spilt not only contained "something of the power of the gods" but was also 'for the Gods': "the sacrificial meal was a communion where the blood was the gods' part and the horse-liver the king's part."[609]

607 Daniel Bray, "Sacrifice and Sacrificial Ideology in Old Norse Religion," in The Dark Side: Proceedings of the Seventh Australian and International Religion, Literature and the Arts Conference, ed. Christopher Hartney and Andrew McGarrity (Sydney: RLA Press, 2004), 125.

608 Ibid, 126.

609 Olof Sundqvist, The Demise of Old Norse Religion, Dismantling and

It's clear that there was something specifically sacred about blood in Old Norse religious practices. The act of reddening something with blood was no doubt seen as blending the line between the sacred and the mundane, which can also be seen when it comes to creating something magical. Within *Völsunga saga* we have a magical drink that is "mixed with the strength of the earth and the blood of her son, and on the horn were carved all kinds of runes and reddened with blood".[610]

This is echoed within *Guðrúnarkviða II* [The Second Lay of Gudrun], with the drink being mixed with the "strength of the earth, the cold of the sea and the blood of sons",[611] incorporating the "bowels of sacrifices" into the process of its creation.[612] I would go as far as to suggest that the presence of blood, plentiful and over the top, with feminine figures is indicative of a Valkyrie, to the degree that we can use that alongside weaponry and armour as an identifying marker. There are no other figures that appear with the sprinkling and spilling of blood in such frequency as the slaughter maidens.

Referring to an interpretation put forward by **Luke John Murphy** that suggests that two kennings found in *Hákonarmál*: "Skglar veðr" and "Óðins veðri" ["Skögul's storm" and "Odin's storm"] "serves to combine the effects of the two 'storms' ... rather than two separate storms/battles, the exact repetition merges the two.... Haakon received his death-wound, suggesting that Skögul formed a channel through which Óðinn's power (or will?) could manifest."[613]

I would suggest that, rather than Odin's power or will being manifested, we are seeing through the spilling of blood a sacrificial act, and a notion of Odin witnessing the actions of the Valkyries in that moment. Almost akin to an oath being made, or, indeed, a transaction being finalised. Blood is shed as the Valkyrie wills, and the Gods bear witness. Of course, we could also be seeing here Odin acting in a manner we would expect him to, with his associations of frenzied bloodshed and war.

Defending the Old Order in Viking Age Scandinavia (De Gruyter, 2023), 275. https://doi.org/10.1515/9783111198750

610 Rodriguez, Old Norse Drinking Culture, 323.
611 Ibid
612 Ibid.
613 Murphy, Herjans Dísir, 139.

Regardless of the perspective I have put forth here, the idea that Odin was the master of the Valkyries isn't one that emerged apropos of nothing. It was an image that was reinforced, reiterated, and stated time and time again over centuries of written work. Yet, the literature also, so often, acts to undermine that very image, suggesting that the 'truth' was far more complex and nuanced than it so often reaffirmed as fact in the modern day. For every example that pushes the Valkyries into the role of servant, we have another that breaks that mould, and defies that characterisation. As **David Varley** writes, Odin "is a being subject to fate who nevertheless seeks mastery of it,"[614] and through the Valkyries' power he arguably achieves that goal.

If I've achieved anything with this work, it is to realign the narrative of the Valkyries away from the image of servant manifest, and into a presentation defined by nuance and depth. The Valkyrie is a figure with lingering presentations even before the Viking Age, and we can safely gather, had an inception that was older still. Her elements were incorporated into the Nordic world, often becoming the perceived image of the servant, but with language that hinted at a lingering mastery and agency that predates that cultural presentation, and even thrived within it. While the centuries since, born from both Christian and masculine biases, have emphasised the Valkyrie within the servant dynamic, she has persevered as a symbol of potent feminine power regardless, echoing that of her origination. Shining bright and effervescent still.

---

614 Varley, The whirling wheel, 239.

IN SUMMARY

Over the course of the last few hundred pages, I have posited various arguments that I hope will have re-framed the reader's perspective on the Valkyries and their role in the greater sphere of Nordic mythology.

The Valkyries personify a wildness made tame by civilisation, by man. Something Pagan, something of the natural world, all red in tooth and claw, incorporated into a more domesticated shape to fit into an ever-changing world. Like all tamed creatures, however, there's a risk of becoming wild once more. A danger, an unpredictability, an externality that longs to return.

From the very beginning, the Valkyrie has been fundamentally tied to the battlefield and to the battle dead. Here, they are often depicted covered in blood, wearing armour, wielding weapons, and flying above the battlefield. In the earliest Nordic attestations, we have a connection to ravens - birds that feast on carrion - and we have a connection to Odin, in being able to converse with those creatures. From these attestations too, we have the Valkyries being assigned to a task: to choose the slain.

Even when that duty is not being actively described, such as in *Hrafnsmal* and *Eiriksmal*, we have the Valkyrie being clearly identified. Here then, Skalds were beginning to weave in behaviours outside of simply 'choosing the slain', leading the way for future appearances to explore those outside behaviours. We therefore have the presentation and emergence of the 'noble Valkyrie', still riding on horseback, still wearing armour, but less defined by choosing the slain, and more into the realm of protecting certain individuals from death.

It's the other side of the coin, the mirrored image. These Valkyries are prevalent throughout the Heroic sagas. They showcase other skills associated with both Odin and Freyja equally. Occasionally, they are given mortal origins. These later depictions coincide with the explicit references to swan-coats or garments, and thus the identification with the greater Germanic *Swan Maiden.*

The conflation and identification with the *Disir*, *Fylgjur*, and *Hamingjur* seems likely fuelled by the ongoing evolution of the Valkyrie into areas outside of their original core duty, though even there, we see natural threads that tie into the manipulation of fate and in acting as guardians of individuals, able to navigate liminal, supernatural spaces. The nebulous use of '*Disir*' in period literature played a significant role during this period also, lending itself to describing similar figures that are 'supernatural feminities' that work within the sphere of fate, and as a result, the sphere of death.

Over time, the nuances of their differences became diluted until, apparently, they became meaningless or lost entirely. That dilution has, from our modern perspective, confused the overall image, as the later texts have survived in largely complete forms, where the earlier texts and the oral material they were based on are more likely to be fragmented, presented to us in a diluted form, or lost entirely. The Valkyrie is older than her dressings, older than Valhalla and the *Einherjar*, but she has adapted within those dressings, strongly associated with the afterlife and the movement of the afterlife, the travel between realms.

In large part due to this apparent evolution, or rather *adaptation* to the needs of the audience and culture, the Valkyrie has been seen as a confusing artefact of skaldic tradition, a contradiction of presentation and behaviours and appearances. But, as I have demonstrated, the Valkyrie perseveres. She is a figure defined by apparent contradiction from the outset, defying the environment she was 'born' into and thrived in. She is defined by liminality, aggression, bloodthirst, nobility, protection, power, and ever-crossing boundaries.

The Valkyries are of the wild, they are masters of the battlefield, itself a place of wildness and disorder. They choose the slain; they decide who has victory and who does not. They operate in an arena that few can challenge and, all in all, interact with us humans in a way that few beings and deities do. They see us at our worst and revel in it. They appear at times of importance with a hand on the wheel, influencing us. They appear to us at our best, empowering us to change our lives in turn.

They thrive in those spaces, and guide and protect those that have great destinies ahead of them. The Valkyries should not be seen as a mere servant, but akin to a master over fate in the environment they control: the battlefield. Places of violent interaction, of the crossover of the animalistic within the confines of civilisation. They are the culmination of so many other threads, the combined effort of various deities leading to the refinement of a force that is so often overlooked in modern Heathenry.

MOVING FORWARDS, WHERE DO WE GO FROM HERE?

The title of this book posed a question for the reader that, previously, may have been an easy one to answer. Whether I have put forward an analysis that has convinced you, or not, I hope to have added more considerations into the discussion, illuminating a faction that has been overlooked by academic, educational and Pagan materials alike.

As highlighted in the opening segments, the motivating force behind this work is to generate discussion and analysis. Perhaps continuing with elements posited here or moving in alternative directions still. For those finding themselves in disagreement, I would urge further comment, if only to have more material to read that discusses the Valkyries at all. I'm eager and open to evolve my understanding, and for this to be a springboard for conversation. The Valkyries are far from explored and seem largely defined through ongoing misconceptions and outdated scholarly work. While recent years have resulted in a resurgence in Valkyric research, there's still much to be done, especially in terms of undoing some of the mistakes of the past, as there is in many areas within the study of the Viking Age.

For Heathens, I hope to offer a source of well-researched material should you wish to know more about the Valkyries and how they may fit into your own practice and path. While I have framed that research from a specific angle, towards re-empowerment of the Valkyries, I hope I have outlined my reasoning to such a degree that you can parse where and how conclusions have been made. For students, should you bump into this work, I hope I have covered the topic to a thorough degree in order to form a platform for further study and helped point you in other directions to explore.

We can safely conclude that the 'Valkyrie' as a figure predates Valhalla, and thus predates many of her core associations, especially regarding serving Odin and serving the *Einherjar* in the afterlife. Yet, it is within the Nordic context that the Valkyrie has flourished, even if she has endured a noted degradation and erosion over the centuries since. There's room for further discussion on the shared Germanic heritage of the Valkyrie including and beyond that of the *Waelcyrge,* and for analysis on breaking down the moment of 'transfer' to highlight cultural exchange during this period. There's extensive room for further linguistic analyses into kennings and language variance across the corpus, and a variety of other avenues besides. The board is wide open, and rich with possibility.

As the culmination of several years of research, this book represents a complete argument to best reflect my perspective of the topic. I fully expect, over future revisions, for my position to shift, though not dramatically, to include further avenues of research. In this, there were many, to the point that I feared the book had the potential to become unwieldy and distracted. My list of Shield-Maidens in the relevant chapter is far from exhaustive, while my approach to ruminating on gender expression within the period merely a footnote in the shadow of a colossal amount of work that has been conducted, and no doubt is being worked on as I write.

There's more to be done on the practice of historical *seiðr* as the field continues to build momentum and snowball, and the endeavour of unravelling wayward influences on numerous topics - mostly Victorian or dated beliefs around gender expression and identity – remains something that will be relevant and built upon for many years to come. The Viking Age still holds many secrets, and many questions. Many will likely go unanswered, while we may be travelling in the right direction for others, getting ever closer to better understanding those that lived and died before us.

THE VALKYRIES
FROM A MODERN HEATHEN PERSPECTIVE

In this closing chapter, we reach a point that I wanted to cover within this book to offer a complete image, travelling from the world of a thousand years ago, through the veil of Christianity and through time to a modern Heathen perspective. Generations have lived and died, and almost 400,000 days later we reach this moment, right here and now. The Valkyries persevere, the Eddas and sagas have stayed with us, fragmented of course, but still diligently studied, enthralling more and more people with each passing year.

I am certainly enthralled with these maidens of slaughter, wisdom, war, battle, and protection. I fell into the Heathen path and in turn fell in love with all its nuances and freedoms. It has been a springboard for further research while also reaffirming my own personal morals and ethical values. There's a deep reverence for nature within Heathenry, alongside a focus on giving your time and energy into building community and helping that community to thrive.

There's a focus on keeping 'frith': acting to keep peace within spaces to ensure productivity and hospitality as much as there is in standing up for what you believe in, and showing loyalty to those you trust and cherish. It's about honouring the Gods, the ancestors and the *vaettir* [spirits] to build reciprocity and show respect. It's about knowing that you will leave an impact on the world, even if you can't see it. Every interaction, every word said to another, every action, holds consequences and ripples outwards.

I do want to also dedicate some space to clarifying a position that may generate conflict. As a reconstructive Heathen, I personally cherish having a better grasp on what the practices of the 'old ways' were really like. Many times in this book I have stated that certain things have been incorrectly seen as authentic practices or beliefs, such as the Northern Lights being associated with the Valkyries, or that keys were particularly associated with women. I do not want to invalidate the perspective of those that hold these elements as true within their belief structure. Indeed, efforts towards reconstruction can only go so far before we hit quite the barrier: inconsistencies, discrepancies, and so much missing information.

One of the benefits of Paganism is that there are no rules, no dogma, no structure, and we borrow elements that, in essence, work towards betterment and refinement within our own spiritual journey. A similar point can be made when we tackle the presentation of the Gods within the material I have analysed. The readings I have suggested, for example the unflattering and unsavoury nature of Freyr condoning violence against Gerdr, are from a literature-first view, not a Pagan-first view. As Heathens we should always be aware that our sources are not infallible and shouldn't be considered wholly factual. At times, quite the opposite!

They are not sacred texts of absolute truth, but writing we should criticise from an almost disembodied point, using them to inform our understanding of the Gods in terms of their associations and relationships. Considering the way the people of the time may have seen the Gods, or whatever lingering sentiment existed within the Christian world they were recorded in.

Despite a lack of physical evidence for Valkyrie worship, the Valkyries remain a central pillar of my personal Heathen practice, vibrant and impactful. While I approached the process of researching and writing this book as a devotional act, I also wanted to end in a place that takes all of what you've read so far and embeds it into something real, tangible, physical and modern. These beings aren't just whispers of history, words on a page, or distant echoes of a time long past. Not by any measure. I worship the Valkyries, as do others, and they have changed me, and no doubt will continue to change me, for the better.

As you may imagine from the commentary presented from the outset in this work, there are not many sources at all that offer advice for those looking to worship these entities or offer insight from someone who does worship them in a modern Pagan practice. Not to mention that, with everything I've mentioned above, it might be easy to dismiss the notion entirely with one question: Why would someone worship the Valkyries?

I've referenced, time and time again over the course of this work, the idea that the Valkyries at their earliest incarnation were something feral and animalistic. Something almost primordial, and utterly uncontrollable. They delight in bloodshed and inspire conflict. They reap, and feast on those bloody battlefields. It's not the sort of imagery that invites eager worship, though I'm certainly not one to judge!

Whilst we have no uncontested historical evidence for Valkyrie worship, they nonetheless play an important role in the balance of life and death, and the ever-enticing aspect of the 'afterlife'. I hold the position that some of the archaeological figurines we've found were probably understood to be Valkyries by their owner and may have been used as a token for good luck in battle. A devotional object to inspire success, or to draw the Valkyrie to them should death be on the cards.

They are present at our most animalistic, conflict-driven state, playing a key role in resolving those conflicts one way or another. If we align ourselves with the later literature, they were human once, born of mortals, but made other through circumstance or talent. They are, themselves, a duality much akin to how we perceive ourselves as humans. We see ourselves as dignified, civilised beings, but under the right conditions - almost too easily at times - we can be transformed into something that many would describe as quite the opposite. Returning to our animalistic roots, shedding the image of civilisation as easily as we would discard an item of clothing.

We are animals, and I think it's easily forgotten when we drape ourselves in the finery we've created. The Valkyries are our reflections but made grand, divine and exaggerated. Embodying that careful balance within all of us, that call of the wild, and the call of order, and everything in between. They exist entirely on that spear edge, all power and wildness, and feral brutality, and wisdom, and guidance, and beauty, and empowerment. From a Pagan and Heathen perspective, they are entities who occupy the space between worlds, purposefully avoiding easy classification.

They are, arguably, the 'closest' to us, in terms of how they interact with humanity, and in dealing in an area that Gods – as immortal, undying beings that so often seem to embody power and victory and vitality – could struggle to understand and empathise with. Except for, perhaps, Freyja, Hel, Ran and like death deities, including Skuld if we are to run with the argument I have presented above. These are the deities that I feel closest to in turn, those that host and care over the dead for far, far longer than we inhabit the world of the living, that ephemeral blink of an eye that goes by so fast. The Valkyries are interwoven in human deeds, human activity, and human nature, stepping side by side with us through history.

In other ways, they are undoubtedly wise, possessing sought after knowledge or offering guidance and a purpose. They are the product of Freyja and Odin, of Vanir and Aesir, of human and godly efforts coalesced into one potent and effective force.

The battlefield can be seen as a sacred space, a crucible of life and death and sacrifice. The Valkyries are the masters of that space, acting as the guardian of the threshold between the world of the living and the world of the dead. They are also beyond that space, integrated and integral to both worlds.

> We call to the Corpse-Maidens,
> To the victory-eager goddesses of enmity,
> Who gift life and deploy death on the standard-road.
> Flying on swan wings to the hall of the slain,
> And to the gloried hall of many seats.
> We hail the Guardians of the shield-rim and the slaughter fields,
> As you delight and dance in your realm, revelling in your duty.
> We call to the disir of blood jewels,
> To the sisters of spears, shields and swords.
> Hail to the Valkyries![615]

There's one element of researching and reviving Old Norse religion that makes itself obvious quite quickly: we can conclude very little when it comes to comparing it to the greater whole. We don't have many answers, and so there is freedom in that to explore those elements that are most intriguing to you. That approach creates a veritable kaleidoscope of practices all huddled together under the umbrella of 'Norse Paganism'.

For those finding themselves at this threshold peering in, it's an unusual and often overwhelming landscape, filled to the brim with answers such as "we don't know", "do what feels right for you", and "we can infer this, but *that* contradicts it". I imagine the often started "Here are the myths, but they're stories, don't take them too literally" makes for a confusing introductory line, as often as the *Poetic* and *Prose Edda* are suggested as beginner texts.

---

615 Sif Brookes and Dan Coultas, The Wyrd Less Woven: An Alternative Heathen Prayer Book (2024), 134.

Akin to "here are the core texts, but here are all the reasons we don't trust them at all".[616] For those coming from more dogmatic practices, this uncertainty is sure to be baffling, making for unsteady foundations to build any sort of belief structure. It also makes things interesting, and once you settle into the lack of rules, freeing. Worship how you want to, whatever feels right to you. If you want more historical grounding, there are some sources to point you in a good direction. From there, you can follow the rabbit holes as you see fit, maybe even find a passion for research, or a particular subject, like I did.

Equally, worshipping the Valkyries is not for everybody, nor would I ever say that it should be. In my experience, they can be overwhelming in every way imaginable. They can be a cacophony, louder than life, louder than anything, all encompassing. They are death, and battle, and screaming, and war, as much as they can be quiet, and contemplative, and calming. Their collective variety cannot be anticipated, and that is often disruptive. Yet, again in my experience, they're always empowering and potent in their primal essence. A wild force unleashed onto the world, running rampant and chaotic. Unbound, indomitable, and unstoppable.

⸱When I conduct a blot or ritual, I call to the Valkyries to hallow and protect, for that is one thing they are attested to doing most frequently. They defend and deflect and tear asunder those that would threaten to reject their will and whim.

⸱When I offer to the Valkyries, I serve mead as they are said to do and offer them a drink as they revel in their realm. I offer food for them to partake in, acting as a grateful host to their number, inviting them into my home.

⸱I offer water, invoking the idea of the liminal spaces that they so frequently inhabit.

⸱I approach them with honesty and humility, understanding that they can be as changeable as the wind and entirely unpredictable in their approach.

---

616 I reaffirm that these texts should be used to inform you about the Gods, their relationships, associations, internal dynamics etc., and as a rough scaffolding to further flesh out your individual practice. They should be questioned, analysed and critiqued – they are not infallible, and we shouldn't consider them so.

They give me bravery and courage when I need it and remind me that I should be unashamedly *me*. To do things with all my effort, to believe what I believe in, and stand up to corruption, wrongdoing or injustice, and when needed, embrace understanding, communication, and peaceful resolution. Building connections and community is vital to Heathenry, now, then, and in the future.

Of course, I'm still learning, I still make mistakes, I can judge too quickly and act without all the information, but from the Valkyries I learn to grow, always. To be both passionate and compassionate. They have helped me grow more confident in myself, and to slowly overcome my anxiety disorder. The me of the past would be astounded that I voluntarily do public speaking now, that I put myself out there and talk to people. Not only that, but I enjoy it!

I also work to incorporate them into group worship, in groups that are open to incorporating them, to make sure that there is a moment of recognition for their number. For so often do they get diminished to that of servant and mortal mead-maiden. In August of 2024, I will lead a blot to the Valkyries at *The Great Heathen Gathering Helsmoot*, hosted by Asatru UK, which, as far as I know, is the first time a blot of that size will be conducted to the Valkyries on UK soil. It is an honour, but I'm all too aware that this will be a strange occasion for many - hopefully it will in turn contribute to the normalisation of the worship of the slaughter maidens within Heathenry and Paganism as a whole.

Appendix A

Translation by Lee M. Hollander, Viga-Glum's Saga and The Story of Ogmund Dytt. Translated From the Old Icelandic. (New York: Twayne, 1972), 46-7.

Methinks, that huge and helm-clad,
Hitherward a woman
Proceeded swiftly, heading,
Silver-dis, towards þvera,
High as the hills towering,
Head-dress Frigg, in my
Dream I deemed her Oðinn's
Daughter, warrior-choosing

Hollander removes the ambiguity around the nature of the figure, making her a Valkyrie outright ("warrior-choosing" would only be referring to a Valkyrie here), rather than the '*Hamingja*-woman' seen in other translations. This attested entity follows all the conventions of her Valkyrie sisters, employing a common descriptor of 'Dis' alongside metallic imagery. This is also the only mention that I could find of a Valkyrie being called "Oðinn's [Odin's] - Daughter", though the nature of kennings being as they are, this perhaps shouldn't be taken too literally.

We have explicit references to Valkyrie parentage that is decidedly not Odin, even with thought given to the plethora of heiti that he possesses throughout the literature. In the larger discussion of violent actions in relation to the Valkyries, it's interesting that Glum's potential exposure to a Valkyrie figure is so dramatic, even considering the rather dramatic ways in which the Valkyries often appear in poetry and prose. Glum, after all, is given the nickname Viga-Glum due to his propensity for bloodshed.

The Valkyrie being mountainous in size could be a reference to how prominent those behaviours are in his life, how influential the Valkyrie and her bloodlust are in his life. Naturally, of course, her size marks her as otherworldly, and emphasises the dream-state this scene occurs in. If we're to take a literal interpretation of her name, this could be Skögul, 'high-towering', though again few translations of the saga contain this specific verse.

APPENDIX B
A LIST OF COMMONLY AGREED VALKYRIE FIGURES AND POTENTIAL VALKYRIE FIGURES

For the most part, I agree with the list and rationality presented by **Neil Price** in *The Viking Way*,[617] but I've deviated somewhat when it comes to specific details. As such, I have also listed potential figures with my personal rationalisation and comments at each instance.

Brynhildr	Potentially identical to Sigrdrifa. Possesses a swan-coat. Human origins. States she has 'sisters' (gather not biological?) who also possess swan coats – who are they? Brynhildr may be a continental Germanic 'import' to the Nordic world, bringing the Swan Maiden iconography with her.
Eir	Potentially the same figure as the Goddess, the Handmaiden of Frigg, with that in mind we can presumably conclude Aesir origins. Her name is associated with healing and mercy, and her inclusion alongside other named Valkyries reinforces the idea of a role involved with choosing the slain, and choosing those who will live and return to the world of civilisation.
Geirahöð	
Geiravör	
Geirdriful	
Geirönul	
Geirskögul	Is once used as an alternative name for Skögul, though in the *Voluspa* is clearly a separate individual. *Grimnismal* includes a Valkyrie named 'Geirölul', though it's largely believed this is a copy error, with Geirskögul replacing her.

---

617   Price, The Viking Way, 281.

Göll	
Göndul	Equated with Freyja in a later source – though her being mentioned among other Valkyries without comment or distinction suggests that other writers/skalds over the course of her attestations saw her as separate.
Gunnr	Potentially also Guðr – Bek-Pedersen substitutes Gunnr's name for Guðr in her translation of *Darraðarljoð*.[618]
	Gunnr being a noted wolf-rider may identify her as a Jotunn.
Herfjötur	
Herja	
Hlaðguðr svanhvít	Possesses a swan-coat. Human origins.
Hildr	Human origins, called Hildr Hǫgnadóttir in *Hjaðningavíg* [The Battle of the Heodenings].
Hjalmþrimul	
Hervör alvitr	Possesses a swan-coat. Human origins.
Herþǫgn	Defined by Price as 'army hostess', I suggest 'battle silence'.
Hjörþrimul	
Hlökk	
Hrist	
Hrund	
Kára	Reincarnated from Sigrún. Presumably human origins, due to reincarnation.
Mist	
Nipt	
Ölrún	Possesses a swan-coat. Human origins.
Randgríðr	
Ráðgríðr	
Randgniðr	
Reginleifr	
Róta	Potentially also the 'Ruta' presented in Grammaticus' *Gesta Danorum*.
Sanngriðr	

---

618   Bek-Pedersen, The Norns in Old Norse Mythology, 137

Sigrdrifa	Potentially identical to Brynhildr – though *Grípisspá* infers she is reincarnated from Sváva. Brynhildr is given human parentage without this association.
Sigrún	Reincarnated from Sváva. Human origins.
Skalmöld	
Skeggjöld	'sword-time', which is similar to Skeggjöld, 'axe-age'. Potentially discussing war/battle, a time of swords and axes
Skögul	The 'high-towering/shaker'.
Skuld	Snorri specifically equates the Valkyrie Skuld with the "Youngest Norn".
Sváva	Potentially reincarnated into Sigrún and then later, Kára. Human origins.
Sveið	
Svipul	
Tanngriðr	
Þögn	
Þrima	
ValÞögn	
Þrúðr	Potentially the same being as the daughter of Sif and Thor, with that assumption we can presume Aesir origins.

POTENTIAL AND DISPUTED VALKYRIES IN PERIOD LITERATURE

Viga-Glum's Unnamed 'Hamingja-woman'	Potentially Skögul, based on a literal translation of her name, or another Valkyrie, potentially known or otherwise.
Hjlóð	Daughter of a Jotunn, presumably a Jotunn herself. She is described as "óskmey" [wish-girl] in Völsunga saga, which – while largely agreed to refer to a Valkyrie – remains up for debate. She is more subservient and submissive than other Valkyries and is never described as engaging in martial activities or within a battlefield[619]

---

619 As such, I largely agree with Luke John Murphy, that Hjlóð may better fit into the larger category of "supernatural female", rather than a Valkyrie specifically. Murphy, Herjans Dísir: Valkyrjur, Supernatural Feminities, and Elite

Ilmr	A persuasive argument has been made by Joseph Hopkins,[620] among other earlier scholars, which suggests that Ilmr is a Valkyrie largely due to a kenning found in *Landnámabók* – "Jalmr Ilmar" ['Racket of Ilmr'] which fits the kenning conventions of other Valkyrie figures, such as "glaumr Gunnar" ['din of Gunnr'], and notably not of other Asynjur.
The 18 unnamed 'Disir' in Flateyjarbók, see also the unnamed 'dream women' that are depicted alongside blood, such as we see in Gisla Saga.	Their description and behaviour seem identical to that of other Valkyries, but at a time when *'Disir'* was a catch-all term for any supernatural feminine force that dealt in death and fate. Note also that it is also in *Flateyjarbók* that we find Göndul being identified with Freyja – there's potentially an effort to minimise the Valkyries within this work, reflecting a larger cultural and religious trend.
Þorgerðr Hölgabrúðr	Displays the behaviours and follows the conventions of a Valkyrie. See applicable chapter for further notes.
Geir-Rota	With consideration of the rationale presented with Geirskögul, it may be that this is another name for Rota, or it could be a separate Valkyrie entirely.
Irpa	Frequently appears alongside Þorgerðr.
Fenja and Menja	The Giantesses of *Grottasǫngr* – more of a reach, but their potential Valkyrie status should be acknowledged.
Guðr	May be the same figure as Gunnr, or a separate entity.

Warrior Culture in the Late Pre-Christian Iron Age, 123-4.

620 Joseph S. Hopkins, Goddesses Unknown II: On the Apparent Old Norse Goddess Ilmr (RMN Newsletter, 2014), 34.

TRANSLATIONS OF PRIMARY SOURCES

Andersson, T.M. and W.I. Miller. "The Saga of the People of Ljosavatn". In The Complete Sagas of Icelanders Including 49 Tales Volume IV, edited by Viðar Hreinsson, 193-255. Reykjavik, Iceland: Leif Eriksson Publishing, 1997.

Attwood, Katrina. "Anonymous Poems, Gyðingsvísur 5". In Poetry on Christian Subjects. Skaldic Poetry of the Scandinavian Middle Ages 7, edited by Margaret Clunies Ross. Turnhout, Belgium: Brepols, 2007.

Bede, Ecclesiastical History of the English People. Translated by Leo Sherley-Price. England: Penguin Group, 1990.

Bellows, Henry Adams. "The Ballad of Hamther (1936)". Sacred Texts. Accessed April 3, 2024. https://sacred-texts.com/neu/poe/poe37.htm

Bellows, Henry Adams. The Poetic Edda: The Mythological Poems. Garden City, New York: Dover Publications Inc, 2004.

Bellows, Henry Adams. The Poetic Edda: The Heroic Poems. Mineola, New York: Dover Publications Inc, 2007.

Beowulf: Translation and Commentary (Expanded Edition). Translated by Tom Shippey, edited by Leonard Neidorf. London, England: Uppsala Books, 2023.

Clement of Alexandria. "The Exhortation to the Greeks. The Rich Man's Salvation. To the Newly Baptized". Loeb Classical Library 92. Translated by G. W. Butterworth. Cambridge, MA: Harvard University Press, 1919.

Cogadh Gaedhel re Gallaibh. Translated by James Henthorn Todd. London: Longmans, Green, Reader, and Dyer, 1867.

Cook, Albert S. Judith, An Old English Epic Fragment. Boston, USA: D.C. Heath & Co, 1889.

Dronke, Ursula. The Poetic Edda: Volume II: Mythological Poems. Oxford: OUP, 1997.

Ellwood, T. The Book of the Settlement of Iceland. Kendal: T.Wilson, 1898.

Eyrbyggja Saga. Translated by Hermann Pálsson and Paul Edwards. London: Penguin Classics, 1989.

Faḍlān, Ahmad ibn. Ibn Fadlan and the Land of Darkness: Arab Travellers in the Far North. Translated by Paul Lunde and Caroline E.M. Stone. London: Penguin Classics, 2011.

Finlay, Alison. "Glúmr Geirason, Gráfeldardrápa". In Poetry from the Kings' Sagas 1: From Mythical Times to c. 1035. Skaldic Poetry of the Scandinavian Middle Ages 1, edited by Diana Whaley. Turnhout, Belgium: Brepols, 2012.

Fulk, R.D. "Anonymous, Eiríksmál". In Poetry from the Kings' Sagas 1: From Mythical Times to c. 1035. Skaldic Poetry of the Scandinavian Middle Ages 1, edited by Diana Whaley. Turnhout, Belgium: Brepols, 2012.

Fulk, R.D. "Sigvatr Þórðarson, Austrfararvísur". In Poetry from the Kings' Sagas 1: From Mythical Times to c. 1035. Skaldic Poetry of the Scandinavian Middle Ages 1, edited by Diana Whaley. Turnhout, Belgium: Brepols, 2012.

Fulk, R.D. "Eyvindr skáldaspillir Finnsson, Hákonarmál". In Poetry from the Kings' Sagas 1: From Mythical Times to c. 1035. Skaldic Poetry of the Scandinavian Middle Ages 1, edited by Diana Whaley. Turnhout, Belgium: Brepols. 2012.

Fulk, R.D. "Þorbjǫrn hornklofi, Haraldskvæði (Hrafnsmál)". In Poetry from the Kings' Sagas 1: From Mythical Times to c. 1035. Skaldic Poetry of the Scandinavian Middle Ages 1, edited by Diana Whaley. Turnhout, Belgium: Brepols, 2012.

Gade, Kari Ellen. "Einarr Skúlason, Sigurðardrápa I 2". In Poetry from the Kings' Sagas 2: From c. 1035 to c. 1300. Skaldic Poetry of the Scandinavian Middle Ages 2, edited by Kari Ellen Gade. Turnhout, Belgium: Brepols, 2009.

Gade, Kari Ellen. "Halldórr ókristni, Eiríksflokkr". In Poetry from the Kings' Sagas 1: From Mythical Times to c. 1035. Skaldic Poetry of the Scandinavian Middle Ages 1, edited by Diana Whaley. Turnhout, Belgium: Brepols, 2012.

Gade, Kari Ellen. "Einarr Skúlason, Fragments 4". In Poetry from Treatises on Poetics. Skaldic Poetry of the Scandinavian Middle Ages 3, edited by Kari Ellen Gade and Edith Marold. Turnhout, Belgium: Brepols, 2017.

Gisli the Outlaw. Translated by George Webbe Dasent. 1866.

Gudrun, a Mediaeval Epic. Translated by Mary Pickering Nichols. Boston and New York: Houghton, Mifflin and company, 1889.

Grammaticus, Saxo. The History of the Danes, Books I-IX. Translated by Peter Fisher, edited by Hilda Ellis Davidson. UK: D.S. Brewer, 1996.

Greenfield, S. B. "Exodus (Lines 1–275)." Old English Newsletter 21 (1987), 15–20

Grimm, Jakob. Teutonic Mythology. Translated by James Steven Stallybrass. London: Routledge, 1999.

Hartmann, Jacob Wittmer. The Göngu-Hrólfssaga: A Study in Old Norse Philology. New York: Columbia University Press, 1912.

Heslop, Kate. "Anonymous Poems, Óláfs drápa Tryggvasonar 8". In Poetry from the Kings' Sagas 1: From Mythical Times to c. 1035. Skaldic Poetry of the Scandinavian Middle Ages 1, edited by Diana Whaley. Turnhout: Brepols, 2012.

Historia Langobardorum. Translated by William Dudley Foulke. 1907. Germanic Mythology. "Historica Langobardorum". Accessed March 19, 2024. https://germanicmythology.com/works/HistoriaLangobardum.html

Hollander, Lee M. Viga-Glum's Saga and The Story of Ogmund Dytt Translated From the Old Icelandic. New York: Twayne, 1972.

Hopkins, Joseph S. "Nigon Wyrta Galdor". Mimisbrunner.info. Accessed October 15, 2023, https://www.mimisbrunnr.info/nigon-wyrta-galdor.

Kershaw, Nora. "The Tháttur of Sörli". The Complete Fornaldarsögur Norðurlanda: Legendary Sagas of the Northland. 1921. "The Tháttur of Sörli". Germanic Mythology. Accessed June 25, 2024. https://www.germanicmythology.com/FORNALDARSAGAS/SORLATHATTURKERSHAW.html

Kunz, Keneva. The Saga of the People of Laxardal and Bolli Bollason's Tale. Penguin Classics Edition. Penguin Group, 2008.

Larrington, Carolyne. The Poetic Edda. (Revised Edition). UK: Oxford University Press, 2014.

MacFirbis, Duald. On the Fomorians and the Norsemen. Translated by Alexander Brugge. Norway: J. C. Gundersens bogtrykkeri, 1966.

Marold, Edith. "Einarr skálaglamm Helgason, Vellekla 7". In Poetry from the Kings' Sagas 1: From Mythical Times to c. 1035. Skaldic Poetry of the Scandinavian Middle Ages 1, edited by Diana Whaley. Turnhout, Belgium: Brepols, 2012.

Marold, Edith with Vivian Busch, Jana Krüger, Ann-Dörte Kyas and Katharina Seidel, "Eilífr Goðrúnarson, Þórsdrápa". In Poetry from Treatises on Poetics. Skaldic Poetry of the Scandinavian Middle Ages 3. Translation by John Foulks, edited by Kari Ellen Gade and Edith Marold. Turnhout, Belgium: Brepols, 2017.

Morris, William and Eirikr Magnússon. The Saga Library vol. II, The Story of the Ere-Dwellers with The Story of the Heath-Slayings. London: Bernard Quaritch Ltd, 1892.

The Nibelungenlied; The Lay of the Nibelungs. Translated by Cyril Edwards. Oxford, UK: Oxford University Press, 2010.

Njal's Saga. Translated by Robert Cook. London, England: Penguin Group, 2001.

Njál's Saga. Translated by Lee M. Hollander. UK: Wordsworth Classics, 2007.

Pálsson, Herman and Paul Edwards. Seven Viking Romances. New York: Penguin Random House, 1986.

Pettit, Edward. The Poetic Edda. A Dual-Language Edition. Open Book Publishers, 2023. https://doi.org/10.11647/OBP.0308

Poole, Russell. "Guthormr sindri, Hákonardrápa 1". In Poetry from the Kings' Sagas 1: From Mythical Times to c. 1035. Skaldic Poetry of the Scandinavian Middle Ages 1, edited by Diana Whaley. Turnhout, Belgium: Brepols, 2012.

Poole, Russell. "Anonymous Poems, Liðsmannaflokkr 1". In Poetry from the Kings' Sagas 1: From Mythical Times to c. 1035. Skaldic Poetry of the Scandinavian Middle Ages 1, edited by Diana Whaley. Turnhout, Belgium: Brepols, 2012.

Poole, Russell. "Tindr Hallkelsson, Hákonardrápa 5". In Poetry from the Kings' Sagas 1: From Mythical Times to c. 1035. Skaldic Poetry of the Scandinavian Middle Ages, edited by Diana Whaley. Turnhout, Belgium: Brepols, 2012.

Ross, Margaret Clunies. "Bragi inn gamli Boddason, Ragnarsdrápa". In Poetry from Treatises on Poetics. Skaldic Poetry of the Scandinavian Middle Ages 3, edited by Kari Ellen Gade and Edith Marold. Turnhout, Belgium: Brepols, 2017.

Ross, Margaret Clunies. "Þjóðólfr ór Hvini, Haustlǫng". In Poetry from Treatises on Poetics. Skaldic Poetry of the Scandinavian Middle Ages 3, edited by Kari Ellen Gade and Edith Marold. Turnhout, Belgium: Brepols, 2017.

Sacred Texts. "Hakon the Good's Saga". Accessed June 23, 2024. https://sacred-texts.com/neu/heim/05hakon.htm

The Saga of the Jomsvikings. Translated by Lee M. Hollander. USA: University of Texas Press, 1988.

The Saga of King Hrolf Kraki. Translated by Jesse Byock. London, England, UK: Penguin Group, 1998.

The Saga of the Volsungs. Translated by R.G. Finch. London: Nelson, 1965.

The Saga of the Volsungs. The Norse Epic of Sigurd the Dragon Slayer. Translated by Jesse Byock. London, England: Penguin Classics, 1999.

Stasinus of Cyprus. Homerica: The Cypria Fragment 1. Translated by Hugh G. Evelyn-White. 1914. Accessed Jun 24, 2024. https://www.theoi.com/Olympios/ArtemisWrath2.html#Agamemnon

The Story of Viga-Glum (Illustrated Edition). Translated by Edmund Walker Head. 1866.

Sturluson, Snorri. Edda. Translated by Anthony Faulkes. London and Vermont: W&N Everyman, 2008.

Sturluson, Snorri. The Prose Edda. Translated by Jesse Byock. London: Penguin Books Ltd, 2005.

Sturluson, Snorri. Heimskringla: History of the Kings of Norway. Translated by Lee M. Hollander. Texas, USA: University of Texas Press, 2007.

Tacitus. Agricola and Germania. Translated by Harold Mattingly, edited by James Rivers. London: Penguin Classics, 2010.

Three Icelandic Outlaw Sagas: The Saga of Gisli, The Saga of Grettir, and The Saga of Hord. Translated by George Johnston, edited by Anthony Faulkes. London: University College London, Viking Society for Northern Research, 2004.

Tolkien, Christopher. The Saga of King Heidrek the Wise. London: Thomas Nelson and Sons Ltd. 1960.

Tolley, Clive. Grottasõngr, the Song of Grotti. London, UK: University College of London, Viking Society for Northern Research, 2008.

Townend, Matthew. "Óttarr svarti, Hǫfuðlausn". In Poetry from the Kings' Sagas 1: From Mythical Times to c. 1035. Skaldic Poetry of the Scandinavian Middle Ages 1, edited by Diana Whaley. Turnhout, Belgium: Brepols, 2012.

Townend, Matthew. "Hallvarðr háreksblesi, Knútsdrápa". In Poetry from Treatises on Poetics. Skaldic Poetry of the Scandinavian Middle Ages 3, edited by Kari Ellen Gade and Edith Marold. Turnhout, Belgium: Brepols, 2017.

Various. The Sagas of the Icelanders (World of the Sagas). USA: Penguin Group, Penguin Classics Deluxe Edition, 2005.

Vatnsdœla saga, Íslenzk fornrit VIII. Edited by Einar Ól. Sveinsson. Reykjavík: Hið íslenzka fornritafélag, 1939.

Vigfusson, Gudbrand. Sturlunga Saga including The Islendinga Saga of Lawman Sturla Thordsson and Other Works. Oxford: Oxford Clarendon Press, 1878.

BIBLIOGRAPHY

Acker, Paul and Carolyne Larrington. The Poetic Edda: Essays on Old Norse Mythology. New York and London: Routledge, 2002.

Aðalsteinsson, Jon Hnefill. Blót í norrænum sið. Reykjavik: Háskólaútgáfan Félagsvísindastofnun, 1997.

Aðalsteinsson, Jon Hnefill. A Piece of Horse Liver: Myth, Ritual and Folklore in Old Icelandic Sources. Reykjavik: Háskólaútgáfan, 2012.

Anderson, Carl Edlund. Formation and Resolution of Ideological Contrast in the Early History of Scandinavia. PhD diss., University of Cambridge, 1999.

The Anthology of English Folk Tales, edited by Nicola Guy. Gloucestershire, UK: The History Press, 2019.

Bagge, Sverre. Society and Politics in Snorri Sturluson's Heimskringla. Berkeley: University of California Press, 1991.

Barnes, Terri L. "The Intrigue of the Female Warrior: Lagertha, Joan of Arc, and Matilda of Tuscany". Medieval Warfare (2019).

Bassil-Morozow, Helena. "Loki then and now: the trickster against civilization". International Journal of Jungian Studies vol 9, no. 2 (Glasgow, UK: Glasgow Caledonian University, 2017): 84-96.

Bek-Pedersen, Karen. The Norns in Old Norse Mythology. Scotland, UK: Dunedin Academic Press, 2011.

Bennett, Judith and Ruth Karras, ed. The Oxford Handbook of Women and Gender in Medieval Europe. Oxford: Oxford University Press, 2013.

Berg, Heidi Lund. "'Truth' and reproduction of knowledge. Critical thoughts on the interpretation and understanding of Iron-Age keys". In Viking Worlds. Things, Spaces and Movement, edited by Marianne Hem Eriksen, Unn Pedersen, Berndt Rundberget, Irmelin Axelsen and Heidi Lund Berg, 124-43. Oxford and Philadelphia: Oxbow Books, 2015.

Bintley, Michael D. J. "Where the Wild Things Are in Old English Poetry", in Representing Beasts in Early Medieval England and Scandinavia, edited by Michael D. J. Bintley and Thomas J. T. Williams, 205-28. Woodbridge, Boydell & Brewer, 2015.

Blain, Jenny and Robert J. Wallis. "The 'Ergi' Seidman: Contestations of Gender, Shamanism and Sexuality in Northern Religion Past and Present". Journal of Contemporary Religion vol 15, no. 3 (2000): 395-411.

Blain, Jenny. Nine Worlds of Seid-Magic, Ecstasy and Neo-Shamanism in North European Paganism. London and New York: Routledge, 2002.

Bourns, Timothy J.S. Between Nature and Culture: Animals and Humans in Old Norse Literature. PhD.diss. Oxford: Oxford University, 2017.

Bray, Daniel. "Sacrifice and Sacrificial Ideology". In The Dark Side: Proceedings of the Seventh Australian and International Religion, Literature and the Arts Conference (2002), edited by Christopher Hartney and Andrew McGarrity (Sydney: RLA Press, 2008), 123-35.

Britannica Kids. "Valkyries". Accessed November 18, 2023. https://kids.britannica.com/students/article/Valkyries/313973

Brookes, Sif and Dan Coultas. The Wyrd Less Woven: An Alternative Heathen Prayer Book. 2024.

Brown, Nancy Marie. The Real Valkyrie. The Hidden History of Viking Warrior Women. New York: St. Martin's Press, 2021.

Broz, Vlatko. 'Kennings as blends and prisms.' Jezikoslovlje 12, no. 2 (2011): 165-86.

Bulfinch, Thomas. Bulfinch's Mythology: The Age of Fable or Stories of Gods and Heroes. Boston: Sanborn, Carter, and Bazin, 1855.

Burdick, Ceilidh Elisabeth. Women of Fate in the Viking Age: Völur, Valkyries, and the Angel of Death. Ma thesis., University of Oslo, 2022.

Byock, Jesse. "Feuding in Viking-Age Iceland's great village." In Conflict in Medieval Europe: Changing Perspective in Society and Culture, edited by W.C. Brown and P. Gorecki, 229-41. Aldershot: Ashgate, 2003.

Caffey, Erin M. Femininity in Medieval Scandinavia: How Paganism Forged Gender Equality. Grad diss., Winthrop University, 2023.

Cairo, Samantha J. The Significance of Shape-Shifting and Transformation in Medieval Welsh and Icelandic Literature: The Ingenuity of Medieval Writers. MA thesis., Western Michigan University, 1999.

Carver, Martin., Alex Sanmark and Sarah Semple. Signals of Belief in Early England: Anglo-Saxon Paganism Revisited. Oxford: Oxbow Books, 2010.

Caywood, Judith. Rædende Iudithðe: The Heroic, Mythological and Christian Elements in the Old English Poem Judith. Undergrad thesis., University of San Diego, 2015.

Chadwick, H. Munro. The Heroic Age. Cambridge: Cambridge University Press, 1926.

Chadwick. Nora K. "The Monsters and Beowulf". In The Anglo-Saxons: Studies in Some Aspects of Their History: 171-203. London, UK: Bowes & Bowes, 1959.

Clover, Carol J., "Maiden Warriors and Other Sons." Journal of English and Germanic Philology 85,1 (1986), 35–49.

Clunies-Ross, Margaret. Prolonged echoes: Old Norse myths in Medieval Northern Society. Odense, Denmark: Odense University Press, 1994.

Colum, Padraic. The Children of Odin (also published as 'Nordic Gods and Heroes'). New York: Macmillan, 1920.

Coultas, Dan. Heathenry & The Sea. 2021.

Coultas, Dan. Perceptions of Male Queerness in Early Medieval Scandinavia. MA diss., University of Leeds, 2023.

Crawford, Jackson. "Valkyries (Valkyrjur)", Jan 23, 2019. YouTube video. https://www.youtube.com/watch?v=VMrYEq_jNVs

Dale, Roderick. The Myths and Realities of the Viking Berserkr. London and New York: Routledge, 2022.

Damico, Helen and Alexandra Hennessey Olsen, ed. New Readings on Women in Old English Literature. USA: Indiana University Press, 1990.

Davidson, Hilda Roderick Ellis. Gods and Myths of Northern Europe. Harmondsworth: Pelican, 1964.

Davidson, Hilda Roderick Ellis. Myths and Symbols in Pagan Europe. Early Scandinavian and Celtic Religions. USA: Syracuse University Press, 1988.

Davidson, Hilda Ellis. Roles of the Northern Goddess. London and New York: Routledge, 1998.

Dobat, Andres Siegfried. "Viking Age functional culture as a reflection of the belief in divine intervention". In Old Norse Religion in Long-Term Perspectives: Origins, Changes & Interactions, edited by Anders Andrén, Kristina Jennbert, and Catharina Raudvere, 184-8. Lund, Sweden: Nordic Academic Press, 2006.

Double, Isabella. "Women and their Roles in Early Christianity". Dies Legibiles II vol 2 (2022): 41-6.

Drake, Michael. The Great Shift and How to Navigate It. USA: Talking Drum Publications, 2018.

Dronke, Ursula. Myth and Fiction in Early Norse Lands (Variorum Collected Studies). London: Routledge, 1996.

Dunlop, D. M. "Zeki Validi's Ibn Faḍlān." Die Welt des Orients 1, no. 4 (1950): 307-12.

Eliade, Mircea. Occultism, Witchcraft and Cultural Fashions: Essays in Comparative Religions. Chicago and London: The University of Chicago Press, 1976.

Eliade, M. Shamanism: Archaic Techniques of Ecstasy. London: Arkana, 1989.

Ellis, Hilda Roderick. The Road to Hel. UK: Cambridge University Press, 1943.

Faulkes, Anthony. "The sources of Skáldskaparmál: Snorri's intellectual background". In Snorri Sturluson. Kolloquium anläßlich der 750. Wiederkehr seines Todestages, ScriptOralia vol 51, edited by Alois Wolf, 59-76. Germany: Gunter Narr Verlag, 1993.

Faulkes, Anthony. Poetical Inspiration in Old Norse and Old English Poetry. London: University College London, 1997.

Ferrari, Fulvio. "Gods, Warlocks and Monsters in Örvar-Odds saga." In The Fantastic in Old Norse/Icelandic Literature: Sagas and the British Isles; Preprint Papers of The 13th International Saga Conference; Durham and York, 6th-12th August, 2006, edited by John McKinnell, David Ashurst and Donata Kick. Durham: The Centre for Medieval and Renaissance Studies, Durham University, 2006: 241-47.

Franks, Amy Jefford. "Valfǫðr, Vǫlur, and Valkyrjur: Óðinn as a Queer Deity Mediating the Warrior Halls of Viking Age Scandinavia." Scandia, 2 (2019): 28-65.

Freud, Sigmund. On Sexuality: Three Essays on the Theory of Sexuality and Other Works. Translated by James Strachey, edited by Angela Richards. Middlesex, England: Penguin Books, 1977.

Friðriksdóttir, Jóhanna Katrín. Valkyrie, the Women of the Viking World. UK: Bloomsbury Academic, 2020.

Gardeła, Leszek. "Into Viking Minds: Reinterpreting the Staffs of Sorcery and Unravelling Seiðr," Viking and Medieval Scandinavia 4 (2008): 45-84.

Gardeła, Leszek. "A Biography of the Seiðr-Staffs. Towards an Archaeology of Emotions". In Between Paganism and Christianity in the North, edited by L. P. Słupecki and J. Morawiec, 190-219. Rzeszów: Rzeszów University, 2009.

Gardeła, Leszek. Women and Weapons in the Viking World: Amazons of the North. Oxford: Oxbow Books, 2021.

Gardeła, Leszek, Peter Pentz, and Neil Price. "Revisiting the 'Valkyries': Armed Females in Viking Age Figurative Metalwork". Current Swedish Archaeology 30 (2022): 95-151.

Gardeła, Leszek., Sophie Bønding and Peter Pentz, eds. The Norse Sorceress: Mind and Materiality in the Viking World. Oxford: Oxbow Books, 2023. https://doi.org/10.2307/jj.5699282.

Ginzburg, Carlo. Ecstasies: Deciphering the Witches' Sabbath. Translated by Raymond Rosenthal. London: Hutchinson Radius, 1990.

Glosecki, Stephen O. Shamanism and Old English Poetry (Garland Reference Library of the Humanities). Garland Publishing, 1989.

Grant, Tom. "A Problem of Giant Proportions: Distinguishing Risar and Jötnar in old Icelandic saga material". Gripla 30 (2019): 77-106.

Gräslund, Anne-Sofie. "The position of Iron age Scandinavian women: Evidence from graves and rune stones." In Gender and the archaeology of death, edited by Bettina Arnold and Nancy L. Wicker, 81-104. Walnut Creek, CA: Altamira Press, 2001.

Green, Amanda. L. Knocking on Death's Door. A Re-examination of the Old Norse Worlds of Death. Félagsvísindasvið Háskóla Íslands, 2022.

Greenwood, Susan, "The wild hunt: A mythological language of magic". Handbook of Contemporary Paganism (2008): 195-222.

Grundy, Stephan. "Shapeshifting and Berserkergang". Disuptatio, 3 (1998): 104-22.

Guerber, H. A. The Myths of the Norsemen: From the Eddas and Sagas. Loki Publishing, 2013.

Gunnell, Terry. The Origins of Drama in Scandinavia. Cambridge: D.S. Brewer, 1995.

Gunnell, Terry. "The Season of the Dísir: The Winter Nights and the Dísarblót in Early Scandinavian Belief". Cosmos 16 (2005): 117-49.

Gvarishvili, Zeinab. Kenning and Kend Heiti as the base model of the modern cognitive metaphor. 2018.

Hadley, Dawn. "Ethnicity and Identity in Context: The Material Culture of Scandinavian Settlement in England in the Ninth and Tenth Centuries." In Identité et ethnicité: concepts, débats historiographiques, exemples (Ve-XIIe siècles), edited by V. Gazeau and P. Badouin. Caen: Publications du Centre de Recherches Archéologiques et Historiques Médiévales (2008), 167-83.

Hagen, Rune Blix. ""I Hurl the Spirits of Gandul'. Pleasure, Jealousy, and Magic: The Witchcraft Trial of Ragnhild Tregagaas in 1325." In Myths and Magic in the Medieval Far North: Realities and Representations of a Region on the Edge of Europe. Norway: The Arctic University of Norway, 2020.

Hayeur Smith, Michèle. The Valkyries' Loom: The Archaeology of Cloth Production and Female Power in the North Atlantic. USA: University Press of Florida, 2020.

Heartfield, Kate. The Valkyrie. London, UK: Harper Voyager, 2023.

Hedenstierna-Jonson, Charlotte et al.'A female Viking Warrior Confirmed by Genomics', American Journal of Physical Anthropology, 164.4, (2017): 853–60.

Heide, Eldar. 'Spinning Seiðr'. In Old Norse Religion in Long-Term Perspectives: Origins, Changes, and Interactions. Edited by Anders Andrén, Kristina Jennbert, and Catharina Raudvere, 164-70. Lund, Sweden: Nordic Academic Press, 2004.

Hermann, Pernille. "Concepts of Memory. Approaches to the Past in Medieval Icelandic Literature." Scandinavian Studies 81, no. 3 (2009): 287-308.

Hines, John. Old-Norse Sources for Gaelic History. UK: University of Cambridge, 2002.

Hohmann, Kurt. Skaði and Freyja: Females of Power amongst the Aesir. "Academic.edu": https://www.academia.edu/15301723/Ska%C3%B0i_and_Freyja_Females_of_Power_amongst_the_Aesir

Holland, Lucy. Song of the Huntress. London, UK: Tor, 2024.

Hopkins, Joseph S. Goddesses Unknown II: On the Apparent Old Norse Goddess Ilmr. RMN Newsletter. 2014.

Hopkins, Joseph S. "Gesta Danorum in English Translations." Mimisbrunnr. Accessed November 27, 2023. https://www.mimisbrunnr.info/gesta-danorum-english-translations

Hutton, Ronald. "The Wild Hunt and the Witches' Sabbath." Folklore 125 (2014): 161–78.

Jakobsson, Ármann. "The Trollish Acts of Þorgrímr the Witch: The Meanings of Troll and Ergi in Medieval Iceland." Saga-Book, vol 32 (2008): 39–68.

Jakobsson, Ármann. "A contest of cosmic fathers: God and giant in Vafþrúðnismál". Neophilologus 92 (2008): 263-77.

Jakobsson, Ármann. "Laxdæla Dreaming: A Saga Heroine Invents Her Own Life". Leeds Studies in English 39 (2008): 33-51.

Jennbert, Kristina. Animals and Humans: Recurrent Symbiosis in archaeology and Old Norse Religion. Lund, Sweden: Nordic Academic Press. 2011.

Jesch, Judith. Women in the Viking Age. Woodbridge: Boydell, 1991.

Jesch, Judith. "Viking women, warriors, and Valkyries". The British Museum. Published April 19, 2014. https://www.britishmuseum.org/blog/viking-women-warriors-and-valkyries

Jesch, Judith. The Viking Diaspora. UK: Routledge, 2015.

Jesch, Judith. "Women, War and Words: a Verbal Archaeology of Shield-maidens". Viking Wars (2021): 127-142.

Jochens, Jenny. Old Norse Images of Women. Philadelphia: University of Pennsylvania Press, 1996.

Johnson, Joy L. and Robin Repta. "Sex and Gender: Beyond the Binaries." In Designing and Conducting Gender, Sex, and Health Research, edited by J.L Olife and L.Greaves, 17-37. Thousand Oaks, California: Sage, 2012.

Jones, Julia Clinton. Valhalla: The Myths of Norseland; A Saga, in Twelve Parts. New York, USA: R. Worthington, 1880.

Keens, Lucy Anne. Scenes of a sexual nature: theorising representations of sex and the sexual body in the sagas of the Icelanders. PhD thesis., London: University College London, 2016.

Kelly, Shaun B. An Examination of The Representations of Magic in The Saga of Hrolf Kraki. 2012

Kershaw, Priscilla K. "The One-eyed God: Odin and the (Indo-) Germanic Männerbünde". Journal of Indo-European Studies, 36 (1997).

Kiernan, Kevin. "Grendel's Heroic Mother". Geardagum 6 (1984): 13-33.

Kress, Helga. "Taming the Shrew: The Rise of Patriarchy and the Subordination of the Feminine in Old Norse Literature". In The Cold Counsel. The Women in Old Norse Literature and Myth, edited by Sarah M Anderson and Karen Swenson, 81-92. New York: Routledge, 2001.

Kure, Henning. I begyndelsen var skriget -- Vikingetidens myter om skabelsen. København: Gyldendal, 2010.

Kvilhaug, Maria. The Maiden with the Mead. Norway: University of Oslo, 2004.

Kvilhaug, Maria Christine. The Seed of Yggdrasill: Deciphering the Hidden Messages in Old Norse Myths. Copenhagen: Whyte Tracks, 2015.

Kvilhaug, Maria. The Great Knowledge. USA: The Three Little Sisters LLC, 2023.

Lafayllve, Patricia.M. Freyja, Lady, Vanadis. USA: Outskirts Press, 2006.

Larrington, Carolyne. The Norse Myths That Shape the Way We Think. London: Thames & Hudson Ltd, 2023.

Lecouteux, Claude. Phantom Armies of the Night, The Wild Hunt and the Ghostly Processions of the Undead. USA: Inner Traditions, 2011.

Leyser, Henrietta. Medieval Women: A Social History of Women in England 450-1500. UK: Palgrave Macmillan, 1995.

Lindow, John. Norse Mythology: A Guide to Gods, Heroes, Rituals, and Beliefs. Oxford: Oxford University Press, 2001.

Lund, Julie. "Banks, Borders and Bodies of Water in a Viking Age Mentality". Journal of Wetland Archaeology, vol 8 (2008): 53 - 72.
Lund, Julie. "At the Water's Edge". In Signals of Belief in Early England: Anglo-Saxon Paganism Revisited, edited by Martin Carver, Alexandra Sanmark and Sarah Semple, 49-66. Oxford and Philadelphia: Oxbow Books, 2010.

Lund Berg, Heidi. "'Truth' and reproduction of knowledge. Critical thoughts on the interpretation and understanding of Iron-Age keys". In Viking Worlds. Things, Spaces and Movement, edited by Marianne Hem Eriksen, Unn Pedersen, Berndt Rundberget, Irmelin Axelsen and Heidi Lund Berg, 124-43. Oxford and Philadelphia: Oxbow Books, 2015.

Malone, Kemp. "An Anglo-Latin Version of the Hjaðningavíg". Speculum Vol. 39, No. 1 (1964): 35-44.

Mayburd, Miriam. "Helzt þóttumk nú heima í millim..." A reassessment of Hervör in light of seiðr's supernatural gender dynamics. Arkiv för nordisk filologi, vol. 129. (2014)

McKinnell, John. "Þórgerðr Hölgabrúðr and Hyndluljóð". In Mythological Women. Studies in Memory of Lotte Motz 1922-1997, edited by Rudolf Simek and Wilhelm Heizmann, 265-290. Wien: Fassbaender, 2002.

McKinnell, John. Meeting the other in Norse myth and legend. Woodbridge, Suffolk, UK: D.S. Brewer, 2005.

McKinnell, John. "The Trouble with Father: Hervararkviða and the Adaptation of Traditional Story-Patterns". In Essays on Eddic Poetry, edited by Donata Kick and John D. Shafer, 292 – 316. Toronto: University of Toronto Press, 2014.

Mees, Bernard. "Þrymskviða, Vígja, and the Canterbury Charm." Viking and Medieval Scandinavia 9 (2013): 133–53. http://www.jstor.org/stable/45020173.

Meissner, Rudolf. Die Kenningar der Skalden: ein Beitrag zur skaldischen Poetik. Bonn and Leipzig: Kurt Schroeder, 1921.

Mitchell, Stephen. A. Witchcraft and Magic in the Nordic Middle Ages. USA: University of Pennsylvania Press, 2011.

Moen, M. The Gendered Landscape, A discussion on gender, status and power expressed in the Viking Age mortuary landscape. Oslo: University of Oslo, 2010.

Moen, Marianne and Matthew J. Walsh. "Agents of Death: Reassessing Social Agency and Gendered Narratives of Human Sacrifice in the Viking Age." In Cambridge Archaeological Journal. Cambridge University Press, 2021: 597 – 611

Moore, Meredith Catherine. Dread Sisterhood: Conceptions of the Feminine in Norse Depictions of Death. MA thesis., Háskóli Íslands, 2015.

Munch, Peter Andreas. Norse Mythology. Legends of Gods and Heroes. Translated by Sigurd Bernhard Hustvedt. New York: The American-Scandinavian Foundation, 1926.

Mundal, Else. Fylgjemotiva i norrøn litteratur. Oslo: Norway: Universitetsforlaget, 1974.

Mundal, Else. "Austr sat in aldna... Giantesses and Female Powers in Voluspa."In Mythological Women: Studies in Memory of Lotte Motz (1922-1997), edited by Rudolf Simek and Wilhelm Heizmann, 185-96. Vienna: Fassbaender, 2002.

Murphy, Luke John. Herjans Dísir: Valkyrjur, Supernatural Feminities, and Elite Warrior Culture in the Late Pre-Christian Iron Age. MA Thesis. Félagsvísindasvið Háskóla Íslands. 2013.

Nässtrom, Britt-Mari. Freyja, the Great Goddess of the North. Harwich Port, USA: Clock & Rose Press. 2003.

Ney, Agneta. "Genus och ideologi i Völsunga saga." In Fornaldarsagornas struktur och ideologi, edited by Ármann Jakobsson, Annette Lassen and Agneta Ney, 113-22. Uppsala: Uppsala universitet, 2003.

Norrman, Lena. "Woman or Warrior? The Construction of Gender in Old Norse Myth". 11th International Saga Conference (2000).

North, Richard. Heathen Gods in Old English Literature. Cambridge and New York: Cambridge University Press, 1997.

O'Donoghue, Heather. From Asgard to Valhalla. The Remarkable History of the Norse Myths (2nd Edition). London, UK: Bloomsbury Academic, 2024.

Oestigaard, T. "Water." In The Oxford Handbook of the Archaeology of Ritual and Religion, edited by T. Insoll, 38-50. Oxford, Oxford University Press, 2011.

Orchard, Andy. Dictionary of Norse Myth and Legend. Great Britain: Cassell, 1997.

Pantmann, Pernille. "The symbolism of keys in female graves on Zealand during the Viking Age". In The Iron Age on Zealand, Status and Perspectives, edited by Linda Boye, 75-80. Royal Society of Northern Antiquities, 2011.

Pintar, Andrea. Valkyries or Valiant Women: The World of Women, Weapons and War in Viking Age Scandinavia. University of Amsterdam/VU University, 2016.

Platz, Amanda. Autonomous Power and Profound Agency: Women and Magic in the Icelandic Legendary Sagas. Ma thesis: Clemson University, 2021

Pluskowski, A. "Animal Magic." In Signals of Belief in Early England: Anglo-Saxon Paganism Revisited, edited by M. Carver, A. Sanmark, and S. Semple, 103-27. Oxford: Oxbow Books, 2010.

Pluskowski, Aleks. "Conjuring Canids: Wolves and Dogs in Viking Age Sorcery", in The Norse Sorceress: Mind and Materiality in the Viking World, edited by Leszek Gardeła, Sophie Bønding, and Peter Pentz, 229-38. Oxford: Oxbow Books, 2023.

Pollington, Stephen. 'The mead-hall community'. Journal of Medieval History 37 (2011): 19-33.

Pollington, Stephen. The Elder Gods: The Otherworld of Early England. Ely, Cambridgeshire, UK: Anglo-Saxon Books, 2022.

Pollington, Stephen. Woden, A Historical Companion. London: Uppsala Books, 2024.

Price, Neil. The Viking Way: Religion and War in Late Iron Age Scandinavia (Revised Edition). Uppsala, Sweden: Uppsala University, 2019.

Price, Neil. The Children of Ash of Elm, A History of the Vikings. UK: Penguin Random House, 2020.

Psaki, F. Regina. "Women's Counsel in the Riddarasögur: The Case of Parcevals saga." In The Cold Counsel. The Woman in Old Norse Literature and Myth, edited by Sarah M. Anderson and Karen Swenson, 201-24. New York: Routledge, 2001.

Purser, Philip A. Her Syndan Wælcyrian: Illuminating the Form and Function of the Valkyrie-Figure in the Literature, Mythology, and Social Consciousness of Anglo-Saxon England. Ph.D dissertation, Georgia State University, 2013.

Odin's Cave. "Freya Norse Goddess | The Queen of Valkyries". Accessed June 18, 2024. https://www.odinscave.com/blogs/norse-mythology-gods/introducing-freya-the-queen-of-valkyries

Oehrl, Sigmund. "'I am Eagle" – Depictions of raptors and their meaning in the art of Late Iron Age and Viking Age Scandinavia (c. AD 400–1100).' Raptor on the fist – falconry, its imagery and similar motifs throughout the millennia on a global scale. Wachholtz, 2020.

Old Icelandic Dictionary. "Vigr". Accessed June 24, 2024. https://old-icelandic.vercel.app/word/vigr-2

Quinn, Judy. "The Use of Eddic Poetry in Contemporary Sagas". In The Australian-Icelandic Cultural Society (Melbourne) Volume 3 (1987): 54-72.

Quinn, Judy. "The 'Wind of the Giantess': Snorri Sturluson, Rudolf Meissner, and the Interpretation of Mythological Kennings along Taxonomic Lines". Viking and Medieval Scandinavia 8 (2012): 207-59.

Redon, Antonio. Females Warriors of the Viking Age: Fact or Fiction. MA diss., Iceland: University of Iceland School of Humanities, 2017.

Reinicke, Tamás. Bound by Gold and Blood: Power Structure in the Viking Age. Norway, University of Oslo, 2017.

Riseley, Charles. Ceremonial Drinking in the Viking Age. Dissertation, University of Oslo, 2014.

Rodriguez, Jesus Fernando Guerrero. Old Norse Drinking Culture. Ph.D thesis, University of York, 2007.

Røthe, Gunnhild. The Fictitious Figure of Þorgerðr Hölgabrúðr in the Saga Tradition. The Fantastic in Old Norse/Icelandic Literature: Preprint Papers of the 13th International Saga Conference, Durham and York 6th-12th August 2006, I-II, edited by John McKinnell, David Ashurst and Donata Kick, 836-45. Durham: Centre for Medieval and Renaissance Studies, 2006.

Rowe, Elizabeth Ashman. "Sǫrla þáttr: The Literary Adaptation of Myth and Legend." Saga-Book, 26 (2002): 38–66.

Sanmark, Alexandra. "Living On: Ancestors and the Soul". In Signals of Belief in Early England: Anglo-Saxon Paganism Revisited, edited by Martin Carver, Alexandra Sanmark and Sarah Semple, 158-80. Oxford and Philadelphia: Oxbow Books, 2010.

Santa Monica Studio. God of War. PlayStation 4 ed. Sony Interactive Entertainment, 2018.

Santa Monica Studio. God of War Ragnarök. PlayStation 5 ed. Sony Interactive Entertainment, 2022.

Sawyer, Birgit Strand. "Women in Gesta Danorum." In Saxo Grammaticus: A Medieval Author between Norse and Latin Culture, edited by K. Friis-Jensen. Danish Medieval History and Saxo Grammaticus, 2. Copenhagen: Museum Tusculanum (1981): 135-67.

Schulz, Katja. Riesen: Von Wissenshütern und Wildnisbewohnern in Edda und Saga. Skandinavistische Arbeiten 20. Heidelberg: Winter (2004): 24-49

Self, Kathleen M. "The Valkyrie's Gender: Old Norse Shield-Maidens and Valkyries as a Third Gender". Feminist Foundations, Vol.26, No.1 (2014): 143 -72.

Sheeha, Iman. 'Mistress, look out at window': Women, Servants and Liminal Domestic Spaces on the Early Modern Stage. London: Brunel University, 2020.

Short, William and Óskarson, Reynir. Men of Terror: A Comprehensive Analysis of Viking Combat. USA: Westholme Publishing, 2021.

Sikora, Maeve. "Diversity in Viking Age Horse Burial: A comparative study of Norway, Iceland, Scotland and Ireland". The Journal of Irish Archaeology 12 & 13 (2004).

Silber, Patricie. 'Gold and its Significance in Beowulf'. Annuale Medievale, vol.18 (1977): 5-19.

Simek, Rudolf. "The use and abuse of Old Norse religion: Its beginnings in high medieval Iceland". In Old Norse Religion in Long-Term Perspectives: Origins, Changes & Interactions, edited by Anders Andrén, Kristina Jennbert, and Catharina Raudvere, 377 – 80. Lund. Sweden: Nordic Academic Press, 2006.

Simek, Rudolf. Dictionary of Northern Mythology. Translated by Angela Hall. Cambridge: D.S. Brewer. 2007.

The Skaldic Project. "Kennings for type WOLF." Accessed November 19, 2023. https://skaldic.org/db.php?if=default&table=kenning&val=90&view=meiss

The Skaldic Project. "Kennings for Woman." Accessed February 2, 2024. https://skaldic.org/db.php?if=default&table=kenning&val=WOMAN#

Solli, Brit. "The Norse God Odin and "Holy White Stones": A Queer Interpretation". In Facets of Archaeology: Essays in Honour of Lotte Hedeager on her 60th Birthday, ed. by Konstantinos Chilidis, Julie Lund and Christopher Prescott, Oslo Archaeological Series, 10 (Oslo: Unipub, 2008): 275-89.

Spence, Marguerita and Marian E. Everatt. A Short History of York. London: A. Brown & Sons, LTD, 1948.

Ström, Folke. Níð, Ergi and Old Norse Moral Attitudes. London: University College London, 1974.

Sundqvist, Olof. The Demise of Old Norse Religion, Dismantling and Defending the Old Order in Viking Age Scandinavia. De Gruyter, 2023. https://doi.org/10.1515/9783111198750

Surrisi, C.M. The Bones of Birka: Unravelling the Mystery of a Female Viking Warrior. USA: Chicago Review Press, 2023.

Taggart, Declan. "Fate and Cosmogony in Völuspá: Shaping History in a Moment". Northern Studies, vol 44 (2013): 21–35.

Thysse, Arwen. Men and Trolls: A Discussion of Race and the Depiction of the Sámi in the Hrafnistumannasögur. Edmonton, Canada: Scandinavian-Canadian Studies Scandinavian-Canadian Studies, 2022. https://doi.org/10.29173/scancan221

Tolley, Clive. Vǫrðr and Gandr: Helping Spirits in Norse Magic. Arkiv For Nordisk Filologi, 1995.

Turville-Petre, E.O.G. Myth and Religion of the North: The Religion of Ancient Scandinavia. Westport, Connecticut, USA: Greenwood Press, 1964.

Upham, Tonicha Mae. Equal Rites: Parsing Rus' Gender Values Through an Arabic Lens. MA thesis, University of Iceland, 2019.

Varley, David Hugh. The whirling wheel: the male construction of empowered female identities in Old Norse myth and legend. Durham theses, Durham University, 2015.

Visit Norway. "Facts about the Northern Lights." Accessed March 19, 2024. https://www.visitnorway.com/things-to-do/nature-attractions/northern-lights/facts-about-the-northern-lights/

Walsh, Matthew J., Sean O'Neill, and Lasse Sørensen, ed. In the Darkest of Days: Exploring Human Sacrifice and Value in Southern Scandinavian Prehistory. Oxford: Oxbow Books, 2023.

Wellendorf, Jonas. Gods and Humans in Medieval Scandinavia: Retying the Bonds. Cambridge: Cambridge University Press, 2018.

Wihlborg, Julia. "Last Ride of the Valkyries: To (re)interpret Viking Age Female Figurines according to Gender and Queer Theory". Kyngervi 2 (2020): 22-39.

Wikström af Edholm, Klas. "Human sacrifice in Old Norse Skaldic Poetry". In In the Darkest of Days: Exploring Human Sacrifice and Value in Southern Scandinavian Prehistory, edited by Matthew J. Walsh, Sean O'Neill and Lasse Sørensen, 111-8. Oxford, UK: Oxbow Books, 2023.

Williams, Kirstina. Of Thralls and Freemen: Norse social structure during the Viking Age. Seattle: University of Washington, 2015. DOI: 10.13140/RG.2.1.3161.5209.

Williams, Thomas J. T. "For the Sake of Bravado in the Wilderness': Confronting the Bestial in Anglo-Saxon Warfare". In Representing Beasts in Early Medieval England and Scandinavia, edited by Thomas J. T. Williams and Michael D. J. Bintley, 176-204. Suffolk: Boydell & Brewer, 2015.

Wolf, Kirsten. Transvestism in the Sagas of the Icelanders. Canada: University of Manitoba, 1997.

Woodward, Robert H. "Swanrad in Beowulf". Modern Language Notes 69:8 (1954): 544-6.

World History Encyclopedia. "Valkyries". Accessed January 24, 2024. https://www.worldhistory.org/Valkyrie/

Zoëga, Geir T. A Concise Dictionary of Old Icelandic. Oxford: Clarendon, 1910.

RECOMMENDED READING

Aðalsteinsson, Jon Hnefill. A Piece of Horse Liver: Myth, Ritual and Folklore in Old Icelandic Sources. Reykjavik: Háskólaútgáfan, 2012.

Bek-Pedersen, Karen. The Norns in Old Norse Mythology. Scotland, UK: Dunedin Academic Press, 2011.

Bourns, Timothy J.S. Between Nature and Culture: Animals and Humans in Old Norse Literature. PhD.diss. Oxford: Oxford University. 2017.

Carver, Martin., Alex Sanmark and Sarah Semple. Signals of Belief in Early England: Anglo-Saxon Paganism Revisited. Oxford: Oxbow Books, 2010.

Ellis, Hilda Roderick. The Road to Hel. UK: Cambridge University Press, 1943.

Friðriksdóttir, Jóhanna Katrín. Valkyrie, the Women of the Viking World. UK: Bloomsbury Academic, 2020.

Gardeła, Leszek. Women and Weapons in the Viking World: Amazons of the North. Oxford: Oxbow Books, 2021.

Gardeła, Leszek., Sophie Bønding and Peter Pentz, eds. The Norse Sorceress: Mind and Materiality in the Viking World. Oxford: Oxbow Books, 2023. https://doi.org/10.2307/jj.5699282.

Hayeur Smith, Michèle. The Valkyries' Loom: The Archaeology of Cloth Production and Female Power in the North Atlantic. USA: University Press of Florida, 2020.

Jesch, Judith. Women in the Viking Age. Woodbridge: Boydell, 1991.

Jochens, Jenny. Old Norse Images of Women. Philadelphia: University of Pennsylvania Press, 1996.

Leyser, Henrietta. Medieval Women: A Social History of Women in England 450-1500. UK: Palgrave Macmillan, 1995.

Lindow, John. Norse Mythology: A Guide to Gods, Heroes, Rituals, and Beliefs. Oxford: Oxford University Press, 2001.

Lund, Julie. "Banks, Borders and Bodies of Water in a Viking Age Mentality". Journal of Wetland Archaeology, vol 8 (2008): 53 - 72.

Mitchell, Stephen. A. Witchcraft and Magic in the Nordic Middle Ages. USA: University of Pennsylvania Press, 2011.

Murphy, Luke John. Herjans Dísir: Valkyrjur, Supernatural Feminities, and Elite Warrior Culture in the Late Pre-Christian Iron Age. MA Thesis. Félagsvísindasvið Háskóla Íslands, 2013.

Pollington, Stephen. The Elder Gods: The Otherworld of Early England. Ely, Cambridgeshire: Anglo-Saxon Books, 2022.

Pollington, Stephen. Woden, A Historical Companion. London: Uppsala Books, 2024.

Poole, Russell Gilbert. Viking Poems on War and Peace: A Study in Skaldic Narrative. U of Toronto P, 1991.

Price, Neil. The Viking Way: Religion and War in Late Iron Age Scandinavia (Revised Edition). Uppsala, Sweden: Uppsala University, 2019.

Price, Neil. The Children of Ash of Elm, A History of the Vikings. UK: Penguin Random House, 2020.

Purser, Philip A. Her Syndan Wælcyrian: Illuminating the Form and Function of the Valkyrie-Figure in the Literature, Mythology, and Social Consciousness of Anglo-Saxon England. Ph.D dissertation, Georgia State University, 2013.

Simek, Rudolf. Dictionary of Northern Mythology. Cambridge: D.S. Brewer, 2007.

Sundqvist, Olof. The Demise of Old Norse Religion, Dismantling and Defending the Old Order in Viking Age Scandinavia. De Gruyter, 2023.

Sif Brookes is a reconstructive Nordic Heathen fascinated with the Valkyries, with a supplementary academic interest around historical seiðr, the role of women in the early Medieval period, Viking Age weaponry and armour, and the study of death and burial in pre-Christian Germanic civilisations.

She is frequently invited to speak at events of all sizes on all the above and is currently working alongside museums and academic centres to broaden Pagan inclusion. She is the co-author and illustrator of The Wyrd Less Woven, an Alternative Heathen Prayer Book, alongside being a committee member of various Pagan organisations within the UK.

She was a founding host of the Heathen Wyrdos podcast (now called Wyrdcraft), before leaving that project in April 2023 to pursue writing, art, and content creation. She currently creates content under Valsif on Youtube (a work in progress) and on Twitch as LadyValsif (more of a work in progress).

The Three Little Sisters

The Three Little Sisters is an indie publisher that puts authors first. We specialize in the strange and unusual. Our books are written by long time practitioners, academics and more.

 https://shop.the3littlesisters.com